BATTER UP!
Are you fan enough to face a mound of tough trivia questions?

1. Who was the youngest manager ever to win a pennant?
2. Who was the Dodger pitcher who finished a record six games against the Yankees in the 1947 World Series?
3. Who was the left-handed batter who hit four consecutive home runs in a nine-inning game?
4. What was John Odom's nickname?
5. What physical adversity did Pete Gray overcome in order to become a professional baseball player?
6. Who is the only player who has won batting titles in both leagues?

W0010346

ANSWERS
1. Joe Cronin (26)
2. Hugh Casey
3. Lou Gehrig (1932 Yankees)
4. "Blue Moon"
5. A missing arm
6. Ed Delahanty (.410 with 1899 Phillies and .376 with 1902 Senators)

⊘ SIGNET (0451)

THE WORLD OF SPORTS

☐ **THE MOST EXTRAORDINARY BASEBALL QUIZ BOOK, EVER by David Nemec.**
Are you a true baseball fanatic? Do you study every niche and nuance of
the game? Well, watch out for curveballs as you test your knowledge on
over 700 tantalizing questions that will prove what a true baseball scholar
you are. (165504—$4.95)

☐ **GREAT BASEBAL FEATS, FACTS & FIRSTS by David Nemec.** Thousands of
scores, stats and stories in one amazingly complete volume! Discover the
unconventional records, the offbeat feats, the historic scores and the one-
of-a-kind characters that keep baseball flying—in this comprehensive up-
to-the-minute encyclopedia. (183428—$4.99)

☐ **THE BASEBALL CHALLENGE QUIZ BOOK by David Nemec.** For the fun of
competition and a mother lode of the game's golden lore, this is a book to
make every fan stand up and cheer! (169433—$3.99)

☐ **THE ULTIMATE BASEBALL QUIZ BOOK by Don Forker.** You're up against a
full count of questions about the American national pastime. See if you can
touch all the bases, but look out! This newly revised edition just might
throw you a curve! (152360—$4.99)

☐ **THE SIGNET ULTIMATE BASKETBALL QUIZ BOOK by Patrick Mullooly.** Here
is a brain-teasing quiz book that covers every aspect of the great game of
basketball from the early days of the NBA to today. Find out how much you
really know about the game, the teams, and the players, the records.
(177649—$3.99)

Prices slightly higher in Canada

Buy them at your local bookstore or use this convenient coupon for ordering.

PENGUIN USA
P.O. Box 999 — Dept. #17109
Bergenfield, New Jersey 07621

Please send me the books I have checked above.
I am enclosing $_____ (please add $2.00 to cover postage and handling). Send
check or money order (no cash or C.O.D.'s) or charge by Mastercard or VISA (with a $15.00
minimum). Prices and numbers are subject to change without notice.

Card #_____ Exp. Date _____
Signature_____
Name_____
Address_____
City _____ State _____ Zip Code _____

For faster service when ordering by credit card call **1-800-253-6476**

Allow a minimum of 4-6 weeks for delivery. This offer is subject to change without notice.

The Ultimate Baseball Quiz Book

Second Revised Edition

Dom Forker

A SIGNET BOOK

SIGNET
Published by the Penguin Group
Penguin Books USA Inc., 375 Hudson Street,
New York, New York 10014, U.S.A.
Penguin Books Ltd, 27 Wrights Lane,
London W8 5TZ, England
Penguin Books Australia Ltd, Ringwood,
Victoria, Australia
Penguin Books Canada Ltd, 10 Alcorn Avenue,
Toronto, Ontario, Canada M4V 3B2
Penguin Books (N.Z.) Ltd, 182–190 Wairau Road,
Auckland 10, New Zealand

Penguin Books Ltd, Registered Offices:
Harmondsworth, Middlesex, England

First published by Signet, an imprint of Dutton Signet,
a division of Penguin Books USA Inc.

First Printing, March, 1981
First Printing (Second Revised Edition), March, 1996
10 9 8 7 6 5 4 3

Copyright © Dom Forker, 1981, 1988, 1996
All rights reserved

 REGISTERED TRADEMARK—MARCA REGISTRADA

Printed in the United States of America

Without limiting the rights under copyright reserved above, no part of this publi-
cation may be reproduced, stored in or introduced into a retrieval system, or
transmitted, in any form, or by any means (electronic, mechanical, photocopying,
recording, or otherwise), without the prior written permission of both the copyright owner and the above publisher of this book.

BOOKS ARE AVAILABLE AT QUANTITY DISCOUNTS WHEN USED TO PROMOTE PROD-
UCTS OR SERVICES. FOR INFORMATION PLEASE WRITE TO PREMIUM MARKETING DIVI-
SION, PENGUIN BOOKS USA INC., 375 HUDSON STREET, NEW YORK, NEW YORK 10014.

If you purchased this book without a cover you should be aware that this book
is stolen property. It was reported as "unsold and destroyed" to the publisher
and neither the author nor the publisher has received any payment for this
"stripped book."

To my lifetime heroes:
Ellen Gallagher Forker, my mother,
and Columb Forker, my father

Contents

Introduction

Fifty summers have rolled by since that sudden spring when Jackie Robinson broke the color barrier of "organized" baseball, but I still fondly remember, as though it were yesterday, that unusually warm April afternoon of 1946 when he first crossed the foul line of a "white" diamond.

At the time I was an avid fan of Frank Hague, the larcenous mayor of Jersey City, and a bitter foe of Jackie Robinson, the felonious base thief of the Montreal Royals.

Looking back to that eventful day, however, I find it easy to justify the prejudices of my nine-year-old self.

First, Mayor Hague had indirectly provided me with the ticket that gained me access to Roosevelt Stadium, which was filled with 26,000 pennant-waving fans on that historic occasion.

Little did I know, at the time, that Mayor Hague expected every city employee in Jersey City to buy a quota of tickets for the opening-day game every year in order to insure a sellout. He sold so many tickets, it seemed, that he could have turned people away from the Los Angeles Coliseum.

Fortunately for the grade-school baseball fans in the Jersey City–Bayonne area, not all of the people who bought tickets for the opener wished to attend it. Better still, many of them felt that they were getting at least part of their money's worth if they could give them away to appreciative young boys who would put them to their proper use. I was just one of the many grateful youths who received free tickets for the 1946 opening-day game. We proudly presented our prized possessions to the good Sisters of St. Joseph's, and we promptly got excused from all afternoon classes on that special day.

Second, I was an ardent fan of the Jersey City Giants, the Triple-A International League farm team of the parent New York Giants.

Manager Mel Ott's players were, of course, the bitter rivals of the Brooklyn Dodgers, who just happened to be the parent organization of the Montreal Royals. If you rooted for the Big Giants, you rooted for the Little Giants; if you cheered for the Dodgers, you cheered for the Royals. The rivalry was as simple as that.

So, when Jackie Robinson stepped into the batter's box in the first inning, I cheered the Jersey City Giants' pitcher and booed the Montreal Royals' second baseman. But Robinson, leaning forward like a cobra with his bat held straight up and down, seemed eager to give me a reception of his own.

And he did!

He led the Royals to a 14–1 victory with four hits, including a home run, two stolen bases, and four runs scored. By the time the game had ended, there seemed to be a lot of converts and very few Giants' fans left in the sparsely populated park.

That's the way it was back then, and in the 1950s, when we were growing up on the streets of Bayonne. From morning to night, we would form baseball comparisons that would inevitably lead to disputed deadlocks. Who's the best center fielder in New York: Joe DiMaggio, Willie Mays, or Duke Snider? Wow! Who's the best team in New York: the Yankees, the Dodgers, or the Giants? Dynamite! Who's the best manager in New York: Casey Stengel, Leo Durocher, or Charlie Dressen? Division!

I've never grown tired of talking about baseball: arguing the indefensible, conjuring up the possible, and predicting the might-have-beens. Facts, patterns, and ironic twists have always been especially appealing to me. Somehow none of it seems trivial. Anything that is connected with baseball is just too important to me.

Maybe you feel the same way! If you do, maybe you can help me. Who was that Jersey City Giants' pitcher whom I wanted to strike out Jackie Robinson, when I was young?

(Answer appears on page 343.)

Dom Forker
July 1, 1995

Chapter One

THE PRESENT-DAY PLAYERS

1. NATIONAL LEAGUE

How well do you know the accomplishments of the present-day National League players? Let's see how many of the following questions you can answer.

1. _____ Who in 1994 became the first Brave right fielder since Hank Aaron in 1973 to bat .300?

2. _____ Name the Pirate infielder who wears number 13 in honor of Venezuelan countryman Dave Concepcion?

3. _____ Whose first-year average of .318 was the highest by any National League Rookie of the Year winner since the honor was initiated in 1947? He was also the first winner to drive home 100 runs (112) in a season.

4. _____ Who in 1994 became the first Padre pitcher to lead the league in strikeouts?

5. _____ Identify the West Coast pitcher who finished runner-up in saves in both 1993 and 1994.

6. _____ Which 1994 San Francisco Giant pitcher hit .354, the highest average by a Giant moundsman since Joe Genewich of the 1929 club hit .375?

7. _____ Who in 1992 became only the second player to cop four-base crowns in both leagues?

8. _____ Who was the Expo who finished third in the 1994 batting race?

9. _____ Identify the outfielder who scored 143 runs in 1993, the most in the National League since Chuck Klein of the 1932 Phillies plated 152.

10. _____ Who in 1993 became the first Red pitcher since Ewell Blackwell in 1947 to lead the league in strikeouts?

11. _____ Which Astro pitcher no-hit the Mets in 1993?

12. _____ Name the player who tied two major league records when he hit four home runs and drove home 12 runs in a 1993 game against the Reds.

13. _____ Which player in 1994 became the third consecutive Los Angeles Dodger to win the Rookie of the Year Award?

14. _____ Identify the San Francisco Giant infielder who has driven home more runs in a season than any other club player at his position.

15. _____ Can you remember the 1994 pitcher who broke his arm while delivering a pitch against the Padres?

16. _____ Who in 1994 became only the fourth hurler since 1900 to record more wins (14) than walks (13) in a minimum of 150 innings?

17. _____ Name the 1994 Expo moundsman who amassed 15 wins quicker than any other hurler in team history.

18. _____ Identify the 1994 player who became only the ninth man in big-league history to clout 30 or more homers in seven consecutive seasons.

19. _____ Who was the youngest defending batting champ (.330 in 1992) ever to be traded?

20. _____ Can you recall the fleet-footed outfielder who led the league in stolen bases in both 1991 and 1992, his second and third full seasons in the majors?

21. _____ Who averaged 32 saves a season for the 1986–89 Reds?

22. _____ Identify the Phillie infielder who had a 66-game errorless streak in 1993.

23. _____ Who pitched the first perfect game in Reds' history?

24. _____ Which player has won six batting titles?

25. _____ Whose 40 home runs by the end of July in 1994 set a league mark?

26. _____ Name the all-time Met career home run leader.

27. _____ Can you recall the first Astro to win the Rookie of the Year Award?

28. _____ Identify the player going into the 1995 season who had led league shortstops in chances for five consecutive years.

29. _____ Who became the first player to suit up for clubs in two professional sports on the same day?

30. _____ Identify the only shortstop in the last 40 years to bat better than .300 in five consecutive (1989–93) years.

31. _____ Name the present-day National League outfielder who led the major leagues in assists with the 1991 Baltimore Orioles.

32. _____ Who set a Marlin club record by homering in four consecutive games in 1994?

33. _____ Can you recall the 1993 pitcher who became the first moundsman to win 20 games three years in a row since Ferguson Jenkins of the 1967–72 Cubs turned the trick six seasons in succession?

34. _____ Name the Marlin pitcher whose four wins in 1994 were all shutouts.

35. _____ Identify the player during the 1994 strike who lost $31,148 per day, the most of any player in the game.

36. _____ Name the Phillie infielder who, in his first major league game, played all 20 innings of a 7–6 win over the Los Angeles Dodgers.

37. _____ Which Cubbie became the first 30–30 player in team history?

38. _____ Which Red player has had .340 and .335 seasons since being dealt by the Yankees prior to the 1990 season?

39. _____ Name the first player in history to be selected to the All-Star Game at both catcher (1991) and second base (1992).

40. _____ Identify the shortstop who broke Ozzie Smith's 13-year reign as Gold Glove Award winner.

41. _____ Who became baseball's all-time career assist leader at shortstop in 1994, breaking Luis Aparicio's prior mark?

42. _____ Name the Rockie who set career highs in both homers (27) and RBI (95) in 1994.

43. _____ Whose 35 home runs in his rookie year was second only to Wally Berger (1930 Boston Braves) and Frank Robinson (1956 Reds), who each hit 38?

44. _____ Can you name the player who has hit .300 for 13 consecutive seasons, the longest string since Stan Musial topped the .300 mark for 16 successive seasons?

45. _____ Name the outfielder who didn't make an error in his first 392 games and 938 chances.

46. _____ Who became the youngest catcher to call a no-hitter since Ted Simmons received Bob Gibson's in 1971?

47. _____ Identify the 1993 Brave shortstop who became the first club player at that position to bat .300 (.305) since Alvin Dark stroked .322 in 1948.

48. _____ Who is the Expos' reliever who broke Steve Howe's rookie record for most contests (65) in 1973?

49. _____ Which Met second baseman set club records for home runs and RBI at his position in 1993?

50. _____ Can you pinpoint the Phillie who set a team mark for home runs (27) and RBI (93) by a switch-hitter?

51. _____ Which 1992–93 Phillie hit 20-plus homers and drove home 100-plus runs in back-to-back years?

52. _____ Who batted .342 and .325 in his two seasons with the Cardinals?

53. _____ Who became the first player since Carl Yastrzemski in 1967 to finish first or second in his league in batting average (.368), home runs (39), runs (104), and RBI (116)?

54. _____ Whose 18 home runs in 1993 was the most by a Pirate rookie since Ralph Kiner slugged 23 in 1946?

55. _____ Identify the Cardinal who came to the plate 416 official times in 1993 and never grounded into a double play.

56. _____ Name the Rockie who was a Rookie of the Year with the Oakland Athletics.

57. _____ Who in 1994 batted .306, hit 16 home runs, and led all major league outfielders with 16 assists?

58. _____ Whose .394 batting average was the highest league mark since Bill Terry of the New York Giants hit .401 in 1930?

59. _____ Identify the right-handed batter who averaged 34 home runs per year from 1990 to 1994.

60. _____ Which Astro pitcher went 18–4 with an .818 winning percentage in 1993?

61. _____ Name the player who has won three MVP awards.

62. _____ Whose 23-game hitting streak in 1994 was the longest in the league since Jerome Walton of the 1989 Cubs batted safely in 30 consecutive contests?

63. _____ Who in 1990 became the youngest Dodger pitcher to win 20 games since Ralph Branca did it with Brooklyn in 1947?

64. _____ Identify the Rockie who was the first player to be selected in the expansion draft, from the Braves.

65. _____ Name the Cardinal who saved a club-high 40 games for the Rangers in 1993.

66. _____ Who in 1993 became the first rookie to lead the Pirates in strikeouts since Bill Werle in 1949?

67. _____ Identify the 1994 rookie who became just the fifth player in major league history to begin the season in the minors, yet be selected to the All-Star team.

68. _____ Can you recall the pitcher who went from 20–8 with the 1991 Pirates to 3–9 with the 1993 Reds?

69. _____ Who is the grandson of Ray and the son of Bob, both of whom were major league players?

70. _____ Whose 53 saves in 1993 set a league record?

71. _____ Name the Phillie who pitched a complete game shutout against the Blue Jays in the 1993 World Series.

72. _____ Can you pinpoint the pitcher who set the modern-day record by granting just 0.7 walks per nine innings in 1994?

73. _____ Identify the Expo pitcher who was signed by his uncle, Jesus Alou, in 1985.

74. _____ Do you know the only pitcher to save 45 games in a season in both leagues?

75. _____ Name the youngest hurler in Brave history to record 50 career wins.

76. _____ Whose 17 home runs in 1994 all came off right-handed pitching?

77. _____ Name the 1994 Phillie who recorded his 1,000th career strikeout and his 100th career win.

78. _____ Name the Expo shortstop who set a club record for home runs in 1994.

79. _____ Who in 1993 set a club record for catchers by playing in 113 consecutive errorless games?

80. _____ Name the .320 hitter with six home runs and 11 RBI in 13 World Series games.

81. _____ Can you recall the Bruin who 12 times has had consecutive-game hitting streaks in double digits?

82. _____ Who in 1985 became the first rookie pitcher to win 20 games since Bob Grim of the Yankees in 1954?

83. _____ Whose three intentional passes by the Pirates in one game in 1994 set a league mark?

84. _____ Identify the player who won the league batting title while grounding into a league-high 20 double plays.

85. _____ Name the infielder who started in a record 10 consecutive All-Star games at his position.

86. _____ Do you know the 1994 Rookie pitcher who paced the circuit with an .833 winning percentage?

87. _____ Who became the first Dodger to hit 20 or more home runs in each of his first two seasons?

88. _____ Name the left-handed hitter who slugged 34 home runs in his first National League season.

89. _____ Who along with his father is a partner in the all-time father-son homer record? (Going into the 1995 season, they had combined for 591.)

90. _____ Identify the player who twice hit a club-high 39 home runs in a season for the Mets.

91. _____ Whose 18 strikeouts in a single game tied Sandy Koufax's prior team mark?

92. _____ Can you recall the Cardinal pitcher who won his first six major league decisions and then dropped his next seven verdicts to end the year with a 6–7 mark?

93. _____ Name the former American Leaguer who fired eight and two-thirds innings of no-hit ball in his first National League game.

94. _____ Who has hit .300 with the Indians, Giants, and Dodgers?

95. _____ Who is the National League catcher who turned in a .999 fielding percentage in 1992?

96. _____ Identify the former Expo reliever who broke Jeff Reardon's club record (41) for saves.

97. _____ Do you recall the Marlin reliever who converted his first 15 save chances?

98. _____ Who is the Brave pitcher who is 5 in ten post-season starts?

99. _____ Whose 1.56 ERA was a record 1.0 lower than the next major league pitcher?

100. _____ Name the pitcher whose 16 sac-bunts tied for the league lead in 1994.

2. THE AMERICAN LEAGUE

1. _____ Who tied the major league record of Dale Long and Don Mattingly when he hit a home run in each of eight consecutive games?

2. _____ Whose father was an outstanding wide receiver for the Los Angeles Rams?

3. _____ Name the first baseman who had 100 RBI seasons his first two years in the majors.

4. _____ Which pitcher won Cy Young awards in back-to-back seasons?

5. _____ Identify the pitcher who threw a perfect game in 1994.

6. _____ Can you recall the Oakland A pitcher who once won 12 games in a row with another team?

7 _____ Name the Twin pitcher who threw a no-hitter in 1994.

8. _____ Who going into the 1995 season had led the Brewers in home runs four years in a row?

9. _____ Can you pinpoint the certain Hall of Famer who going into the 1995 season had been on the roster of five different organizations in five years?

_____ Name the pitcher who was 35–10 in ?2–94.

_____ Identify the last player to hit 50 ?e runs in a season.

_____ Who is the former Seton Hall player who led the American League with 20 intentional walks in 1994?

13. _____ Which Oriole has been the only Bird to win two MVP awards?

14. _____ Which player stole 31 bases in 32 attempts in 1994, the best mark in history for a base sleuth with at least 25 steals?

15. _____ Name the player who converted the tenth unassisted triple play in major league history in 1994.

8

_____ Identify the player, who now plays for the St. Louis Cardinals, whom the Red Sox kept in place of Wade Boggs and Jeff Bagwell.

_____ Who won the 1995 Rookie of the Year Award?

_____ Which player was a .259 hitter in six seasons in the National League before he became a .335 batter in his first two years in the American League?

_____ Who holds the league record for hitting three home runs in a game five times?

_____ Who became the first back-to-back MVP winner since Roger Maris of the Yankees in 1960 and 1961?

_____ Name the only present-day second baseman to twice hit 20 home runs and drive home 100 runs in a season.

_____ Which Rookie of the Year Award winner was sent to the minors early in the following season?

_____ Identify the Brewer pitcher who once won ten games in a row.

_____ Who is the Red Sox reliever who saved two games and won one in the 1991 World Series?

_____ Which pitcher has won six Gold Gloves?

_____ Can you name the pitcher who has thrown a no-hitter, posted a 20-win season, and saved more than 300 games?

_____ Name the only pitcher of today to strike out 300 batters in a season.

_____ Who in 1995 became the only player in either league to hit 50 home runs and 50 doubles in the same season?

_____ Name the 24-year-old catcher who has played in four All-Star games in his five-year major league career.

_____ Name the batting champ whose average dipped 66 points to .297 the following year?

_____ Who is the only Mariner to win a batting title?

32. _____ Identify the MVP and Cy Youn⟩ Award winner who once saved 51 of 54 games in ⟨ season.

33. _____ Who in 1995 became the first Ya⟨ kee since Bobby Murcer to hit for the cycle?

34. _____ Which Twin once won a batting titl⟨

35. _____ Identify the first Brewer startin⟩ pitcher since Teddy Higuera in 1986 to make the A⟨ Star team.

36. _____ Can you zero in on the Royal r⟨ liever who saved 45 games in 1993?

37. _____ Who is one of six pitchers to win ⟨ least 100 games in each league?

38. _____ Can you recall the 1993–94 Whi⟨ Sox pitcher who went 24–7 in his first two years in th⟨ majors?

39. _____ Which pitcher in 1993 set the leagu⟨ record for wild pitches in one season with 26?

40. _____ Name the former White Sox pitche⟨ who won 20 games in back-to-back years with th⟨ Pale Hose.

41. _____ Identify the Tigers' all-time caree⟨ save leader.

42. _____ Who is the only 40-home run, 4⟨ base theft man in history?

43. _____ Which Oriole catcher became onl⟨ one of five receivers in league history to hit 25 home⟨ and bat .300?

44. _____ One other catcher belongs to th⟨ above group. Who is he?

45. _____ Identify the all-time career home ru⟨ king at shortstop in the junior circuit.

46. _____ Can you recall the outfielder wh⟨ was drafted by an owner who admired his Littl⟨ League play?

47. _____ Whose lifetime .712 winning percent⟨ age going into the 1995 season was the best in Oriol⟨ history for a pitcher with a minimum of 50 decisions?

48. _____ Name the player who had a fly bal⟨ bounce off his head and over the fence for a home ru⟨ against Cleveland in 1993.

9. _____ He averaged 38 home runs a season from 1990 to 1994, but he hasn't stolen a base in his nine-year career. Who is he?

0. _____ Who is the Yankee who won a batting title one year and an MVP Award the following season?

1. _____ Who is the shortstop who fielded a league-record .996 in 1990?

2. _____ Identify the player who has hit more home runs in one season than any other White Sox player.

3. _____ Name the player who became the first Indian to hit 30-plus home runs for four straight seasons.

4. _____ Who in 1995 finished runner-up in the closest Rookie of the Year Award contest in 16 years?

5. _____ Who tied a league mark by gaining his 20th career win in only his 30th appearance?

6. _____ Can you recall the Mariner pitcher who was traded to the Expos for Randy Johnson?

7. _____ Which player hit a rookie-record 49 home runs in one year?

8. _____ Name the only man to play in a major league game with his father.

9. _____ Can you name the player whose home run production fell from 46 in 1993 to 19 in 1994?

0. _____ Whose 42 steals in 1994 were the most by a Red Sox since Tommy Harper of the 1973 BoSox pilfered a club-record 54?

1. _____ Which Mariner pitcher no-hit the Red Sox in 1994?

2. _____ Who has stolen 100 or more bases three times?

3. _____ Name the reliever who combined to save 46 games for the Cardinals and Yankees in 1993.

4. _____ Identify the Twin who won the Rookie of the Year Award in 1991.

5. _____ Can you name the 1994 Cy Young Award winner?

6. _____ Which pitcher goes by the nickname "El Presidente"?

67. _____ Who topped the 3,000-hit mark 1993?

68. _____ Do you remember the 1994 play who was suspended for six games for corking his bat

69. _____ Name the center fielder who we from one home run in 1993 to 12 in 1994.

70. _____ Identify the player who in 1995 w closing in on 800 career stolen bases.

71. _____ Which Blue Jay pitcher going in the 1995 season had more career strikeouts than i nings pitched?

72. _____ Who holds the Yankee single-seas stolen base record?

73. _____ Whose Gold Glove in 1994 was the fi over a 14-year career? (He's always had some silver in bat.)

74. _____ Name the player who is one of on two Tigers to play 2,000 games, collect 2,000 hits, a slug 200 homers. (The other Bengal is Al Kaline.)

75. _____ Whose 6–0 start in 1993 tied a R Sox club record?

76. _____ Who is the Oriole slugger who ave aged 27 home runs a season from 1991 to 1994?

77. _____ Which versatile Red Sox infielde played all four positions in 1994?

78. _____ Identify the only player to win tl MVP, the All-Star Game MVP, and the Cy Your Award in the same season.

79. _____ Can you recollect the only player t hit 50 home runs in his first full season?

80. _____ Who is the Mariner who in 1993 h a grand slam in back-to-back games?

81. _____ Who stroked 200 or more hits in a American League record seven consecutive seasons?

82. _____ Name the former Tiger (and currer California Angel) who has played every position excep catcher and pitcher.

83. _____ Identify the Yankee whose .359 bat ting average was the highest by a Pinstriper sinc Mickey Mantle of the 1957 Bombers hit .365.

. _____ Who batted .500 en route to the World Series MVP Award in 1993?

. _____ Can you zero in on the White Sox infielder who averaged 20 homers and 91 RBI per season from 1991 to 1994?

. _____ Who moved into the select 3,000-Hit Club in 1995?

. _____ Name the player whose autobiography is titled *I Love This Game*.

. _____ Identify the Angel outfielder who hit 54 home runs in his first two major league seasons.

. _____ Do you know the only player to hit 30 or more home runs in each of his first four seasons?

. _____ Whose 32 wins in 1993–94 ranked second in the American League to Jimmy Key's 35?

. _____ Identify the Mariner right-handed hitter who averaged 25 home runs and 81 RBI from 1991 to 1994.

2. _____ Name the Mariner who shares the major league record for sacrifices (4) in a game.

3. _____ Who is the tallest player in major league history?

4. _____ Can you remember the Red Sox pitcher who allowed just one run in 21 road appearances in 1994?

5. _____ Identify the Yankee who got his 1,000th career hit at Yankee Stadium in 1995.

6. _____ Who became the oldest player (36) to hit 20 home runs and steal 20 bases in the same season?

7. _____ Which player became the oldest (36) to drive home 100 runs in a season for the first time?

8. _____ In 1994 he became the tenth player to steal his 200th base and hit his 300th home run. Who is he?

9. _____ Name the Blue Jay who won his sixth Gold Glove in 1994.

0. _____ Who is the American League East pitcher who is 5–0 in League Championship Series?

3. PRESENT-DAY GOLD GLOVE CHAMP

The number in the middle of the column is the numb
of Gold Gloves each present-day leader has. Match t
number with the correct players. The National League h
a tie at four positions during this era. The Americ
League has a tie at one spot. All of the names are list
Both leagues are tied at one position.

1B	Mark Grace Andres Galarraga	(9)	Don Mattingly
2B	Jose Lind Robby Thompson Craig Biggio	(4)	Robby Alomar
3B	Tim Wallach Matt Williams	(4)	Gary Gaetti
SS	Ozzie Smith	(13)	Alan Trammell Tony Fernandez
OF	Andre Dawson	(8)	Dave Winfield*
OF	Tony Gwynn	(6)	Kirby Puckett
OF	Bobby Bonds	(6)	Devon White
C	Tony Pena* Benito Santiago Tom Pagnozzi	(3)	Ivan Rodriguez
P	Greg Maddux	(6)	Mark Langston

* See answer page.

4. THEY WENT TO SCHOOL AT . . .

Match the players in the left-hand column with the colleges and universities for which they played in the right-hand column.

1. _____ Mo Vaughn	a.	U. of Arkansas
2. _____ Roger Clemens	b.	Seton Hall
3. _____ Kirk Gibson	c.	U. of Nevada–Las
4. _____ Robin Ventura		Vegas
5. _____ Mike Stanley	d.	U. of Texas
6. _____ John Olerud	e.	Yale
7. _____ Frank Thomas	f.	Mississippi State
8. _____ Albert Belle	g.	San Diego State
9. _____ Kenny Lofton	h.	U. of Tennessee
0. _____ Dave Winfield	i.	Texas A&M
1. _____ Eric Karros	j.	U. of Georgia
2. _____ Chuck Knoblauch	k.	Michigan State
3. _____ Mike Bordick	l.	Auburn
4. _____ Ron Darling	m.	San Jose State
5. _____ Tino Martinez	n.	Florida State
6. _____ Dave Fleming	o.	St. John's
7. _____ Will Clark	p.	Washington State
8. _____ John Franco	q.	Oklahoma State U.
9. _____ Deion Sanders	r.	LSU
0. _____ Barry Larkin	s.	U. of Tampa
1. _____ Ken Caminiti	t.	U. of Maine
2. _____ Jeff King	u.	U. of Arizona
3. _____ Delino DeShields	v.	U. of Florida
4. _____ Tony Gwynn	w.	U. of Minnesota
5. _____ Matt Williams	x.	UCLA
	y.	U. of Michigan

Ruth's Shadow

Babe Ruth captured the attention of the nation on October 2, 1932, for on that historic day he allegedly "called his shot."

The Yankees had won the first two games of the World Series before traveling to Chicago's Wrigley Field. The Cub fans and players were riding Ruth unmercifully for criticizing the Bruin players for failing to award former Yankee infielder Mark Koenig a full share of their series cut.

But Ruth relished the attention.

In the first inning Earle Combs reached second on a two-base throwing error by shortstop Billy Jurges. Bruin pitcher Charlie Root, obviously upset, proceeded to walk Joe Sewell, something he did not want to do with Ruth coming to the plate. On a 2–0 count, Ruth cracked a three-run homer.

The third time that Ruth came to the plate, in the fifth inning, the Yankees were leading, 4–3. In the interim, he had misplayed a ball in right field, much to the delight of the Cub supporters. Before Root got a chance to pitch to the Babe in the fifth, Ruth allegedly pointed his bat toward the center-field bleachers, saying, in effect, "This is where the ball is going to land." The stage had been set for one of the most dramatic moments in baseball history.

Ruth deliberately took two strikes, which he dutifully noted by raising first one finger and then a second one after the calls. Then he proceeded to deposit the ball in the exact spot to which he had pointed his bat. Coincidentally, that was the 15th and last home run that Ruth hit in series play.

Lost in the fanfare of that day were the exploits of another Yankee, who hit two home runs, including the game-winner.

Who was this Yankee great who played in the shadow of Ruth?

(Answer appears on page 343.)

Chapter Two

THE HITTERS

5. HOW GOOD IS .300?

Twenty of the following 40 players have won at least one
batting title, though they have lifetime averages of less than
.300; the other twenty players have lifetime averages of .300
or better, though they have never won a batting title. Put
the batting champs in the left-hand column and the .300
hitters in the right-hand column.

Mickey Mantle	Lou Boudreau
Johnny Pesky	Mickey Vernon
Enos Slaughter	Debs Garms
Tommy Davis	Sam Rice
Norm Cash	Heinie Zimmerman
Joe Cronin	Dale Mitchell
Hal Chase	Pete Reiser
George Stirnweiss	Larry Doyle
Carl Yastrzemski	Hank Greenberg
Mel Ott	Ferris Fain
Bill Dickey	Alex Johnson
Pete Runnels	Eddie Collins
Bobby Avila	Phil Cavarretta
Lloyd Waner	Earle Combs
Harry Walker	Carl Furillo
Bob Meusel	Babe Herman
Joe Jackson	Kiki Cuyler
Hack Wilson	Frankie Frisch
Earl Averill	Pie Traynor
Dick Groat	Mickey Cochrane

Batting Champs

1. _____
2. _____
3. _____
4. _____
5. _____
6. _____
7. _____
8. _____
9. _____
10. _____
11. _____
12. _____
13. _____
14. _____
15. _____
16. _____
17. _____
18. _____
19. _____
20. _____

.300 Hitters

1. _____
2. _____
3. _____
4. _____
5. _____
6. _____
7. _____
8. _____
9. _____
10. _____
11. _____
12. _____
13. _____
14. _____
15. _____
16. _____
17. _____
18. _____
19. _____
20. _____

6. WHO DID IT TWICE?

National League

Five of the following ten players have won one National League batting title; the other five have won two. List the one-time winners in the left-hand column and the two-time winners in the right-hand column: Willie Mays, Lefty O'Doul, Tommy Davis, Harry Walker, Dixie Walker, Henry Aaron, Carl Furillo, Jackie Robinson, Ernie Lombardi, and Richie Ashburn.

_____	1. _____
_____	2. _____
_____	3. _____
_____	4. _____
_____	5. _____

American League

Five of the following ten players have won one American League batting title; the other five have won two. List the one-time winners in the left-hand column and the two-time winners in the right-hand column: George Kell, Al Kaline, Jimmie Foxx, Norm Cash, Luke Appling, Mickey Vernon, Mickey Mantle, Pete Runnels, Ferris Fain, and Harvey Kuenn.

_____	1. _____
_____	2. _____
_____	3. _____
_____	4. _____
_____	5. _____

7. THE FABULOUS FIFTIES

Twelve players have hit a total of 50 or more home run in one season: Cecil Fielder, Willie Mays, Mickey Mantle Hank Greenberg, George Foster, Jimmie Foxx, Roge Maris, Johnny Mize, Ralph Kiner, Hack Wilson, Alber Belle, and Babe Ruth. They have done it a total of 1 times. One of them accomplished the feat four times. Fou of them achieved it twice. Place them in the order of thei single-season rank. Totals, years, and leagues are given a clues.

1. _____ (61) 1961 (AL)
2. _____ (60) 1927 (AL)
3. _____ (59) 1921 (AL)
4. _____ (58) 1932 (AL)
5. _____ (58) 1938 (AL)
6. _____ (56) 1930 (NL)
7. _____ (54) 1920 (AL)
8. _____ (54) 1928 (AL)
9. _____ (54) 1949 (NL)
10. _____ (54) 1961 (AL)
11. _____ (52) 1956 (AL)
12. _____ (52) 1965 (NL)
13. _____ (52) 1977 (NL)
14. _____ (51) 1947 (NL)
15. _____ (51) 1947 (NL)
16. _____ (51) 1955 (NL)
17. _____ (51) 1990 (AL)
18. _____ (50) 1938 (NL)
19. _____ (50) 1995 (AL)

8. THE (500) HOME RUN CLUB

There have been 14 players who have hit more than 500 home runs in their careers. See how many of them you can name. Their respective totals are listed in parentheses. None of them is active.

1. _____ (755)
2. _____ (714)
3. _____ (660)
4. _____ (586)
5. _____ (573)
6. _____ (563)
7. _____ (548)
8. _____ (536)
9. _____ (534)
10. _____ (521)
11. _____ (521)
12. _____ (512)
13. _____ (512)
14. _____ (511)

9. THEY HIT FOR POWER AND AVERAGE

National League

Five National League players have won both the home run crown and the batting title in the same year. One of them did it twice. Match the following players with the year(s) in which they performed the feat: Joe Medwick, Johnny Mize, Heinie Zimmerman, Rogers Hornsby (2), and Chuck Klein.

1. _____ (1912)
2. _____ (1922)
3. _____ (1925)
4. _____ (1933)
5. _____ (1937)
6. _____ (1939)

American League

Do the same with the following nine American Leaguers: Ted Williams (3), Lou Gehrig, Nap Lajoie, Mickey Mantle, Babe Ruth, Ty Cobb, Jimmie Foxx, Carl Yastrzemski, and Frank Robinson.

1. _____ (1901)
2. _____ (1909)
3. _____ (1924)
4. _____ (1933)
5. _____ (1934)
6. _____ (1941)
7. _____ (1942)
8. _____ (1947)
9. _____ (1956)
10. _____ (1966)
11. _____ (1967)

10. THE 3,000-HIT CLUB

The following 20 players have accumulated 3,000 or more, major league hits: Rod Carew, Robin Yount, Al Kaline, Tris Speaker, Carl Yastrzemski, Ty Cobb, Honus Wagner, Roberto Clemente, Eddie Collins, Stan Musial, Hank Aaron, Nap Lajoie, Pete Rose, Paul Waner, Cap Anson, Lou Brock, Willie Mays, Dave Winfield, Eddie Murray, and George Brett. Their respective totals are included. Place the players in their proper order.

1. _____ (4,256)
2. _____ (4,189)
3. _____ (3,771)
4. _____ (3,630)
5. _____ (3,514)
6. _____ (3,419)
7. _____ (3,415)
8. _____ (3,415)
9. _____ (3,312)
10. _____ (3,283)
11. _____ (3,242)
12. _____ (3,154)
13. _____ (3,152)
14. _____ (3,142)
15. _____ (3,110)
16. _____ (3,071)
17. _____ (3,053)
18. _____ (3,023)
19. _____ (3,007)
20. _____ (3,000)

11. TRIPLE CROWN WINNERS

Eleven players have won the Triple Crown a total of 13 times: Ted Williams (2), Rogers Hornsby (2), Carl Yastrzemski, Mickey Mantle, Ty Cobb, Frank Robinson, Jimmie Foxx, Joe Medwick, Lou Gehrig, Chuck Klein, and Nap Lajoie. Fit them into the respective years in which they won the select award.

1. _____ (1901)
2. _____ (1909)
3. _____ (1922)
4. _____ (1925)
5. _____ (1933)
6. _____ (1933)
7. _____ (1934)
8. _____ (1937)
9. _____ (1942)
10. _____ (1947)
11. _____ (1956)
12. _____ (1966)
13. _____ (1967)

12. HIGHEST LIFETIME AVERAGE FOR POSITION

Identify the player, from the three listed at each position, who has hit for the highest lifetime average. At one position two players are tied for the lead.

National League

1B	_____	(.341) Bill Terry, Johnny Mize, or Stan Musial
2B	_____	(.359) Frankie Frisch, Jackie Robinson or Rogers Hornsby
SS	_____	(.327) Arky Vaughan, Honus Wagner, or Travis Jackson
3B	_____	(.320) Joe Torre, Heinie Zimmerman, or Pie Traynor
OF	_____	(.336) Chuck Klein, Harry Walker, or Riggs Stephenson
OF	_____	(.333) Paul Waner, Babe Herman, or Zack Wheat
OF	_____	(.349) Kiki Cuyler, Stan Musial, or Lefty O'Doul
C	_____	(.310) Eugene Hargrave, Gabby Hartnett, or Roy Campanella

American League

1B	_____	(.340) Lou Gehrig, Jimmie Foxx, or George Sisler
2B	_____	(.338) Nap Lajoie, Charlie Gehringer, or Eddie Collins
SS	_____	(.314) Joe Cronin, Cecil Travis, or Luke Appling
3B	_____	(.307) George Kell, Frank Baker, or Jimmy Collins

OF _____ (.367) Harry Heilmann, Tris Speaker, or Ty Cobb

OF _____ (.356) Babe Ruth, Al Simmons, or Joe Jackson

OF _____ (.344) Joe DiMaggio, Ted Williams, or Heinie Manush

C _____ (.320) Mickey Cochrane, Yogi Berra, or Bill Dickey

13. HIGHEST SINGLE SEASON AVERAGE FOR POSITION

Identify the player, from the three listed at each position, who has hit for the highest average in a single season.

National League

1B _____ (.401) Bill Terry, Johnny Mize, or Stan Musial

2B _____ (.424) Frankie Frisch, Jackie Robinson, or Rogers Hornsby

SS _____ (.385) Arky Vaughan, Honus Wagner, or Travis Jackson

3B _____ (.379) Joe Torre, Fred Lindstrom, or Pie Traynor

OF _____ (.398) Paul Waner, Fred Lindstrom, or Lefty O'Doul

OF _____ (.394) Tony Gwynn, Chuck Klein, or Zack Wheat

OF _____ (.393) Stan Musial, Babe Herman, or Roberto Clemente

C _____ (.358) Ernie Lombardi, Gabby Hartnett, or Chief Meyers

American League

1B _____ (.420) Lou Gehrig, Jimmie Foxx, or George Sisler

2B _____ (.422) Nap Lajoie, Charlie Gehringer, or Eddie Collins

SS _____ (.388) Joe Cronin, Cecil Travis, or Luke Appling

3B _____ (.390) George Kell, Frank Baker, or George Brett

OF _____ (.420) Harry Heilmann, Tris Speaker, or Ty Cobb
OF _____ (.408) Babe Ruth, Al Simmons, or Joe Jackson
OF _____ (.406) Sam Crawford, Ted Williams, or Heinie Manush
C _____ (.362) Mickey Cochrane, Yogi Berra, or Bill Dickey

14. THE YEAR THEY HIT THE HEIGHTS

Take the following ten hitters and match them up with their highest respective season's batting average: Babe Ruth, Jackie Robinson, Stan Musial, Rogers Hornsby, Charlie Keller, Ted Williams, Roberto Clemente, Ty Cobb, Joe DiMaggio, and Mickey Mantle.

1. _____ (.424)		6. _____ (.376)
2. _____ (.420)		7. _____ (.365)
3. _____ (.406)		8. _____ (.357)
4. _____ (.393)		9. _____ (.342)
5. _____ (.381)		10. _____ (.334)

15. MATCHING AVERAGES

Match the following ten players with their corresponding lifetime averages listed below: Rogers Hornsby, Babe Ruth, Honus Wagner, Ty Cobb, Stan Musial, Jimmie Foxx, Tris Speaker, Mickey Cochrane, Mel Ott, and Bill Terry.

1. _____ (.367)		6. _____ (.331)
2. _____ (.359)		7. _____ (.327)
3. _____ (.344)		8. _____ (.325)
4. _____ (.342)		9. _____ (.320)
5. _____ (.341)		10. _____ (.304)

16. ONCE IS NOT ENOUGH

Nine of the following sluggers have hit four home runs in a major league game: Babe Ruth, Lou Gehrig, Rocky Colavito, Mark Whiten, Hank Aaron, Gil Hodges, Pat Seerey, Mickey Mantle, Jimmie Foxx, Joe Adcock, Mike Schmidt, Willie Mays, Joe DiMaggio, Bob Horner, Hank Greenberg, and Reggie Jackson. Who are they?

1. _____   6. _____
2. _____   7. _____
3. _____   8. _____
4. _____   9. _____
5. _____

17. NATIONAL LEAGUE HOME RUN KINGS

Match the following National League home run champs with the number of times they have won the crown: Barry Bonds, Johnny Mize, Ralph Kiner, Duke Snider, Eddie Mathews, Johnny Bench, Mike Schmidt, Mel Ott, and Fred McGriff.

1. _____ (8)   6. _____ (2)
2. _____ (7)   7. _____ (1)
3. _____ (6)   8. _____ (1)
4. _____ (4)   9. _____ (1)
5. _____ (2)

18. AMERICAN LEAGUE HOME RUN KINGS

Match the following American League home run champs with the number of times they have won the crown: Roger Maris, Lou Gehrig, Frank Howard, Babe Ruth, Jose Canseco, Carl Yastrzemski, Jimmie Foxx, Joe DiMaggio, Jim Rice, Harmon Killebrew, Frank Baker, Hank Greenberg, George Scott, Reggie Jackson, Graig Nettles, Ted Williams, Gorman Thomas, Juan Gonzalez, Mickey Mantle, and Dick Allen.

1. _____ (12)   11. _____ (2)
2. _____ (6)   12. _____ (2)
3. _____ (4)   13. _____ (2)
4. _____ (4)   14. _____ (2)
5. _____ (4)   15. _____ (2)
6. _____ (4)   16. _____ (2)
7. _____ (4)   17. _____ (1)
8. _____ (4)   18. _____ (1)
9. _____ (3)   19. _____ (1)
10. _____ (3)   20. _____ (1)

19. WOULD YOU PINCH-HIT?

Some of the best pinch-hitters in the history of the game are listed with their averages as substitute batters. Were their lifetime averages higher (Yes-No) than their pinch-hitting marks? One of the player's lifetime average and pinch-hitting average were the same.

1. _____ (.320) Tommy Davis
2. _____ (.312) Frenchy Bordagaray
3. _____ (.307) Frankie Baumholtz
4. _____ (.303) Red Schoendienst
5. _____ (.300) Bob Fothergill
6. _____ (.299) Dave Philley
7. _____ (.297) Manny Mota
8. _____ (.286) Steve Braun
9. _____ (.283) Johnny Mize
10. _____ (.280) Don Mueller
11. _____ (.279) Mickey Vernon
12. _____ (.278) Gene Woodling
13. _____ (.277) Bobby Adams
14. _____ (.277) Ed Kranepool
15. _____ (.276) Jose Morales
16. _____ (.276) Ron Northey
17. _____ (.273) Sam Leslie
18. _____ (.273) Pat Kelly
19. _____ (.273) Debs Garms
20. _____ (.270) Peanuts Lowrey

20. DECADES OF BATTING CHAMPS

Listed below is one batting champ from each decade and the year in which he led the league. All you have to provide is the team for which he did it.

National League

1. _____ (1908) Honus Wagner
2. _____ (1917) Edd Roush
3. _____ (1929) Lefty O'Doul
4. _____ (1938) Ernie Lombardi
5. _____ (1945) Phil Cavarretta
6. _____ (1953) Carl Furillo
7. _____ (1968) Pete Rose
8. _____ (1970) Rico Carty
9. _____ (1982) Al Oliver
10. _____ (1992) Gary Sheffield

American League

1. _____ (1902) Ed Delahanty
2. _____ (1916) Tris Speaker
3. _____ (1923) Harry Heilmann
4. _____ (1936) Luke Appling
5. _____ (1945) George Stirnweiss
6. _____ (1951) Ferris Fain
7. _____ (1962) Pete Runnels
8. _____ (1970) Alex Johnson
9. _____ (1981) Carney Lansford
10. _____ (1991) Julio Franco

21. SUB-.320 BATTING LEADERS

Name the seven players from the following 14 who have won batting titles with averages that were less than .320: George Stirnweiss, Tony Oliva, Roberto Clemente, Rod Carew, Carl Yastrzemski, Ted Williams, Pete Runnels, Frank Robinson, Alex Johnson, Elmer Flick, Kirby Puckett, Terry Pendleton, Tony Gwynn, and Bobby Bonds. Match the players with the respective averages and years.

1. _____ (.319) 1991
2. _____ (.318) 1972
3. _____ (.316) 1966
4. _____ (.313) 1988
5. _____ (.309) 1945
6. _____ (.306) 1905
7. _____ (.301) 1968

22. .390-PLUS RUNNERS-UP

Name the five players from the following ten who have failed to win batting titles with averages that were better than .390: Harry Heilmann, George Sisler, Babe Ruth, Joe Jackson, Ted Williams, Rogers Hornsby, Al Simmons, Ty Cobb, Babe Herman, and Bill Terry.

1. _____ (.408) 1911
2. _____ (.401) 1922
3. _____ (.393) 1923
4. _____ (.393) 1930
5. _____ (.392) 1927

23. STEPPING INTO THE BOX

In front of the 30 players who are listed, mark an "L" (left-handed), "R" (right-handed), or "S" (switch-hitter) for the way in which they hit.

1. _____ Mel Ott
2. _____ Ernie Lombardi
3. _____ Tom Tresh
4. _____ Tony Lazzeri
5. _____ Pete Rose
6. _____ Willard Marshall
7. _____ Jim Gilliam
8. _____ Wally Westlake
9. _____ Jim Gentile
10. _____ Bud Harrelson
11. _____ Granny Hamner
12. _____ Tommy Holmes
13. _____ George McQuinn
14. _____ Hector Lopez
15. _____ Smoky Burgess
16. _____ Wes Covington
17. _____ Phil Masi
18. _____ Sid Gordon
19. _____ Willie Miranda
20. _____ Maury Wills
21. _____ Nellie Fox
22. _____ Jimmie Foxx
23. _____ Red Schoendienst
24. _____ Eddie Waitkus
25. _____ Sam Mele
26. _____ Frankie Frisch
27. _____ Gino Cimoli
28. _____ Jim Rivera
29. _____ Mickey Mantle
30. _____ Roy White

The Shot Heard 'Round the World

Bobby Thomson's game-winning home run in the final playoff game of the 1951 season gave the Giants the most dramatic come-from-behind title in the history of baseball. It also provided trivia buffs with a gold mine of facts and questions.

Sal Maglie started the game for the Giants; Don Newcombe toed the mound for the Dodgers. They hooked up in a classic pitching duel until the eighth inning when the visiting Dodgers scored three runs to take a 4–1 lead. With Maglie departed from the scene and Newcombe mowing down the Giants in the bottom of the eighth, the Dodgers seemed virtually assured of winning their sixth National League pennant. But the Giants, who had fought back from a 13½-game deficit during the regular season, were not about to give up.

Al Dark led off the bottom of the ninth by singling to center. Charlie Dressen, the manager of the Dodgers, made a tactical mistake when he did not tell first baseman Gil Hodges to play behind the runner, for Don Mueller ripped a single to right, sending Dark to third. If Hodges had been playing deep, Mueller would have hit into a double play, and the Dodgers would have cinched the pennant, for Monte Irvin, the following batter, popped out. Whitey Lockman then ripped a double, scoring Dark and sending Mueller to third. Sliding into the base, Mueller broke his ankle and was replaced by pinch-runner Clint Hartung. That brought Thomson up to the plate with a free base at first. Had Dressen chosen to put the potential winning run on base, the Giants would have had to send a rookie up to the plate—Willie Mays.

Instead Dressen decided to change pitchers. He had Carl Erskine and Ralph Branca warming up in the bull pen. Erskine had looked the sharper of the two, but just before bull pen Coach Clyde Sukeforth made his recommendation to Dressen, Erskine bounced a curve. That settled the matter: Branca got the call. When Branca walked in from the bull pen, some of the superstitious "faithful" from Flatbush must have got an ominous feeling when they noted the number "13" on the back of the pitcher's uniform. Coincidentally, Branca had 13 wins at the time. He also had 12 losses. After his second pitch to Thomson, which the "Staten Island Scot" hit for the pennant-winning homer, the 13's were balanced, all the way across.

Almost all of baseball's avid followers of the sport know that Branca was the losing pitcher in that fateful game. But I've run across very few baseball aficionados who know who the winning pitcher was. Do you?

(Answer appears on page 343.)

Chapter Three

THE PITCHERS

24. FAMOUS HOME RUN PITCHES

Match the following pitchers with the batters to whom they threw historic home run pitches: Mitch Williams, Dennis Eckersley, Don Newcombe, Bob Purkey, Bob Lemon, Ralph Terry, Howie Pollett, Robin Roberts, Ralph Branca, Jack Billingham, Al Downing, Barney Schultz, and Charlie Leibrandt.

1. _____ He threw the home run pitch to Bill Mazeroski that gave the Pirates the 1960 World Series. The circuit clout gave Pittsburgh a 10–9 win.
2. _____ He threw the game-winning home run pitch to Joe DiMaggio in the top of the tenth inning in the second game of the 1950 World Series. The Yankees won, 2–1.
3. _____ He threw the home run pitch to Bobby Thomson in the final playoff game of the National League's 1951 season. The Giants outlasted the Dodgers, 5–4.
4. _____ He threw the three-run homer to Dick Sisler in the top of the tenth inning of the final game of the 1950 season. The home run gave Robin Roberts the margin of victory, and it gave the Phillies the National League pennant.
5. _____ He threw the pitch that Hank Aaron hit for home run number 714.
6. _____ He threw the pitch that Hank Aaron hit for home run number 715.

7. _____ He threw the tenth-inning home run pitch to Rudy York in the first game of the 1946 World Series. It gave the Red Sox a 3–2 victory.

8. _____ He threw the ninth-inning home run pitch to Mickey Mantle in the third game of the 1964 World Series. It gave the Yankees a 2–1 victory.

9. _____ He threw the three-run homer to Dusty Rhodes in the bottom of the tenth inning in Game One of the 1954 World Series. The blow gave the Giants a 5–2 victory.

10. _____ He threw the ninth-inning home run pitch to Roger Maris in the third game of the 1961 World Series. The home run gave the Yankees a 3–2 win.

11. _____ He threw the two-out, two-run, pinch-hit home run to Kirk Gibson in the bottom of the ninth inning of Game One of the 1988 World Series to give the Los Angeles Dodgers a dramatic come-from-behind 5–4 win over the A's.

12. _____ He threw the lead-off homer to Kirby Puckett in the bottom of the 11th inning of Game Six in 1992 to give the Twins a 4–3 win that knotted the Series at three against the Braves.

13. _____ He threw the three-run home run to Joe Carter in the bottom of the ninth inning of Game Six in 1993 that gave the Blue Jays an 8–6 win over the Phillies and their second consecutive world title.

25. THE PITCHING MASTERS

The following 14 pitchers won 300 or more games in their careers: Lefty Grove, Cy Young, Gaylord Perry, Early Wynn, Walter Johnson, Steve Carlton, Tom Seaver, Don Sutton, Warren Spahn, Eddie Plank, Phil Niekro, Grover Alexander, Nolan Ryan, Christy Mathewson. Put them in their proper order.

1. _____ (511)   8. _____ (324)
2. _____ (416)   9. _____ (324)
3. _____ (373)   10. _____ (318)
4. _____ (373)   11. _____ (314)
5. _____ (363)   12. _____ (311)
6. _____ (329)   13. _____ (300)
7. _____ (326)   14. _____ (300)

26. THE PERFECT GAME

Thirteen of the following 25 pitchers have thrown perfect games: Tom Browning, Walter Johnson, Tom Seaver, Carl Hubbell, Kenny Rogers, Ernie Shore, Babe Ruth, Jim Hunter, Sal Maglie, Dennis Martinez, Whitey Ford, Jim Bunning, Cy Young, Steve Carlton, Robin Roberts, Bob Feller, Addie Joss, Sandy Koufax, Wes Ferrell, Nolan Ryan, Don Larsen, Charlie Robertson, Mike Witt, Len Barker, and Allie Reynolds. Identify them.

1. _____   8. _____
2. _____   9. _____
3. _____   10. _____
4. _____   11. _____
5. _____   12. _____
6. _____   13. _____
7. _____

27. MULTIPLE NO-HITTERS

All of the 25 pitchers who are listed below have hurled no-hit games. Fifteen of them have done it more than once. In fact, one of them has done it seven times; one of them, four times; two of them, three times; and 11 of them, twice. Match the pitcher with the number that denotes how many times he performed the feat.

Bobo Holloman	Warren Spahn
Mel Parnell	Sam Jones
Johnny Vander Meer	Milt Pappas
Steve Busby	Bill Singer
Rick Wise	Carl Erskine
Ken Holtzman	Sal Maglie
Don Wilson	Bob Feller
Gaylord Perry	Virgil Trucks
Dean Chance	Allie Reynolds
Sandy Koufax	Jim Maloney
Jim Bunning	Don Larsen
Juan Marichal	Nolan Ryan
Bo Belinsky	

1. _____ (7)   9. _____ (2)
2. _____ (4)   10. _____ (2)
3. _____ (3)   11. _____ (2)
4. _____ (3)   12. _____ (2)
5. _____ (2)   13. _____ (2)
6. _____ (2)   14. _____ (2)
7. _____ (2)   15. _____ (2)
8. _____ (2)

28. BACK-TO-BACK 20-GAME WINNERS

Match the pitchers with the span of their careers when they recorded consecutive 20-game winning seasons.

1. _____ Tom Seaver		a.	1969–71
2. _____ Dave McNally		b.	1967–72
3. _____ Lefty Grove		c.	1910–19
4. _____ Paul Derringer		d.	1936–39
5. _____ Hal Newhouser		e.	1911–17
6. _____ Red Ruffing		f.	1968–69
7. _____ Warren Spahn		g.	1965–66
8. _____ Bob Feller		h.	1971–72
9. _____ Carl Hubbell		i.	1968–70
10. _____ Bob Lemon		j.	1963–66
11. _____ Denny McLain		k.	1933–37
12. _____ Vic Raschi		l.	1970–73
13. _____ Christy Mathewson		m.	1948–50
14. _____ Grover Cleveland Alexander		n.	1938–40
		o.	1903–14
15. _____ Roger Clemens		p.	1927–33
16. _____ Juan Marichal		q.	1949–51
17. _____ Mike Cuellar		r.	1942–44
18. _____ Bob Gibson		s.	1968–71
19. _____ Walter Johnson		t.	1939–41, 1946–47*
20. _____ Robin Roberts			
21. _____ Sandy Koufax		u.	1950–55
22. _____ Mort Cooper		v.	1956–61
23. _____ Ferguson Jenkins		w.	1944–46
24. _____ Jim Palmer		x.	1986–87
25. _____ Dizzy Dean		y.	1933–36
26. _____ Tom Glavine		z.	1991–93

* The pitcher's consecutive string of 20-win seasons was interrupted by the war.

29. THE FLAMETHROWERS

Name the 12 flamethrowers from the following 24 who have struck out 300 batters at least once in one season: Nolan Ryan, Roger Clemens, Tom Seaver, Sandy Koufax, Ferguson Jenkins, Mickey Lolich, Sam McDowell, Jim Lonborg, Bob Feller, Steve Carlton, Herb Score, Dwight Gooden, Jim Bunning, Walter Johnson, Don Drysdale, Bob Gibson, Red Ruffing, Rube Waddell, Vida Blue, Bob Turley, Carl Erskine, J. R. Richard, Mike Scott, and Randy Johnson.

1. _____   7. _____
2. _____   8. _____
3. _____   9. _____
4. _____   10. _____
5. _____   11. _____
6. _____   12. _____

30. BLUE-CHIP PITCHERS

Ten of the 20 pitchers who are listed below have recorded winning percentages of .600 or better. Who are they?

Whitey Ford	Jim Perry
Ted Lyons	Vic Raschi
Early Wynn	Jim Kaat
Allie Reynolds	Don Drysdale
Jim Palmer	Sal Maglie
Robin Roberts	Dizzy Dean
Gaylord Perry	Sandy Koufax
Mort Cooper	Mickey Lolich
Tom Seaver	Claude Osteen
Waite Hoyt	Lefty Gomez

1. _____
2. _____
3. _____
4. _____
5. _____
6. _____
7. _____
8. _____
9. _____
10. _____

31. 200 TIMES A LOSER

Ten of the 20 pitchers listed below have lost 200 or more major league games. Name them.

Cy Young	Bob Feller
Billy Pierce	Red Ruffing
Christy Mathewson	Milt Pappas
Bobo Newsom	Carl Hubbell
Walter Johnson	Paul Derringer
Juan Marichal	Robin Roberts
Mel Harder	Bob Gibson
Warren Spahn	Bob Friend
Grover Alexander	Early Wynn
Lefty Grove	Jim Bunning

1. _____
2. _____
3. _____
4. _____
5. _____
6. _____
7. _____
8. _____
9. _____
10. _____

32. WINDING UP

Mark "L" in the space provided for the pitchers who threw left-handed and "R" for the hurlers who threw right-handed. There are an even number of each contained in the list.

1. _____ Hal Newhouser
2. _____ Vernon Gomez
3. _____ Mike Garcia
4. _____ Eddie Lopat
5. _____ Scott Erickson
6. _____ Ellis Kinder
7. _____ Billy Pierce
8. _____ Herb Score
9. _____ Bucky Walters
10. _____ Van Lingle Mungo
11. _____ Vic Raschi
12. _____ Johnny Sain
13. _____ Steve Avery
14. _____ Dave Koslo
15. _____ Billy Loes
16. _____ Pedro Martinez
17. _____ Billy Hoeft
18. _____ Don Mossi
19. _____ Frank Lary
20. _____ Zane Smith
21. _____ Harry Brecheen
22. _____ Johnny Podres
23. _____ Larry Jansen
24. _____ Lew Burdette
25. _____ Kevin Appier
26. _____ Vernon Law
27. _____ Mel Parnell
28. _____ Rip Sewell
29. _____ Tommy Byrne
30. _____ Steve Howe

33. GOOD-HITTING PITCHERS

Match the pitchers who are listed below with their batting feats that are described beneath.

Jim Tobin   Warren Spahn
Tony Cloninger   Bob Lemon
Ken Brett   Jack Bentley
Don Newcombe   Andy Messersmith
Cy Young   Lewis Wiltse
Dave McNally   Vic Raschi
Wes Ferrell   Joe Wood
Don Drysdale   Babe Ruth
Allie Reynolds   Bucky Walters
Red Lucas   Bob Gibson
George Uhle   Mike Cuellar
Walter Johnson   Tom Hughes
Red Ruffing

1. _____ He batted .406, the all-time National League high, in a season.
2. _____ He was the only pitcher to hit three home runs in a game.
3. _____ He hit a home run in each of four consecutive games, which is a record for a pitcher.
4. _____ He batted .300 eight times, he ripped 36 home runs, and he pinch-hit safely 58 times.
5. _____ He batted .359 and hit a senior circuit record seven home runs in 1955.
6. _____ He hit a record two home runs in World Series play, including the only grand slam hit by a pitcher.
7. _____ He hit a home run that decided the longest 1–0 game that was determined by a pitcher's four-base blow.
8. _____ He posted a .671 winning percentage as a pitcher; he registered a .342 lifetime batting average.
9. _____ He hit the only grand slam by a pitcher in League Championship Series play.

0. _____ He drove home seven runs, an American League mark for pitchers, in one game.

1. _____ Three times he hit .500 in World Series play. (No one else has done that.)

2. _____ He hit two grand slams in one game. (He drove home a ninth run that game, too.)

3. _____ He hit a home run in each of the 1967–68 World Series to tie for the most home runs by a pitcher in fall classic play.

4. _____ He won 34 games in 1912, three more in the World Series, but ended up his career as an outfielder for the 1919–20 Indians.

5. _____ He began his big-league career as a third baseman, switched to the mound, where he won 198 career games, but still managed to hit 24 home runs, including one in the 1940 World Series.

6. _____ Twice he hit a league-high seven home runs in a season. (He's a Hall of Famer as a pitcher.)

7. _____ He batted .280 lifetime and hit 38 home runs, the all-time high for pitchers.

8. _____ He batted .281 lifetime and delivered 114 pinch-hits, the all-time high for moundsmen.

9. _____ He won an even 200 games and batted .288, the all-time high for hurlers.

0. _____ He batted .440 in his 19th year, the single-season high for pitchers.

1. _____ He hit three doubles in a 1975 game for the Los Angeles Dodgers.

2. _____ He got the most long hits in a game by a pitcher, two triples and two doubles. (He did it with the 1901 Athletics.)

3. _____ He hit 35 home runs and delivered 363 career hits to match the number of wins he recorded.

4. _____ He hit 37 career homers, second on the all-time pitcher's list, and won 207 big-league games.

5. _____ Three times he won more than 30 games in a season; four times he got 40 or more hits in a year. Overall, he hit safely 623 times.

The Asterisk Pitcher

The pitcher who threw the best game that has ever been spun lost the decision. If you don't believe me, you can look it up.

On May 26, 1959, the Pirates' left-hander, Harvey Haddix, pitched a perfect game for nine innings against the host Braves. That puts him in the select company of Cy Young, Addie Joss, Ernie Shore, Charlie Robertson, Don Larsen, Jim Bunning, Sandy Koufax, Jim Hunter, Len Barker, Mike Witt, Tom Browning, Dennis Martinez, and Kenny Rogers, the only other pitchers who have thrown a nine-inning perfect game in the modern era. But Haddix was not as fortunate as his select peers. Their teams gave them sufficient support to win the games. Haddix's club did not.

So "The Kitten" was forced to prove that he could pitch a game that had never been thrown before. He put the Braves down one, two, three in the tenth; he mowed them down in order in the eleventh; and he sailed through the lineup in sequence in the twelfth. But still his teammates, though they had touched Lew Burdette for 12 hits, could not dent the plate the one time that was needed to give their special southpaw instant immortality.

Inning 13 proved to be unlucky for Haddix. Felix Mantilla, the first batter, reached first when third baseman Don Hoak made a throwing error on an easy ground ball. Eddie Mathews bunted Mantilla into scoring position. Haddix was then forced to intentionally pass Hank Aaron to set up the double play for the slow-running Joe Adcock. But Adcock crossed up the strategy by hitting a three-run homer to right center.

Yet the final score was only 1–0. And Haddix got credit for another out. Technically, he could have been credited with an additional out. If he had, he might have gotten out of the inning without a run being scored.

Can you unravel that strange sequence of circumstances?
(Answer appears on page 343.)

Chapter Four

MULTIPLE CHOICE

34. FOUR BASES TO SCORE

1. _____ Who were the Dodger runners when Cookie Lavagetto's game-winning double with two outs in the bottom of the ninth inning broke up Bill Bevens' no-hitter in the 1947 World Series?
   a. Jackie Robinson and Eddie Stanky
   b. Eddie Miksis and Pete Reiser
   c. Jackie Robinson and Spider Jorgensen
   d. Al Gionfriddo and Eddie Miksis

2. _____ Whom did Don Larsen strike out for the final out in his perfect game in the 1956 World Series?
   a. Gil Hodges   c. Dale Mitchell
   b. Roy Campanella   d. Carl Furillo

3. _____ Against whom did Willie Mays hit his first major league home run?
   a. Bob Buhl   c. Larry Jansen
   b. Warren Spahn   d. Robin Roberts

4. _____ Against whom did Hank Aaron hit his first major league home run?
   a. Curt Simmons   c. Lew Burdette
   b. Vic Raschi   d. Don Newcombe

5. _____ Who hit the first home run in Shea Stadium?
   a. Willie Stargell   c. Stan Musial
   b. Frank Thomas   d. Frank Howard

6. _____ Which team was the last all-white club that won the American League pennant?
   a. 1947 Yankees   c. 1959 White Sox
   b. 1953 Yankees   d. 1965 Twins

7. _____ Who hit .400 in World Series play a record three times?
   a. Ty Cobb   c. Lou Gehrig
   b. Babe Ruth   d. Eddie Collins

8. _____ Who was the only Yankee who has won two batting titles?
   a. Joe DiMaggio   c. Lou Gehrig
   b. Mickey Mantle   d. Babe Ruth

9. _____ Who was doubled off first when Sandy Amoros made the game-saving catch on Yogi Berra's fly ball in the seventh inning of the seventh game of the 1955 World Series between the Dodgers and the Yankees?
   a. Billy Martin   c. Gil McDougald
   b. Elston Howard   d. Hank Bauer

10. _____ Which team holds the American League record of 111 wins in one season?
   a. 1946 Red Sox   c. 1959 White Sox
   b. 1927 Yankees   d. 1954 Indians

11. _____ Which National League team holds the major league record of 116 wins in one season?
   a. 1906 Cubs   c. 1952 Dodgers
   b. 1930 Cardinals   d. 1976 Reds

12. _____ Which of the following players has not recorded 500 putouts in one season?
   a. Joe DiMaggio   c. Vince DiMaggio
   b. Dom DiMaggio   d. Richie Ashburn

13. _____ Who was the last player who hit more than 50 home runs in one season?
   a. Mickey Mantle   c. Albert Belle
   b. Roger Maris   d. Willie McCovey

14. _____ Which of these former Yankees did not play in a World Series with a National League club?
   a. Roger Maris   c. Hank Borowy
   b. Bill Skowron   d. Vic Raschi

15. _____ Which of the following players did not win the RBI title with two teams in the same league?
   a. Orlando Cepeda   c. Johnny Mize
   b. Vern Stephens   d. Ralph Kiner

16. _____ Which of the following pitchers did not lose more games than he won?
   a. Bobo Newsom   c. Bob Friend
   b. Murry Dickson   d. Dizzy Trout

17. _____ Whose line drive, which almost provided the margin of victory, did Bobby Richardson catch for the final out of the 1962 World Series?
   a. Willie McCovey   c. Jose Pagan
   b. Jim Davenport   d. Orlando Cepeda

18. _____ Which of the following pitchers won the first playoff game in American League history?
   a. Denny Galehouse   c. Gene Bearden
   b. Bob Feller   d. Mel Parnell

19. _____ Who was the losing pitcher for the Dodgers on the day that Don Larsen threw his perfect game in the 1956 World Series?
   a. Clem Labine   c. Don Newcombe
   b. Johnny Podres   d. Sal Maglie

20. _____ Which of the following umpires worked his last game behind the plate on the day that Don Larsen pitched his perfect game?
   a. Jocko Conlan   c. Babe Pinelli
   b. Augie Donatelli   d. George Magerkurth

21. _____ Which one of the following players won back-to-back American League batting titles in the 1950s?
   a. Al Rosen   c. Ferris Fain
   b. Bobby Avila   d. Al Kaline

22. _____ Which one of the following players won back-to-back National League batting titles in the 1960s?
   a. Matty Alou   c. Tommy Davis
   b. Dick Groat   d. Richie Ashburn

23. _____ Which one of the following shortstops did not win a batting title?
   a. Dick Groat   c. Luke Appling
   b. Lou Boudreau   d. Luis Aparicio

24. _____ What was the name of the midget whom Bill Veeck sent up to the plate to pinch-hit for the Browns?
   a. Frank Gabler   c. Dick Kokos
   b. Ed Gallagher   d. Eddie Gaedel

25. _____ Which one of the following catchers never won an MVP Award?
   a. Yogi Berra   c. Roy Campanella
   b. Bill Dickey   d. Johnny Bench

26. _____ Which one of the following players did not win the MVP Award three times?
   a. Joe DiMaggio   c. Willie Mays
   b. Stan Musial   d. Roy Campanella

27. _____ Which runner stole home a record two times in World Series play?
   a. Bob Meusel   c. Lou Brock
   b. Ty Cobb   d. Jackie Robinson

28. _____ Which one of the following teams did not win four world's championships in one decade?
   a. 1910 Red Sox   c. 1930 Yankees
   b. 1920 Giants   d. 1940 Yankees

29. _____ Who was the last National League batter who hit .400?
   a. Rogers Hornsby   c. Bill Terry
   b. Lefty O'Doul   d. Arky Vaughan

30. _____ Against whom did Babe Ruth "call his shot" in the 1932 World Series?
   a. Lon Warneke   c. Burleigh Grimes
   b. Guy Bush   d. Charlie Root

31. _____ Who hit the "homer in the dark" for the Cubs in 1938?
   a. Gabby Hartnett   c. Stan Hack
   b. Billy Herman   d. Phil Cavarretta

32. _____ Who misplayed two outfield fly balls for the Cubs when the Athletics rallied with ten runs in the seventh inning of the fourth game of the 1929 World Series to win 10–8?
   a. Kiki Cuyler   c. Cliff Heathcote
   b. Riggs Stephenson   d. Hack Wilson

33. _____ Who has been the only American League player, in addition to Ty Cobb, who twice hit over .400?
   a. Joe Jackson   c. George Sisler
   b. Nap Lajoie   d. Harry Heilmann

34. _____ Who was the last National League pitcher who won 30 games in a season?
a. Carl Hubbell   c. Robin Roberts
b. Dizzy Dean   d. Sandy Koufax

35. _____ Who compiled the highest career batting average for left-handers in the history of the National League?
a. Lefty O'Doul   c. Stan Musial
b. Bill Terry   d. Paul Waner

36. _____ Who holds the National League record for playing in the most consecutive games (1,209)?
a. Gus Suhr   c. Billy Williams
b. Stan Musial   d. Steve Garvey

37. _____ Whose modern-day mark did Joe DiMaggio surpass when he batted safely in 56 consecutive games?
a. George Sisler   c. Ty Cobb
b. Heinie Manush   d. Al Simmons

38. _____ Which one of Babe Ruth's following teammates was the only Yankee to hit more home runs in one season than the "Sultan of Swat" during the 1920s?
a. Bob Meusel   c. Tony Lazzeri
b. Lou Gehrig   d. Bill Dickey

39. _____ Which one of the following catchers did not make an error in 117 games during the 1946 season?
a. Buddy Rosar   c. Del Rice
b. Frank Hayes   d. Mickey Owens

40. _____ Who has been the only left-handed batter in National League history to hit 50 home runs in a season?
a. Roger Maris   c. Mel Ott
b. Johnny Mize   d. Lou Gehrig

41. _____ Who holds the American League record for shutouts in one season by a left-handed pitcher?
a. Babe Ruth and Ron c. Whitey Ford
   Guidry   d. Mel Parnell
b. Lefty Grove

42. _____ Who was the youngest player ever elected to the Hall of Fame?
   a. Ted Williams   c. Sandy Koufax
   b. Roberto Clemente   d. Dizzy Dean

43. _____ Which one of the following players did not hit two grand slams in one game?
   a. Frank Robinson   c. Tony Cloninger
   b. Frank Howard   d. Jim Northrup

44. _____ Who holds the American League record for stealing home the most times (7) in one season?
   a. Ty Cobb   c. Rod Carew
   b. Eddie Collins   d. Bert Campaneris

45. _____ Who holds the National League record for stealing home the most times (7) in one season?
   a. Jackie Robinson   c. Lou Brock
   b. Pete Reiser   d. Maury Wills

46. _____ Who were the three players on the same team who hit more than 40 home runs each in the same season?
   a. Babe Ruth, Lou Gehrig, Bob Meusel
   b. Hank Aaron, Davey Johnson, Darrell Evans
   c. Hank Aaron, Eddie Mathews, Wes Covington
   d. Johnny Mize, Willard Marshall, Walker Cooper

47. _____ Who was the first black coach in the American League?
   a. Larry Doby   c. Minnie Minoso
   b. Elston Howard   d. Satchel Paige

48. _____ Who was the first black coach in the National League?
   a. Ernie Banks   c. Buck O'Neil
   b. Joe Black   d. Willis Mays

49. _____ Who started the double play that ended Joe DiMaggio's 56-game hitting streak?
   a. Ken Keltner   c. Ray Mack
   b. Lou Boudreau   d. Hal Trosky

50. _____ What was the most money that the Yankees ever paid Babe Ruth for a season?
   a. $100,000   c. $75,000
   b. $125,000   d. $80,000

51. _____ Which pair of players did not tie for a National League home run title?
   a. Ralph Kiner-Johnny Mize
   b. Ralph Kiner-Hank Sauer
   c. Willie McCovey-Hank Aaron
   d. Willie Mays-Hank Aaron

52. _____ Which pair of players did not tie for an American League home run title?
   a. Hank Greenberg-Jimmie Foxx
   b. Carl Yastrzemski-Harmon Killebrew
   c. Babe Ruth-Lou Gehrig
   d. Reggie Jackson-Dick Allen

53. _____ Who led the National League in home runs for the most consecutive years (7)?
   a. Chuck Klein   c. Ralph Kiner
   b. Mel Ott   d. Hank Aaron

54. _____ Who has pitched the most consecutive shutouts (6) in one season?
   a. Bob Gibson   c. Walter Johnson
   b. Sal Maglie   d. Don Drysdale

55. _____ Which one of the following pitchers did not strike out 19 batters in one game?
   a. Bob Feller   c. Nolan Ryan
   b. Steve Carlton   d. Tom Seaver

56. _____ Who was the first major leaguer who hit .400 in a season?
   a. Ty Cobb   c. Joe Jackson
   b. Nap Lajoie   d. George Sisler

57. _____ Who broke Ty Cobb's run of nine straight batting titles in 1916?
   a. Tris Speaker   c. Hal Chase
   b. George Sisler   d. Harry Heilmann

58. _____ Who was the only non-Yankee who won a home run title in the 1920s?
   a. Al Simmons   c. Ken Williams
   b. Goose Goslin   d. Jimmie Foxx

59. _____ Which one of the following American Leaguers did not win back-to-back batting titles?
   a. Ted Williams   c. Joe DiMaggio
   b. Pete Runnels   d. Carl Yastrzemski

60. _____ Which one of the following National Leaguers did not win back-to-back batting titles?
   a. Pete Rose   c. Stan Musial
   b. Roberto Clemente   d. Jackie Robinson
61. _____ Against whom did Mickey Mantle hit his last World Series home run?
   a. Curt Simmons   c. Harvey Haddix
   b. Barney Schultz   d. Bob Gibson
62. _____ Which one of the following Cub players was called "Swish"?
   a. Stan Hack   c. Billy Jurges
   b. Phil Cavarretta   d. Bill Nicholson
63. _____ Which one of the following players had a career which did not span four decades?
   a. Stan Musial   c. Mickey Vernon
   b. Ted Williams   d. Early Wynn
64. _____ Which one of the following managers did not win a pennant in both leagues?
   a. Joe McCarthy   c. Yogi Berra
   b. Bill McKechnie   d. Al Dark
65. _____ Which pitcher who won three games in the 1912 World Series later starred in the outfield for another American League team that played in the 1920 autumn classic?
   a. Babe Ruth   c. Duffy Lewis
   b. Joe Wood   d. Harry Hooper
66. _____ Which former Yankee pitcher switched to the outfield and compiled a .349 lifetime average?
   a. Rube Bressler   c. Lefty O'Doul
   b. Dixie Walker   d. Babe Ruth
67. _____ Who was the player who once hit three home runs in one game off Whitey Ford?
   a. Clyde Vollmer   c. Pat Seerey
   b. Dick Gernert   d. Jim Lemon
68. _____ Which one of the following one-two punches had the most home runs on the same team?
   a. Babe Ruth-Lou Gehrig
   b. Mickey Mantle-Roger Maris
   c. Hank Aaron-Eddie Mathews
   d. Ernie Banks-Ron Santo

69. _____ Which pair of the following brothers competed against each other in World Series play?
   a. Dizzy and Daffy Dean   c. Ken and Clete Boyer
   b. Jim and Gaylord Perry   d. Matty and Felipe Alou

70. _____ Which one of the following players was not a member of the "Whiz Kids"?
   a. Andy Seminick   c. Mike Goliat
   b. Russ Meyer   d. Harry Walker

71. _____ Which one of the following pitchers was the only one to lose a World Series game?
   a. Jack Coombs   c. Lefty Gomez
   b. Herb Pennock   d. Catfish Hunter

72. _____ Who was the only Phillie pitcher before 1980 who won a World Series game?
   a. Grover Cleveland   c. Eppa Rixey
      Alexander   d. Jim Konstanty
   b. Robin Roberts

73. _____ Which one of the following players did not "jump" to the Mexican League?
   a. Mickey Owen   c. Johnny Hopp
   b. Luis Olmo   d. Max Lanier

74. _____ Who made a shoestring catch of an infield fly to save a World Series?
   a. Billy Herman   c. Billy Martin
   b. Billy Johnson   d. Bobby Avila

75. _____ Which one of the following players did not win an American League home run title with a total below 30?
   a. Babe Ruth   c. Vern Stephens
   b. Nick Etten   d. Reggie Jackson

76. _____ Which one of the following players did not win a National League home run crown with a total below 30?
   a. Hack Wilson   c. Ralph Kiner
   b. Johnny Mize   d. Mike Schmidt

77. _____ Which one of the following players once hit 54 home runs in a season but did not win the league's home run title?
   a. Ralph Kiner   c. Mickey Mantle
   b. Willie Mays   d. Hank Greenberg

Exceptions to the Rule

Most umpires know the rule book from cover to cover. But occasionally a situation that is not covered by the rule book takes place. Then the umpires are in trouble.

Take, for example, the uproar that Herman "Germany" Schaefer created with his zany base running in a game between the Senators and the White Sox in 1911. With the score tied and two outs in the ninth inning, the Senators put runners on the corners, Clyde Milan on third and Schaefer on first. That's the moment when Schaefer decided to create confusion.

On the first pitch to a weak batter, Schaefer promptly stole second without a throw from the catcher. On the next pitch he proceeded to steal first, once again without a throw, but this time with a storm of protest from the White Sox bench. What base was Schaefer entitled to? the Sox wanted to know. The umpires thumbed through the rule book, but they failed to find any clause that prevented a runner from stealing any base that he had previously occupied. So, on the following pitch, Schaefer did the predictable: he stole second again. The frustrated catcher finally relented and threw the ball to second base. But Schaefer beat the throw and Milan raced home with the winning run.

Shortly thereafter, an amendment to the rule book was made: no base runner could steal a base out of sequence. The rules makers decided that Schaefer had tried to make a travesty of the game.

Another bizarre base running feat took place in 1963. This time it involved a Met runner, Jimmy Piersall, who was coming to the end of a celebrated—and clownish—career. In the game in which he hit his 100th career homer, he did something which indelibly impressed the event in the minds of all the people who saw it: he ran around the bases backwards.

Once again the umpires pored through the fine print of the rule book. But it was of no avail: there was no rule which prevented a runner from circling the bases backwards after he had hit a home run. Shortly thereafter, however, there was. The rules makers once again concluded that the runner (Piersall) had tried to make a mockery of the game. So today, batters who hit home runs have to touch the bases in their proper order.

One more ludicrous baseball situation took place in St. Louis in 1951. In a game between the hometown Browns and the Tigers, the always innovative owner of St. Louis, Bill Veeck, staged a scene that baseball fans still laugh about. In the first inning of the second game of a double-header, Zack Taylor, the manager of St. Louis, sent a midget up to the plate to pinch-hit for the leadoff batter, Frank Saucier. The umpires demanded that Taylor put an end to the farce. But Taylor was ready for them, rule book in hand: there was no provision in the baseball guide that prevented the batter with the number ⅛ on his back from taking his turn at the plate. The next day, you can feel safe to assume, there was.

But before the amendment was made, the batter walked on four consecutive pitches before giving way to a pinch-runner. What most probably comes readily to mind is the name of the midget, Eddie Gaedel. He is the subject of an often-asked trivia question. But what might not come so quickly to mind is the name of the pitcher who threw to the smallest target in baseball history, the name of the catcher who gave the lowest target in the history of the game, and the umpire who had the smallest strike zone in the annals of the sport.

Consider yourself to be in the ranks of a select few if you can name two of the three individuals who figured prominently in one of the most bizarre pitcher-batter confrontations that has ever taken place.

(Answer appears on page 343.)

Chapter Five

FROM RUTH TO REGGIE

35. FROM RUTH TO REGGIE

1. _____ Which slugger (1933–47) missed almost six years of playing time because of the Second World War and injuries and still managed to hit 331 career home runs?

2. _____ Which Indian pitcher, who was 15–0 at the time, lost his only game of the year in his last start?

3. _____ Whose line drive in the 1937 All-Star Game broke Dizzy Dean's toe?

4. _____ Who pitched a no-hitter on the opening day of the 1940 season?

5. _____ Who was the only player to win the Rookie of the Year Award, the Most Valuable Player Award, and the Triple Crown?

6. _____ Whose home run on the final day of the 1945 season won the pennant for the Tigers?

7. _____ Whose home run on the final night of the 1976 season won the pennant for the Yankees?

8. _____ Which pitcher, who was acquired from the Yankees, led the Cubs to the pennant in 1945?

9. _____ Who scored the only run in the first game of the 1948 World Series after Bob Feller "almost" picked him off second base?

10. _____ Who was the manager of the Red Sox in 1948–49 when they lost the pennants on the last day of the season?

11. _____ Who was the name star that the Yankees traded to the Indians for Allie Reynolds in 1948?

12. _____ Who was the American League home run king of 1959 who was traded after the season for batting champ Harvey Kuenn?

13. _____ Which former Giant relief specialist, then with the Orioles, threw the pitch that Mickey Mantle hit for his 500th home run?

14. _____ Who invented the "Williams' Shift"?

15. _____ Which slugging American League outfielder broke his elbow in the 1950 All-Star Game?

16. _____ Which Dodger outfielder did Richie Ashburn throw out at the plate in the ninth inning of the last game of the 1950 season to send the Phillies into extra innings and subsequently the World Series?

17. _____ Who threw a no-hitter in his first major league start?

18. _____ Who threw the pitch that Mickey Mantle hit for his 565-foot home run?

19. _____ Who was the 20-game season winner and the two-game World Series winner for the Giants in 1954 whom they acquired from the Braves for Bobby Thomson?

20. _____ Who took Bobby Thomson's centerfield position for the Giants?

21. _____ Who took Bobby Thomson's leftfield position—when he broke his ankle—for the Milwaukee Braves?

22. _____ Which Indian slugging outfielder–first baseman was afflicted with polio in 1955?

23. _____ , Dave McNally, Jim Palmer, and Mike Cuellar were 20-game winners for the Orioles in 1971.

24. _____ Who was the one-time "Wildman" for the Yankees who lost the final game of the 1955 World Series to the Dodgers' Johnny Podres, 2–0?

25. _____ Which versatile infielder hit the line drive which struck Herb Score in the eye?

26. _____ Which pitcher, picked up on waivers from the Indians, won 13 games down the stretch, in-

cluding a no-hitter against the Phillies, to pitch the Dodgers to the 1956 pennant?

27. _____ Who hit two two-run homers against Don Newcombe in the 1956 World Series finale to lead the Yankees to a 9–0 victory over the Dodgers?

28. _____ Which Yankee infielder was hit in the throat by Bill Virdon's bad-hop ground ball in the 1960 World Series?

29. _____ Which team was the first in history to come back from a 3–1 World Series deficit in games and win the autumn classic?

30. _____ Who, in addition to Rogers Hornsby and Nap Lajoie, was the only right-handed batter to hit .400?

31. _____ Who lost his job as a result of Bill Mazeroski's seventh-game home run in the 1960 World Series?

32. _____ Who threw the 60th home run ball to Babe Ruth in 1927?

33. _____ Who threw the 61st home run pitch to Roger Maris in 1961?

34. _____ Who was Whitey Ford's "save-ior" in 1961?

35. _____ Which of the Yankee reserve catchers hit four consecutive home runs in 1961?

36. _____ Who was the pitcher who was known as the "Yankee Killer" in the early 1960s?

37. _____ Which Hall of Famer wore the uniforms of all four New York teams: Giants, Dodgers, Yankees, and Mets?

38. _____ Which Dodger outfielder committed three errors in one inning in the 1966 World Series?

39. _____ What position did Jackie Robinson play when he first came up with the Dodgers?

40. _____ Who was the Commissioner of Baseball when Jackie Robinson broke the color barrier?

41. _____ Who was the first black manager?

42. _____ Who lost three fly balls in the sun, in the same World Series game for the Yankees, in 1957?

43. _____ Which Indian third baseman drove

home better than 100 runs per season for five consecutive years in the early 1950s?

44. _____ Which Phillie outfielder didn't make an error during 266 consecutive games?

45. _____ Who was Babe Ruth's manager during his final major league season with the Boston Braves?

46. _____ Which free agent (Charley Finley style) did the Red Sox pick up in 1967 to help them win the pennant?

47. _____ Who was the last pitcher to win 30 or more games?

48. _____ Which Brave batter was awarded first base in the 1957 World Series when the black polish on the ball proved that he had been hit with the preceding pitch?

49. _____ Which Met batter was awarded first base in the same manner in the 1969 World Series?

50. _____ Which Senator outfielder filed suit against baseball's reserve system in the early 1970s?

51. _____ Who was the most recent player who won the batting title without hitting a home run?

52. _____ Which second-string catcher, at the time, hit four home runs in a World Series?

53. _____ Which manager resigned after leading his team to two world's championships in the 1970s?

54. _____ Which 35-year-old pitcher, who had appeared in only 11 games all season long, surprised the baseball world by striking out a record 13 batters in the A's opening-game win over the Cubs in the 1929 World Series?

55. _____ Which National League team once posted a .315 team batting average but finished last in the standings?

56. _____ Who won seven games and saved four others in World Series play?

57. _____ What city was the only one to produce two Triple Crown winners in the same year (1933)?

58. _____ Who succeeded John McGraw as manager of the Giants?

59. _____ Which pitching brothers won 49 games in 1934?

60. _____ Who had a career average of .439 for four World Series?

61. _____ Who got the most hits in one season in the National League?

62. _____ Which pitcher chalked up the best winning percentage for hurlers with less than 200 but more than 100 wins?

63. _____ Who lost more games than any other pitcher in World Series play?

64. _____ Who was the last Yankee player before Don Mattingly to amass 200 hits in a season?

65. _____ Who was the last Dodger player to win a home run title?

66. _____ Who was the last Yankee player to win a home run title?

67. _____ Who made nine hits in an 18-inning game?

68. _____ Which Yankee pitcher ended Mickey Cochrane's career when he felled the Tigers' playing manager with a high, hard one?

69. _____ Which slugging Brave outfielder missed the 1948 World Series—he never played in one—because of a broken ankle he sustained in a collision at home plate during the last week of the season?

70. _____ Whom did the Dodgers trade to the Pirates because he "jumped" the team on its tour of Japan after the 1966 World Series?

71. _____ Which famous pitcher had to retire prematurely because of the potentially dire effects which could have been produced by his arthritic elbow?

72. _____ Which National League manager, who was a former first baseman, was fired in August of 1938 when his team, the Cubs, was in third place? The Cubs then went on to win the pennant under Gabby Hartnett.

73. _____ Which Yankee catcher holds the major league record of handling 950 consecutive chances without making an error?

74. _____ Which Astro catcher set a major league record when he played 138 consecutive games without making an error?

75. _____ Who recorded the highest lifetime average (.359) in the history of the National League?

76. _____ Who holds the American League mark of 184 RBIs in a season?

77. _____ Who recorded the most shutouts in one season in the American League?

78. _____ Whose base hit drove home the winning run for the Reds in the 1975 World Series against the Red Sox?

The Mystery Death

Going into the 1940 season, baseball experts would never have believed that the hero of the upcoming World Series would be Jimmie Wilson, for the .284 lifetime hitter had recently settled down to life as a full-time coach with the Reds after donning the "tools of ignorance" for 17 seasons. But fate has been known to throw tricky pitches to a baseball team.

Ernie Lombardi, the team's regular catcher, had won the batting title two years before; he would also win it two years later. Behind him was a .316 lifetime hitter. So there didn't seem to be any need for Wilson's services.

But on August 2 the second-string catcher took his own life in Boston, and in mid-September Lombardi sprained his ankle. So Wilson was rushed back into action.

Down the stretch, "Ace" batted only .234, but he was primed up by World Series time. He handled the serves of two-game winners Bucky Walters and Paul Derringer faultlessly, and he swung a torrid bat, hitting .353 in the six games he played. In addition, the 40-year-old catcher stole the only base of the entire series.

The following season, Wilson went into permanent retirement, Lombardi took over the regular catching chores once again, and the reasons for the substitute catcher's suicide remained a mystery.

The identity of that .316 lifetime hitter is pretty much a mystery, too. Can you solve it?

(Answer appears on page 343.)

Chapter Six

BASEBALL'S DID YOU KNOW

The PHILLIES of 1961 lost a record 23 straight games.

The METS of 1962 lost 120 games, a single-season record.

GAYLORD PERRY was the only pitcher to win the Cy Young Award in both leagues. He won it with the Indians in 1972 and the Padres in 1978.

SATCHEL PAIGE, who was 59 years old when he pitched for Kansas City in 1965, has been the oldest player to perform in the major leagues.

DIOMEDES OLIVO was 41 when he broke in with the 1960 Pirates. Two years later, at 43, he appeared in 62 games and was 5–1.

FRED ODWELL hit only one home run before his nine four-base blows won the title in 1905; afterward, the Red outfielder never hit another major league home run.

THURMAN MUNSON was the only Yankee to win both the Rookie of the Year Award (1970) and the MVP Award (1976).

DAVE McNALLY and Mike Cuellar of the 1970 Orioles were the last two pitchers from the same team to tie for the league lead in victories with 24.

WILLIE MAYS has been the only player to hit four home runs in one game and three triples in another.

DAL MAXVILL of the 1968 Cards had the most official at-bats (22) without collecting a hit in a World Series.

ROGER MARIS, who hit a record 61 home runs in 1961, won only one home run title.

MICKEY MANTLE was the first player to hit a home run in the Astrodome. He did it in an exhibition game between the Yankees and the Astros in 1962.

ERNIE LOMBARDI set a major league mark by grounding into the most double plays in the National League in five different seasons.

LEFTY O'DOUL, a pitcher with the pennant-winning Yankees in 1922, and Rube Bressler, a pitcher with the pennant-winning Athletics of 1914, both gained fame as outfielders: O'Doul won two batting titles in the National League and hit .349 lifetime; Bressler hit .302 for his career.

DAVE KOSLO broke the Yankees' nine-game opening-game World Series winning streak in 1951 when he bested Allie Reynolds, 5–1. The last time that the Bronx Bombers had lost the lead game of the fall classic had been in 1936 when Carl Hubbell, also of the Giants, defeated them, 6–1.

GEORGE KELL of the 1945 Athletics went 0-for-10 in a 24-inning game. His lifetime average, though, was .306.

ADDIE JOSS of the 1908 Indians, on the next-to-last day of the season, pitched a perfect game, besting Ed Walsh of the White Sox, 1–0. Walsh pitched a two-hitter.

WALTER JOHNSON of the 1912–19 Senators set a major league record by copping eight consecutive strikeout titles.

JOE JACKSON, Buck Weaver, Fred McMullin, Claude Williams, Swede Risberg, Happy Felsch, Eddie Cicotte, and Chick Gandil were the eight White Sox players who allegedly were bribed to throw the 1919 World Series.

The INDIANS of 1948 had an infield that averaged 108 RBIs: first baseman Eddie Robinson, 83; second baseman Joe Gordon, 124; shortstop Lou Boudreau, 106; and third baseman Kenny Keltner, 119.

TOM HUGHES, who threw nine-inning no-hitters for the Yankees and the Browns, racked up a 20–3 lifetime record in relief.

ELSTON HOWARD of the Yankees played in the World Series his first four years in the majors. The Yanks won in 1956 and 1958; they lost in 1955 and 1957.

STAN MUSIAL of the 1954 Cards and Nate Colbert of the 1972 Padres each hit a record five home runs in a doubleheader.

ROGERS HORNSBY of the 1922 Cardinals became the first National Leaguer to hit 40 home runs in a season when he hit 42 base-clearing blows.

BURLEIGH GRIMES, winding up his career in 1934 with the Yankees, Pirates, and Cards, was the last of the legal spitball pitchers;* Red Faber of the 1933 White Sox was the last of the legal spitball pitchers in the American League.

HANK GOWDY of the Giants and the Braves was the only major leaguer to serve in both World War I and World War II.

FLOYD GIEBELL shut out Bob Feller and the Indians to win the 1940 pennant for the Tigers, but he never won another big-league game. In fact, he won a total of only three.

BOB GIBSON of the Cardinals didn't steal too often, but when he did, he was usually successful: he stole 13 career bases in 17 attempts.

BOB GIBSON lost his first and last World Series games; in between, he won seven straight, a record.

The GIANTS were the first team to use a public address announcer. They did so at the Polo Grounds on August 25, 1929.

LOU GEHRIG began his consecutive game streak by batting for Pee Wee Wanninger the day before he subbed for ailing first baseman Wally Pipp.

* Commissioner Kenesaw Mountain Landis decreed in 1920 that only existing spitball pitchers could continue to wet the ball. Red Faber of the 1933 White Sox was the last American League pitcher to legally dampen the ball; Burleigh Grimes of the 1934 Giants was the last major league pitcher to legally lubricate the ball.

FRANK BAUMHOLTZ of the 1952 Cubs was the only batter that Stan Musial of the Cards pitched to in the majors.

NEAL BALL, shortstop for the 1904 Indians, pulled off the first unassisted triple play in modern major league history.

BOB ASPROMONTE was the last Brooklyn Dodger to remain active in the major leagues. He faded from the scene with the Mets in 1971.

MIKE ANDREWS of the 1973 A's was fired by owner Charlie Finley because he made two errors in the twelfth inning of a World Series loss to the Mets. Commissioner Bowie Kuhn forced Finley to reinstate his second baseman.

CY YOUNG of the Red Sox, who was 41 when he no-hit the Yankees (Highlanders) in 1908, was the oldest pitcher to throw a no-hit game.

GEORGE SISLER of the 1920 Browns collected a record 257 hits. From 1920–22 he averaged 240 safeties per season.

TRIS SPEAKER was involved in a career-record 135 double plays in his 22-year career as an outfielder for the Red Sox, Indians, Senators, and Athletics.

JIM THORPE, Ernie Nevers, Paddy Driscoll, Ace Parker, and George Halas are football Hall of Famers who once played in the majors.

JIM BUNNING won 19 games a record four times.

MORDECAI "Three Finger" BROWN of the 1909–10 Cubs was the only pitcher to twice lead the league in saves and complete games in the same season.

WILLIE MAYS slammed more than 50 home runs in seasons ten years apart: in 1955, with New York, he ripped 51; in 1965, with San Francisco, he rocketed 52.

WALTER JOHNSON hit a record 206 batters during his 21-year career with the Senators.

ROGERS HORNSBY holds the club-high batting average for three different teams: .424 for the 1924 Cardinals, .387 for the 1928 Braves, and .380 for the 1929 Cubs.

The BRAVES of 1961 hit four home runs in a row in one inning. They were slugged by Eddie Mathews, Hank Aaron, Joe Adcock, and Frank Thomas, respectively.

The BRAVES of 1965 hit four home runs in a row in one inning. They were drilled by Joe Torre, Eddie Mathews, Hank Aaron, and Gene Oliver, respectively.

JACK BILLINGHAM of the Reds, in three World Series, turned in the lowest career ERA (0.36) in World Series history. Harry Brecheen of the Cardinals recorded the second lowest mark (0.83), and Babe Ruth of the Red Sox, the third lowest (0.87).

JIM COMMAND of the 1954 Phillies hit a grand slam off the Dodgers' Carl Erskine for his first major-league hit. He got only three more hits in the big time.

TY COBB (1907–15) won a record nine consecutive batting titles; Rogers Hornsby (1920–25) copped a record six consecutive National League crowns. Both Honus Wagner (1906–09) and Rod Carew (1972–75) dominated the batting averages in their respective leagues for four consecutive years.

TY COBB collected 200 or more hits in a season nine times, the American League mark.

TOM CHENEY of the 1962 Senators struck out 21 Orioles in a 16-inning game.

TOMMY BYRNE of the 1951 Browns walked 16 batters in a 13-inning game.

PHIL CAVARRETTA of the Cubs set the following records for a player before he reached his twentieth birthday: runs, 120; hits, 234; triples, 14; and runs batted in, 117.

BILL CARRIGAN, manager of the Red Sox, retired after he had led Boston to back-to-back world titles in 1915–16; Dick Williams, skipper of the A's, resigned after he had guided Oakland to back-to-back world championships in 1972–73.

STEVE BUSBY of the 1973–74 Royals was the first and only pitcher to throw no-hitters in each of his first two seasons.

PATSY DOUGHERTY of the 1903 Red Sox was the first player to homer twice in the same game of a World Series. He performed the feat in Game Two against the Pirates.

"WILD BILL" DONOVAN has been the only pitcher to post 25 or more win seasons in both leagues. He won 25 for the 1901 Dodgers and 25 for the 1907 Tigers.

JOE DiMAGGIO of the 1950 Yankees became the first player to get paid $100,000 for a season.

FRANK HOWARD of the 1968 Senators hit a record ten home runs in six games.

DOM DiMAGGIO, Joe DiMaggio, and Vince DiMaggio all have the same middle name—Paul.

The CUBS of 1906 won a record 116 games, but they lost the World Series to their intercity rivals, the White Sox, in six games.

GAVVY CRAVATH of the 1919 Phillies won the home run crown despite the fact that he had only 214 official at-bats. He hit 12 four-base blows.

DOC CRAMER of the Red Sox, Rip Radcliff of the Browns, and Barney McCosky of the Tigers each stroked 200 hits to tie for the major league lead in 1940.

JIM COONEY of the White Sox and Johnny Neun of the Tigers pulled off unassisted triple plays on successive days. Cooney, shortstop for the Cubs, recorded his on May 30, 1927; Neun, first baseman for the Tigers, executed his the following day.

JOE DiMAGGIO of the 1936 Yankees was the first rookie to play in an All-Star Game. He went hitless in five at-bats and made an error in the field.

ED COLEMAN of the 1936 Browns, who retired after the season, became the first player to pinch-hit safely 20 times in one season.

STEVE GARVEY of the Padres set the all-time errorless game streak at first base with 193 miscue-free games.

OSCAR FELSCH, outfielder for the 1919 White Sox, participated in a record 15 double plays in one season.

GAYLORD PERRY of the 1978 Padres was 40 years old when he won the Cy Young Award, making him the oldest player ever to win the coveted crown.

DAN DRIESSEN of the 1976 Reds, in the first year that the DH was used in the World Series, hit .357 in his team's sweep of the Yankees.

DAZZY VANCE didn't win his first major league decision until he was 31, but by the time he hung up his spikes in 1935, he registered a career record of 197–140.

BABE RUTH was the only player to twice hit three home runs in a World Series game. He did it in 1926 and 1928, both times against the Cards.

MIKE RYBA of the Cards and the Red Sox was the only player to both pitch and catch in both leagues.

HONUS WAGNER, who was 37 when he won the batting crown in 1911, was the oldest National League player to win the batting title.

RAY SCHALK of the 1914–22 White Sox caught four no-hitters.

JIMMY SEBRING of the 1903 Pirates was the first player to hit a home run in the World Series! He homered in the first game of the initial fall classic and got 11 hits in the classic, two short of the all-time record.

The YANKEES of 1960 lost the World Series to the Pirates in seven games despite recording the highest team batting average (.338) ever.

The YANKEES, paced by Roger Maris' 61 home runs and Mickey Mantle's 54 circuit clouts, hit a record-setting 240 four-base blows in 1961. Maris and Mantle's combined total of 115 home runs by back-to-back sluggers in a lineup broke the former mark of 109, which had been set by Babe Ruth and Lou Gehrig in 1927.

The YANKEES defeated the Tigers, 9–7, in the American League's longest game (24 innings) on June 24, 1962. Jack Reed's home run, the only one that he hit in his career, broke up the game.

JOE WOOD was the first player to appear in one World Series (1912) as a pitcher and another fall classic (1920) as an outfielder. Wood won three games for the Red Sox and batted .200 for the Indians.

RICK WISE of the 1971 Phils pitched a no-hitter and hit two home runs in a game against the Reds.

VIC WILLIS, who eight times won 20 or more games during a season, lost a major league record 29 games for the 1905 Braves.

The WHITE SOX of 1940 had the same batting average at the end of one game as they had before it. That's because Bob Feller no-hit them in the opening game of the season.

BABE RUTH of the 1920 Yankees hit 54 home runs, 35 more than his runner-up, George Sisler (19), in the American League home run derby.

HAM HYATT (1909–18) of the Pirates, Cardinals, and Giants was the first player to amass 50 hits as a pinch-hitter. Career-wise, he batted safely 57 times in 240 pinch-hitting performances for a .238 average.

HONUS WAGNER led the National League in batting a record eight times. Rogers Hornsby and Stan Musial won National League batting titles seven times each.

RED ROLFE of the 1939 Yankees scored a record 30 runs in 18 consecutive games.

PIE TRAYNOR was the only regular named to the all-time team to play his entire career with one club. He played with the Pirates from 1920–37.

TRIS SPEAKER of the 1918 Red Sox executed two unassisted double plays in the month of April.

GEORGE UHLE of the Tigers and Indians, who pitched

or 17 years, had a .288 lifetime batting average, the highest mark of any pitcher.

DAZZY VANCE of the 1922–28 Dodgers set a National League record when he won seven consecutive strikeout titles.

HONUS WAGNER, Christy Mathewson, Ty Cobb, Walter Johnson, and Babe Ruth, in 1936, became the first five players to be inducted into the Baseball Hall of Fame at Cooperstown, N.Y.

The PIRATES of 1925, Yankees of 1958, Tigers of 1968, Pirates of 1979, and Royals of 1985 have won the World Series after trailing in games, three to one.

The PIRATES of 1917 hit nine home runs, the all-time low by a National League team.

The PIRATES of 1960 defeated the Yankees in the World Series despite having a pitching staff that recorded an ERA of 7.11.

The REDS of 1935, the host team, defeated the Phillies, 2–1, in the first night game played in the majors.

The RED SOX, who won four world championships in four tries in the same decade, defeated four different National League teams during a seven-year span: the Giants, 1912; the Phillies, 1915; the Dodgers, 1916; and the Cubs, 1918.

ROBIN ROBERTS' 28 wins for the 1952 Phillies has been the most wins by a National League pitcher since Dizzy Dean won 30 in 1934.

BROOKS ROBINSON hit into four triple plays in his career.

BABE RUTH reached first base safely a record 379 times in one season; Lefty O'Doul reached first base safely a record 334 times in the National League.

JOE DiMAGGIO, who averaged 118 RBIs per season during his 13-year career, won only two titles in that department. In 13 years in the big leagues he averaged just under one RBI per game.

A Checkered Career

The Giants of John McGraw had much good fortune—they won ten pennants and three World Series—but they had great misfortune also: they lost one pennant and three World Series that they could have won.

In 1908 they were victimized by "Merkle's Boner." On September 23, in a key game with the Cubs at the Polo Grounds, Al Bridwell lined a ball to the outfield that chased Moose McCormick home with the apparent winning run. But Merkle, who was on first, did not run out the hit to second. Instead he bolted straight to the clubhouse in center field, a custom of the time when the winning hit was made in the bottom of the ninth inning. Johnny Evers, the Cubs' second baseman, alertly called for the ball; and Hank O'Day, the umpire who saw the entire play, ruled that Merkle was out. He also suspended the 1–1 contest because of darkness. That necessitated a one-game playoff for the pennant. The Cubs behind Mordecai Brown defeated Christy Mathewson of the Giants, 4–2.

In 1912 the Giants muffed the World Series. Leading by one run in the final inning of the eighth-and-decisive game—the second game had ended in a 6–6 tie—they made two costly errors, one of commission and one of omission. Fred Snodgrass dropped Clyde Engle's routine fly ball for a two-base error, and first baseman Merkle and catcher Chief Meyers gave Tris Speaker a second life when they permitted his easy foul pop to drop untouched. Speaker then singled home the tying run and advanced what proved to be the winning run to third. Larry Gardner's sacrifice fly clinched the championship.

In 1917 the Giants made two physical errors and one mental error in the fourth inning of the sixth-and-final game. Heinie Zimmerman, the third baseman for the Giants, made a bad throw on an easy grounder; Dave Robertson, the right fielder, dropped an easy fly ball; and Bill Rariden, the catcher, left home plate unattended in a rundown play that led to the winning run.

In 1924, McGraw's last chance to win a World Series, "Little Napoleon" saw fate intervene once again. In the bottom of the 12th, with the score between the Giants and the host Senators tied at three, Muddy Ruel lifted a high foul behind the plate, but the Giant catcher tripped over his own mask, and Ruel, given another opportunity, doubled. Earl McNeely's hopper to third hit a pebble and bounced over Fred Lindstrom's head, scoring Ruel with the winning run.

The Giants' receiver was naturally distraught over his inability to handle Ruel's pop fly properly, for he was a veteran who was used to crisis situations. Up until that time he had been the only catcher to be on the winning side of a World Series sweep. When World War I erupted, he was the first major leaguer to volunteer for military service. Later, when World War II broke out, he became the only major leaguer to see service in both wars. And in the 1914 World Series he batted .545, the third highest average in the history of the autumn classic.

Who was this player with the checkered career?

(Answer appears on page 343.)

Chapter Seven

BASEBALL'S WHO'S WHO

36. BASEBALL'S WHO'S WHO

1. _____ Who pitched in 65 1–0 games, winning 38 of them and losing 27, even though in 20 of his losses he allowed four or fewer hits?
2. _____ Who was the only manager before Dick Williams to win pennants with three different teams?
3. _____ Who was the youngest player to win a batting title?
4. _____ Who was the oldest player to win a batting title?
5. _____ Who was the first player to hit safely in 12 consecutive official at-bats?
6. _____ Who was the only other player to duplicate the feat?
7. _____ Who hit .382 in his last year (570 at-bats) in the majors?
8. _____ Who, in addition to Joe Jackson (.408), was the only player to bat .400 without winning the hitting crown?
9. _____ Who posted the most wins (12) in one season without losing a game?
10. _____ Who pitched three doubleheaders in one month and won all six games, none of which lasted more than one hour and fifty minutes?
11. _____ Who hit two game-winning home runs for the Giants against the Yankees in the 1923 series?

2. _____ Who was the only player to win the MVP Award for two teams in the same league?

3. _____ Who was the National League right-hander who led the circuit in strikeouts for four consecutive years (1932–35) but failed to whiff as many as 200 batters in a season?

4. _____ Who won four batting titles in alternate years?

5. _____ Who won back-to-back batting titles three times?

6. _____ Who was the first baseman who teamed with Joe Gordon, Lou Boudreau, and Ken Keltner to give the Indians an infield that averaged 108 RBIs?

7. _____ Who was the one-time Yankee manager who neither hit a home run nor stole a base in eight major league seasons?

8. _____ Who was the one-time Yankee manager who never finished worse than fourth in 24 years as a major league skipper?

9. _____ Who was the pennant-winning manager who needed the most time—10 years—to win his first league title?

20. _____ Who hit a record six pinch-hit home runs in one year?

21. _____ Who hit five pinch-hit home runs in one year to set an American League record?

22. _____ Who was the only National League pitcher to lead his league in winning percentage for three consecutive years?

23. _____ Who was the only American League pitcher to lead his circuit in winning percentage for three consecutive years?

24. _____ Who shut out every team in the National League in three different years?

25. _____ Who was the left-handed slugger in the National League who tied for the home run title three times?

26. _____ Who was the right-handed slugger in the National League who tied for the home run crown three times?

27. _____ Who posted a 6–0 opening day record?

28. _____ Who pitched six opening day shutouts?

29. _____ Who was the only White Sox player to win a batting title?

30. _____ Who threw the pennant-winning home run to Chris Chambliss in 1976?

31. _____ Who was the only pitcher to win back-to-back MVP awards?

32. _____ Who was the pitcher for the 191– pennant-winning Athletics who recorded a .302 lifetime mark as an outfielder?

33. _____ Who hit 40 or more home runs in the American League eight times, but never reached the 50 mark?

34. _____ Who hit 40 or more home runs in the National League eight times, but failed to hit the 50 mark?

35. _____ Who was the player who led the American League in batting in 1961 with an average of .361, but never before or after reached the .300 level?

36. _____ Who drove home 108 runs in 1992 at the age of 41, to become the oldest player to deliver that many ribbies?

37. _____ Who was the 273-game winner who hit over .300 eight times and pinch-hit safely 58 times?

38. _____ Who was the pitcher who pinch-hit safely 114 times?

39. _____ Who set a major league record by leading his league in ERA percentage nine times?

40. _____ Who was the only player to win the batting and home run titles with two teams in the same league?

41. _____ Who was the first switch-hitter to win a batting crown?

42. _____ Who was the National League relief pitcher from the 1950s and 1960s who recorded 193 career saves?

43. _____ Who was the player who three times won the batting crown and the home run title in the same year?

4. _____ Who finished 750 of 816 contests for a completion percentage of 92?

5. _____ Who was the only National League player to twice get six hits in six at-bats?

6. _____ Who was the only American League player to twice get six hits in six at-bats?

7. _____ Who was the first National League relief pitcher to win the Cy Young Award?

8. _____ Who was the left-handed pitcher who won the Cy Young Award four times?

9. _____ Who is the present-day pitcher who has won the Cy Young Award four times?

50. _____ Who has been the only player to win both the Rookie of the Year Award and the MVP Award in the same year?

51. _____ Who was the most recent National League relief pitcher to win the Cy Young Award?

52. _____ Who was the last National League player to win three consecutive home run crowns?

53. _____ Who was the last American League player to win back-to-back MVP awards?

54. _____ Who was the last National League player to win back-to-back MVP awards?

55. _____ Who was the only pitcher to win the Cy Young Award in both leagues?

56. _____ Who has hit for the highest average in the National League since Bill Terry's .401 in 1930?

57. _____ Who sprayed 200 or more hits in a record ten seasons?

58. _____ Who is the recent-day Cub pitcher who won 20 or more games in six consecutive seasons?

59. _____ Who was the recent-day pitcher who won 20 or more games with three different teams?

50. _____ Who was the recent-day pitcher who won 20 or more games eight times?

51. _____ Who was the former Yankee relief pitcher who led the American League in saves in 1972 and 1976 with 35 and 23, respectively?

52. _____ Who was the most recent pitcher to both win and lose 20 games in the same season?

63. _____ Who was the former American
League player who holds the club batting mark lead
with two different teams?
64. _____ Who is the recent-day pitcher who
struck out more than 200 batters in nine consecutive
seasons?

Classic Comebacks

They say that good things come in twos. That goes for no-hitters, too.

There have been four pitchers in the modern era to throw two no-hitters in one season: Johnny Vander Meer (1938), Allie Reynolds (1951), Virgil Trucks (1952), and Nolan Ryan (1973). One of them (Vander Meer) was the only pitcher to throw two no-hitters in successive starts.

Up until 1968, however, no two teams had exchanged no-hitters on successive days. Now it's been accomplished twice. The first time, on September 23, 1968, a Giant pitcher performed the feat against the visiting Cardinals. The following day, a St. Louis right-hander duplicated the feat against San Francisco.

One year later, two teams traded no-hitters on successive days for the second time. On April 30 a strong-armed Cincinnati right-hander set back the Astros. The next day an Astro flamethrower returned the favor.

If you could name just two of the four pitchers who were involved in these classic comebacks, you would be pitching in coveted company, too. Can you?

(Answer appears on page 343).

Chapter Eight

BASEBALL'S NUMBER GAME

Just how trivial is baseball "trivia"?

Baseball fans, the most record-conscious of all sports fol
lowers, feel very strongly that names and numbers are
vital part of the national pastime. So do the players.

The numbers 56, 60, 61, 367, 511, 755, and 2,130 instanta
neously draw to the minds of astute baseball fans and play
ers the names of great diamond stars of the past: Jo
DiMaggio, Babe Ruth, Roger Maris, Ty Cobb, Cy Young
Hank Aaron, and Lou Gehrig.

Numbers 300 and 3,000 probably hold the most lure fo
the baseball fan and player. Three hundred represents
batter's season's average and his career mark. It also signi
fies a pitcher's season's strikeouts and career wins. Thre
thousand can stand for either career hits by a batter o
career strikeouts by a pitcher.

There are other magical numbers in baseball, too. Quit
often they affect the longevity of a player's career.

Mickey Mantle, the great Yankee switch-hitter, length
ened his career two years because of the numbers gam
In 1966, when he should have retired, Mantle's RBI tota
dipped to 56. But his batting average of .288 and his hom
run total of 23 were still respectable. It would have been
good time to bow out, while he was still on top. But h
was just four home runs shy of 500. The temptation wa
simply too great. So he played another year. In 1967 he hi
22 home runs to up his total to 518, just three short of Te
Williams' 521 and 16 light of Jimmy Foxx's 534. So, o
course, he played one more year, and he ended up wit
536 home runs. Willie Mays's four-base total, the next run
on the home run ladder, was high above Mantle's. So, wit
no more numbers to catch, he retired.

The numbers game was costly to Mantle, though. His .245 and .237 batting averages during his last two years dragged his lifetime average down from .302 to .298. In Mantle's case a higher home run total was preferable to a higher lifetime batting average.

"It really bothers me that I didn't end up my career with a .300 lifetime average," Mantle said when he was asked about his decision to play those last two years. "I'd like to be remembered as a good hitter. At the time I fooled myself into thinking that I could hit the extra home runs and keep the .300 average. But it didn't work out."

Al Kaline got caught up in the numbers game, too. His situation was similar to Mantle's. He played two extra years in order to wind up in the select 3,000 Hit Club. He made it with a herculean effort in 1974, when he got 146 hits to finish up his career with 3,007. But, in those last two years, he slipped four points, from .301 to .297, in his lifetime average.

Once Kaline reached 3,000 hits, he was faced with another dilemma. He had 399 home runs. Should he play another year in order to end up in another select circle of hitters: the 400 Home Run Club?

"No, I decided not to," Kaline said shortly after his retirement. "It would have been nice to hit 400 home runs. But the toll that would have been exacted from my body by playing another season would have been too much. I had a good career. I'm satisfied with it."

The numbers game was not always as important to the baseball player as it is today, though.

Take the case of Sam Rice, who played the outfield for the Washington Senators from 1915 to 1934. He ended up his career with a lifetime average of .322 and a total of 2,987 hits, just 13 short of the magic 3,000. But Rice, who had hit .293 and collected 98 hits in his final season, elected to retire. Had he been a modern-day performer, he undoubtedly would have played one more year in order to reach the prestigious milestone. Rice's decision to retire, though he didn't know it at the time, cost him baseball immortality. There are not too many modern-day fans who even recognize his name. A mere 13 additional hits would have added luster to his name. The present-day fans would then include him with the greatest hitters of all time.

"We didn't pay too much attention to records in those days," Rice said shortly before his death. "There wasn't so much emphasis put on them at the time. If I had it to do all over again, though, I think I would have hung around for a while. With all of this stress on records today, history has sort of cheated me, you know."

Sam Crawford was another player who looked back and rued the day that he retired. Today he is mostly remembered as an outfielder who played alongside Ty Cobb. But "Wahoo" Sam turned in a .309 lifetime average, led the major leagues in triples with 309, and proved to be the first of only two players to lead both the National and American leagues in home runs in a season. Fred McGriff has done it, too.

But he finished his career with 2,964 hits. He also could have played an extra year, as so many modern baseball players will do, and made the 3,000 Hit Club. Then perhaps he would have moved out of Cobb's shadow. But one hit shy of 3,000 is as distant as 1,000 short of the mark. Most baseball buffs know that Roberto Clemente ended up his career with 3,000 hits on the nose. But few people realize that Rice and Crawford missed the mark by a whisker and could have hit it, if they had elected to do so.

Crawford legally deserves the 3,000 Hit Club recognition anyway. In 1899 he got 87 hits with Grand Rapids in the Western League. When the American League was formed in 1900, the National Commission ruled that any player from the Western League who entered either the National or American leagues would be credited with all the hits that he had made in the Western League. But the statistician who compiled Crawford's lifetime average inadvertently overlooked those hits. So he finished his career with 2,964 hits instead of 3,051, to which he is entitled.

Crawford, it seems, was dealt a double twist of fate: he was victimized by the numbers game and the record book.

Lefty O'Doul was also cheated by the numbers game. The two-time batting champ in the National League finished his career with a .349 average. Yet he is not ranked with the top hitters of all time because the baseball rules makers say that he did not play the required ten years in order to qualify for such exalted distinction. Actually, O'Doul played 11 years in the big leagues. But the first four were spent as a pitcher. The record compilers don't count those years.

But the late, irrepressible Irishman did. "I spent 11 years in the big leagues and ended up with a .349 average," he often said to the surprise of unknowing listeners. "That's lifetime average, not a single season's mark. Only Cobb, Hornsby, and Jackson ever did better. That's pretty good company."

O'Doul was also denied entrance into another elite club—the .400 Hitters—by a single base hit. In 1929 he batted .398, the closest that anyone has come to .400 without hitting it. (Harry Heilmann also hit .398. But in another season, he batted .401.)

"Only eight hitters in the history of baseball ever hit .400," O'Doul said regretfully. "If an official scorer had ruled one of many plays a hit rather than an error, I would have been the ninth."

Babe Ruth didn't miss .400 by too much, either. In 1923 he hit .393 and didn't even win the batting title. (Heilmann did.) When people think of the Babe, they envision the legendary long-ball hitter. But they sometimes forget that he was a .342 lifetime hitter, too. If the Babe had been able to get three more hits in 1923, they would never be able to forget it.

Twelve players in the history of the game have hit 50 or more home runs in one season. You can probably name all of them. But can you recall the six players who did not hit 50, but did smack 49? Well, they are Lou Gehrig, Ted Kluszewski, Frank Robinson, Harmon Killebrew, Mark McGwire, and Andre Dawson.

"Close only counts in horseshoes," they say. So these six sluggers have been relegated to a lower echelon of long-ball hitters.

Billy Goodman wound up his major league career with a lifetime average of .300. Minnie Minoso hit .299. Is there a difference? Well, Minoso prevailed upon Chicago White Sox owner Bill Veeck to reactivate him, at the age of 57, in the final month of the 1976 season. In 1980 he returned for two more at-bats. (His lifetime average dropped a point to .298.) You might say that Minoso thought there was a difference.

Thirteen pitchers have won 30 or more games in one season. "Three-Finger" Brown, George Mullin, Ed Cicotte, and Hal Newhouser did not. They won 29. In the record book that looms as one very important win.

Spud Chandler, like Lefty O'Doul, has been footnoted out of the record book. The Yankees' right-hander won 109 games and lost only 43 for a phenomenal winning percentage of .717. That's the best mark of all time for any pitcher who has won 100 or more games. But the rules makers say that a pitcher has to have recorded 200 victories in order to rank with the all-time best. So Whitey Ford (236–106) tops the list with a mark of .690.

Jim Bunning pitched no-hitters in both leagues. He won over 100 games in each league, too. And he also struck out more than 1,000 batters in each league. Overall, he struck out 2,855 batters. Another 145 would have guaranteed him a bust in Cooperstown. He'll probably never make it, though.

Tom Seaver struck out 200 or more batters in nine consecutive years. That's a record. But his personal high of 289 is still far from the top. Twelve pitchers have gone over 300 strikeouts in a season.

Roy Face still thinks about the one decision in 19 which he dropped in 1959. Nineteen and oh? Wouldn't that be something!

A pitcher with the old Boston Braves might have welcomed one more loss, though. In 1905 he dropped 29 decisions. No one else has ever done that. But 30 losses? That would really single him out!

Early Wynn and Robin Roberts typify the modern-day players' conflict with the numbers game.

Wynn won only one game in 1963. That was his last major league victory. It was also his 300th career win. He got it in relief. That's struggling. With satisfaction, though.

Roberts struggled, too. In vain, though. Eleven years after his last 20-game season, he called it quits, 14 victories short of the coveted 300 Win Club.

Why did those Hall of Famers put so much time and toil

into so few victories at the tail end of their careers? They did so because, competitive as baseball players are prone to be, they played the game to the hilt, until their number(s) were up.

To them, it wasn't any trivial matter!

Speaking of trivia, though, that pitcher with the 1905 Braves, who lost a record 29 games in one year, was singled out recently when he was inducted into the Baseball Hall of Fame. Can you single him out?

(Answer appears on page 343.)

The Fateful Farewell

In the 1947 World Series, three players—Bill Bevens, Cookie Lavagetto, and Al Gionfriddo—came out of relative obscurity to figure prominently in the seven-game set between the Yankees and the Dodgers. Afterward they slipped back into obscurity. But they are still remembered today for the pivotal parts they played in the 1947 Fall Classic, one of the most dramatic series of all time.

In Game Four, with the Yankees holding a one-contest lead, Bevens, a pitcher with a less than enviable 7–13 record during the regular season, made World Series history.

With one out remaining in the game, Bevens held tenuously to a 2–1 lead. Up to that point, Bevens had neutralized the Dodgers' big bats; he had not allowed a single base hit. That is not to say, however, that he hadn't allowed any base runners. As a matter of fact, he yielded ten of them, all via the base-on-balls route. (And that's a record!) Two of them, plus a sacrifice and an infield out, cost him a run in the fifth inning. But it was the last two walks he granted that cost him World Series immortality.

In the ninth inning he walked Carl Furillo for pass number nine. Furillo gave way to a pinch-runner, who proceeded to steal second base off rookie catcher Yogi Berra. Then with two outs and a base open, Yankee manager Bucky Harris decided to walk pinch-hitter Pete Reiser, who also gave way to a pinch-runner. That set the stage for pinch-hitter Harry Lavagetto, who responded with a double off the right-field wall to break up the no-hitter and, more important, to win the game for the Dodgers.

In Game Six, Al Gionfriddo, who played the role of a super-sub in the Series, prevented the tying run from scoring with one of the most memorable defensive plays in World Series history.

The Yankees, who had won Game Five on Joe DiMaggio's home run off Rex Barney, had high hopes of wrapping up the classic in Game Six. Once again, it was DiMaggio who almost provided them with the impetus. But with the

Dodgers leading 8–5 in the sixth inning, Dodger manager Burt Shotton once again went to his bench. He called on Gionfriddo, whom he inserted in left field as a defensive precaution.

Immediately, Gionfriddo justified the move. DiMaggio boomed a 415-foot shot to the bull pen in deep left center field. But Gionfriddo, who had broken with the crack of the bat, made a circus catch to prevent the homer that would have tied the game. The Dodgers then hung on to win, 8–6. But the Yankees came back to win the seventh game (5–2) and the Series (4–3).

One might think that Bevens, Lavagetto, and Gionfriddo got raises the following year. But in fact none of the three ever played another regular-season major league game.

You can earn a bonus, however, if you can identify the pinch-runner for Furillo, the pinch-runner for Reiser, and the left-fielder whom Gionfriddo replaced in the Dodger lineup.

(Answer appears on page 343.)

Chapter Nine

NICKNAMES

37. MATCHING NAMES

Match the following players with their nicknames.

Tommy Henrich	Walter Johnson
Carl Hubbell	Dom DiMaggio
Frankie Frisch	Tris Speaker
Honus Wagner	Ted Williams
Luke Appling	Casey Stengel
Johnny Mize	Vernon Law
Bobby Thomson	Ty Cobb
Allie Reynolds	Babe Ruth
Joe DiMaggio	Lou Gehrig
Paul Waner	Mickey Mantle

1. "Staten Island Scot" _____
2. "Super Chief" _____
3. "Splendid Splinter" _____
4. "Big Cat" _____
5. "Little Professor" _____
6. "Old Professor" _____

7. "Old Reliable"   _____
8. "Deacon"   _____
9. "Yankee Clipper"   _____
10. "Georgia Peach"   _____
11. "Flying Dutchman"   _____
12. "Grey Eagle"   _____
13. "Sultan of Swat"   _____
14. "Big Train"   _____
15. "Iron Horse"   _____
16. "Meal Ticket"   _____
17. "Commerce Comet"   _____
18. "Old Aches and Pains" _____
19. "Big Poison"   _____
20. "Fordham Flash"   _____

38. FIRST NAMES

Substitute the players' first names for their nicknames.

Edwin	Elwin
George	Jerome
Harry	Charles
Edward	Joe
James	Johnny
Leon	Leroy
Fred	Enos
Larry	Robert
Paul	Lynwood
Bill	Charles Dillon

1. "Moose" Skowron   _____
2. "Daffy" Dean   _____
3. "Dizzy" Dean   _____
4. "Yogi" Berra   _____
5. "Preacher" Roe   _____
6. "Snuffy" Stirnweiss   _____
7. "Flash" Gordon   _____
8. "Pepper" Martin   _____
9. "Schoolboy" Rowe   _____
10. "Duke" Snider   _____
11. "Casey" Stengel   _____
12. "Dixie" Walker   _____
13. "Peanuts" Lowrey   _____
14. "Satchel" Paige   _____
15. "Country" Slaughter   _____
16. "Chuck" Dressen   _____
17. "Whitey" Ford   _____
18. "Goose" Goslin   _____
19. "Lefty" Grove   _____
20. "Dusty" Rhodes   _____

39. MIDDLE NAMES

Place the following nicknames between the players' first and last names.

"The Whip"   "The Kid"
"Poosh 'Em Up"   "Birdie"
"Pee Wee"   "The Crow"
"Bobo"   "The Barber"
"Three Finger"   "Home Run"
"Puddin' Head"   "The Lip"
"The Dutch Master"   "King Kong"
"The Man"   "Pie"
"The Hat"   "Twinkletoes"
"The Cat"   "Louisiana Lightning"

 1. Harry _____ Walker
 2. Stan _____ Musial
 3. Harry _____ Brecheen
 4. Johnny _____ Vander Meer
 5. Sal _____ Maglie
 6. Ron _____ Guidry
 7. Leo _____ Durocher
 8. Ewell _____ Blackwell
 9. Charlie _____ Keller
10. Willie _____ Jones
11. Frank _____ Crosetti
12. Frank _____ Baker
13. Tony _____ Lazzeri
14. Billy _____ Martin
15. Harold _____ Traynor
16. Louis _____ Newsom
17. George _____ Tebbetts
18. George _____ Selkirk
19. Mordecai _____ Brown
20. Harold _____ Reese

40. LAST NAMES

Match the players' last names with their nicknames and their first names.

Doby	Reiser
Keeler	Murphy
Jones	Hubbell
Feller	Crawford
Jackson	Dugan
Piniella	Cochrane
Houk	Grimm
Medwick	Bottomley
Wood	Turner
Greenberg	Newhouser

1. "Ducky" Joe _____
2. "Wahoo" Sam _____
3. "Shoeless" Joe _____
4. "Smokey" Joe _____
5. "Jumping" Joe _____
6. "Sweet" Lou _____
7. "Hammerin' " Hank _____
8. "Blackjack" Mickey _____
9. "Rapid" Robert _____
10. "Jolly Cholly" _____
11. "Pistol" Pete _____
12. "Sunny" Jim _____
13. "Larrupin' " Larry _____
14. "Prince" Hal _____
15. "Major" Ralph _____
16. "Wee" Willie _____
17. "Fireman" Johnny _____
18. "Milkman" Jim _____
19. "Sad" Sam _____
20. "King" Carl _____

41. PRESENT-DAY PLAYERS

Match the players in the left-hand column with their nicknames in the right-hand column.

1. _____ Lenny Dykstra		a.	"Tewks"
2. _____ Darren Daulton		b.	"The Thrill"
3. _____ Ozzie Smith		c.	"Nails"
4. _____ Andres Galarraga		d.	"Pudge"
5. _____ Howard Johnson		e.	"The Hammer"
6. _____ Dwight Gooden		f.	"Dutch"
7. _____ Sid Fernandez		g.	"The Wizard of Oz"
8. _____ Bob Tewksbury		h.	"Pags"
9. _____ Deion Sanders		i.	"Black Jack"
10. _____ Will Clark		j.	"El Sid"
11. _____ Cecil Fielder		k.	"Neon"
12. _____ Tim Raines		l.	"Hawk"
13. _____ Dennis Martinez		m.	"Rock"
14. _____ Bob Hamelin		n.	"Big Cat"
15. _____ Charles Davis		o.	"Big Unit"
16. _____ Randy Johnson		p.	"El Presidente"
17. _____ Andre Dawson		q.	"Chili"
18. _____ Jack McDowell		r.	"Doc"
19. _____ Mike Pagliarulo		s.	"Wild Bear"
20. _____ Ivan Rodriguez		t.	"Ho-Jo"

The Iron Horse

There is a touch of irony in respect to the manner in which Lou Gehrig broke into the Yankees' lineup and the way in which he departed from it.

When the 1925 season started, Gehrig was the back-up first baseman. The first-string first sacker was a veteran of 12 years, a two-time home run champion, and the American League's leader in triples (19) the previous year. About one-third of the way through the season, though, the first stringer got hit in the head with a pitch, and he suffered from headaches for the remainder of the season. One day he asked manager Joe McCarthy for a game's rest. Lou Gehrig substituted for him and the rest of the story is history: the "Iron Horse" remained in the lineup for a then-record 2,130 consecutive games. But he died a short two years after he hung up his cleats.

The player whom he replaced lived for 40 years after he departed from the Yankee lineup. Can you name him?

(Answer appears on page 344).

Chapter Ten

BREAKING THE BARRIERS

42. DID THEY OR DIDN'T THEY?

Mark "T" or "F" for "True" or "False" before each statement.

1. _____ Don Newcombe hit more home runs (7) in one season than any other pitcher in the history of the National League.
2. _____ Roy Campanella hit more home runs (242) than any other catcher in National League history.
3. _____ Elston Howard hit a home run in his first World Series at-bat.
4. _____ Bob Gibson was the first black pitcher to win the Cy Young Award.
5. _____ Barry Bonds has won three MVP awards.
6. _____ Richie Allen has been the only black third baseman to be named Rookie of the Year.
7. _____ Willie Mays has been the only black player to twice hit more than 50 home runs in a season.
8. _____ Bob Gibson once played for the Harlem Globetrotters.
9. _____ Elston Howard was the last Yankee to win the MVP Award.
10. _____ Ralph Garr's nickname is "The Road Runner."
11. _____ Roy Campanella won a record-tying three MVP awards.
12. _____ Willie Mays was the first player to collect more than 3,000 hits and 500 home runs.

13. _____ Frank Robinson was a unanimous choice as the American League's MVP in 1966.

14. _____ Matty and Felipe Alou have been the only brothers to finish one-two in a batting race.

15. _____ Jackie Robinson was the only black player to appear in the 1947 World Series.

16. _____ Bobby Bonds four times hit more than 30 home runs and stole more than 40 bases in a season.

17. _____ Reggie Jackson hit .300 in a season.

18. _____ Don Newcombe was the first black pitcher to win a series game.

19. _____ Larry Doby was the first black player to win the American League's MVP Award.

20. _____ Jackie Robinson was the first black player to win the National League's MVP Award.

21. _____ Hank Aaron, Roberto Clemente, and Lou Brock won the MVP Award.

22. _____ Reggie Jackson, when he hit three home runs in the final game of the 1977 series, delivered the four-base blows against three different pitchers.

23. _____ Willie Mays never won an RBI crown.

24. _____ No black player has ever won the Triple Crown.

25. _____ Don Newcombe lost all four of his pitching decisions in series play.

26. _____ Roy Campanella was the first black to hit a home run in series play.

27. _____ Larry Doby was the first black to hit two home runs in the same series.

28. _____ Hank Aaron was the first black to hit three home runs in a series.

29. _____ Jim Rice hit more home runs in one season than any other Red Sox player.

30. _____ Al Downing was the first black to appear in a World Series game for the Yankees.

31. _____ Willie Mays never batted .300 or hit a home run in series play.

32. _____ J. R. Richard has been the only black to strike out more than 300 batters in a season.

33. _____ Bob Gibson won more consecutive World Series games than any other pitcher.

34. _____ Al Downing was the first black pitcher to win a series game for an American League team.

35. _____ The Dodgers opened the 1966 World Series against the Orioles with six black players in their starting lineup.

36. _____ Bob Gibson was the last pitcher to win three games in a series.

37. _____ Dave Cash had more at-bats in one season than any other major leaguer.

38. _____ Ferguson Jenkins won more games than any other black pitcher.

39. _____ Willie McCovey played in four decades of major league ball.

40. _____ Jackie Robinson recorded the highest lifetime average (.311) of any black or hispanic player who finished his career with at least ten years of active service.

41. _____ Curt Flood handled 538 consecutive chances without making an error.

42. _____ Maury Wills ranks number two to Lou Brock in the number of career steals by a National Leaguer.

43. _____ Willie Mays scored the run in the 1962 Series which snapped Whitey Ford's scoreless inning streak at 33⅔ innings.

44. _____ Zoilo Versalles, Rod Carew, and Reggie Jackson have won the MVP Award in the American League.

45. _____ Willie Mays has a higher lifetime batting average than Mickey Mantle.

46. _____ Before Bill Madlock won back-to-back batting titles (1975–76), the last black or hispanic player in the National League to perform the feat was Tommy Davis (1962–63).

47. _____ Jackie Robinson was the last player in the series to execute a steal of home that was not on the front end of a double theft.

48. _____ Dick Allen won home run titles in both leagues.

49. _____ Dwight Gooden was the last black pitcher in the National League to win the Cy Young Award.

50. _____ Bill Buckner was the last non-black or non-hispanic player to win a batting title in the National League.

43. THE TRAILBLAZERS

The following black or hispanic players were the first ones to perform for teams that previously were exclusively white: Larry Doby, Hank Thompson–Willard Brown, Sam Hairston, Bob Trice, Carlos Paula, Valmy Thomas, Jackie Robinson, Curt Roberts, Elston Howard, Hank Thompson–Monte Irvin, Ozzie Virgil, Sam Jethroe, Pumpsie Green, Ernie Banks–Gene Baker, Joe Black, and Tom Alston–Brooks Lawrence. Match the players with their respective teams.

1. _____ Browns
2. _____ Pirates
3. _____ Phillies
4. _____ Yankees
5. _____ Athletics
6. _____ Indians
7. _____ Cubs
8. _____ Reds
9. _____ Red Sox
10. _____ Senators
11. _____ Dodgers
12. _____ Braves
13. _____ Cardinals
14. _____ Giants
15. _____ Tigers
16. _____ White Sox

44. BLACK CLOUTERS

Twenty-two black players have won a total of 42 league home run titles (ties count as wins). Match the following players with the number of times they have won the crown: Fred McGriff, Ken Griffey, Jr., Barry Bonds, George Foster, Ben Oglivie, Jim Rice, Cecil Fielder, Larry Doby, Hank Aaron, Dick Allen, Darryl Strawberry, Kevin Mitchell, Jesse Barfield, Willie Mays, Frank Robinson, Reggie Jackson, Willie McCovey, Willie Stargell, Ernie Banks, George Scott, Albert Belle, and Andre Dawson.

1. _____ (4)		12. _____ (2)	
2. _____ (4)		13. _____ (1)	
3. _____ (4)		14. _____ (1)	
4. _____ (3)		15. _____ (1)	
5. _____ (3)		16. _____ (1)	
6. _____ (2)		17. _____ (1)	
7. _____ (2)		18. _____ (1)	
8. _____ (2)		19. _____ (1)	
9. _____ (2)		20. _____ (1)	
10. _____ (2)		21. _____ (1)	
11. _____ (2)			

45. SINGLE-SEASON SLUGGERS

Fourteen black players hold the single-season high in home runs for their respective club(s). (Two of them are co-holders of a club's mark.) The numbers of home runs and the clubs are provided. The players are not. One of the players holds the top position for two different teams.*

1. _____ (52) San Francisco Giants
2. _____ (52) Cincinnati Reds
3. _____ (51) New York Giants**
4. _____ (49) Baltimore Orioles
5. _____ (47) Atlanta Braves***
6. _____ (47) Toronto Blue Jays
7. _____ (45) Seattle Mariners
8. _____ (41) Chicago White Sox
9. _____ (39) California Angels
10. _____ (39) New York Mets
11. _____ (38) San Diego Padres
12. _____ (32) Montreal Expos
13. _____ (31) Colorado Rockies
14. _____ (27) Florida Marlins

*These marks are inclusive of the 1994 season.
** Johnny Mize is the co-holder of this club record.
*** Eddie Mathews is the co-holder of this club mark.

46. NATIONAL LEAGUE BATTING CHAMPS

Eighteen black or hispanic players have won the National League batting title a total of 33 times: Tony Gwynn, Willie McGee, Bill Madlock, Ralph Garr, Al Oliver, Andres Galarraga, Matty Alou, Roberto Clemente, Terry Pendleton, Gary Sheffield, Jackie Robinson, Billy Williams, Willie Mays, Rico Carty, Tim Raines, Tommy Davis, Dave Parker, and Hank Aaron. Match the players with the years in which they copped the crown(s). Several of the players won the title more than once.

1. _____ (1949)   18. _____ (1978)
2. _____ (1954)   19. _____ (1981)
3. _____ (1956)   20. _____ (1982)
4. _____ (1959)   21. _____ (1983)
5. _____ (1961)   22. _____ (1984)
6. _____ (1962)   23. _____ (1985)
7. _____ (1963)   24. _____ (1986)
8. _____ (1964)   25. _____ (1987)
9. _____ (1965)   26. _____ (1988)
10. _____ (1966)   27. _____ (1989)
11. _____ (1967)   28. _____ (1990)
12. _____ (1970)   29. _____ (1991)
13. _____ (1972)   30. _____ (1992)
14. _____ (1974)   31. _____ (1993)
15. _____ (1975)   32. _____ (1994)
16. _____ (1976)   33. _____ (1995)
17. _____ (1977)

47. AMERICAN LEAGUE BATTING CHAMPS

Eight black or hispanic players—Kirby Puckett, Alex Johnson, Edgar Martinez, Frank Robinson, Rod Carew, Julio Franco, Tony Oliva, and Willie Wilson—have won the American League batting title a total of 17 times. Match the players with the years in which they copped the crown(s). One of them did it seven times, one of them did it three times, and one of them did it twice.

1. _____ (1964)
2. _____ (1965)
3. _____ (1966)
4. _____ (1969)
5. _____ (1970)
6. _____ (1971)
7. _____ (1972)
8. _____ (1973)
9. _____ (1974)
10. _____ (1975)
11. _____ (1977)
12. _____ (1978)
13. _____ (1982)
14. _____ (1989)
15. _____ (1991)
16. _____ (1992)
17. _____ (1995)

48. ROOKIES OF THE YEAR

Six of the first seven Rookie of the Year awards in the National League went to black players: Sam Jethroe, Jim Gilliam, Don Newcombe, Willie Mays, Joe Black, and Jackie Robinson. Can you place them in their proper order?

1. _____ (1947)
2. _____ (1949)
3. _____ (1950)
4. _____ (1951)
5. _____ (1952)
6. _____ (1953)

49. THE HALL OF FAME

Twenty-five black or hispanic players have been elected to the Hall of Fame. You should be able to name at least ten of them. If you name 15, though, you're entitled to a little bit of fame for yourself.

1. _____	10. _____	18. _____
2. _____	11. _____	19. _____
3. _____	12. _____	20. _____
4. _____	13. _____	21. _____
5. _____	14. _____	22. _____
6. _____	15. _____	23. _____
7. _____	16. _____	24. _____
8. _____	17. _____	25. _____
9. _____		

To Catch a Thief

The final game of the 1926 World Series has gone down in baseball history as one of the most exciting finishes in the annals of the fall classic.

It certainly did not lack drama.

With the visiting Cardinals leading the Yankees 3–2 in the bottom of the sixth, Jesse Haines developed a finger blister while the Yankees loaded the bases with two out. Rogers Hornsby, the manager of St. Louis, decided to replace Haines with Grover Alexander, who had already won two games in the series. Alexander, one of the all-time greats of the hill, had to face Tony Lazzeri, a long-ball-hitting rookie. On the second pitch of the confrontation, Lazzeri almost decisively won the duel: he hit a long line drive to left that tailed a few feet left of the foul pole. Three pitches later, Alexander struck Lazzeri out on a sweeping curveball.

In a groove, Alexander mowed the Yankees down in order in both the seventh and the eighth innings. He had retired nine consecutive batters before he faced Babe Ruth, with two outs, in the ninth. Working cautiously, he proceeded to walk the Babe. But Alex was still not out of danger. He had to face Bob Meusel, who had won the home run crown the year before. On the first pitch to Meusel, however, Ruth pulled the unexpected: he tried to steal second base. But the Cardinals' catcher threw a strike to Hornsby to nail Ruth, who became the first and only base runner to make the last out of a World Series on an attempted steal.

After the series ended, owner Sam Breadon traded manager Hornsby to the Giants and named his catcher the team's manager. Maybe the backstop's final throw of the 1926 World Series had something to do with the owner's decision.

Who was that veteran of 21 seasons who stopped the Yankees in 1926 and led the Cardinals in 1927?

(Answer appears on page 344.)

Chapter Eleven

SOUTH OF THE BORDER: YESTERDAY AND TODAY

50. SOUTH OF THE BORDER: YESTERDAY I

Match the ten players in the two columns below with their respective descriptions below.

Bobby Avila	Roger Moret
Al Lopez	Zoilo Versalles
Luis Aparicio	Mike Gonzalez
Orlando Cepeda	Tony Perez
Fernando Valenzuela	Roberto Clemente

1. _____ Who was the first Mexican-born player to win a batting title? (It was taken away from him by the rules committee in 1994.)
2. _____ Which native of Mexico won a Cy Young Award?
3. _____ Who was the hispanic who managed two different teams to pennants?
4. _____ Who was the native of Puerto Rico who posted 13–2 and 14–3 seasons with the Red Sox?
5. _____ Who was the first Latin-born player to be named Rookie of the Year in the American League?
6. _____ Who was the native of Cuba who caught in the major leagues for 17 years. He briefly managed the Cardinals.
7. _____ Who was the first Latin-born player to be named Rookie of the Year in the National League?

8. _____ Who was the native of Cuba who once hit three home runs in a World Series?
9. _____ Who was the first Latin-born player to win an MVP Award?
10. _____ Who was the first Latin-born player to win an MVP Award in the National League?

51. SOUTH OF THE BORDER:
YESTERDAY II

Match the ten players in the two columns below with their respective descriptions beneath.

Luis Tiant   Chico Carasquel
Tony Oliva   Willie Hernandez
Ed Figueroa   Hector Lopez
Juan Marichal   Pedro Ramos
Juan Nieves   Adolph Luque

1. _____ Who was the first native of Puerto Rico to win 20 games in a season?
2. _____ Which native of the Dominican Republic twice led National League pitchers in wins?
3. _____ Who was the first native of Puerto Rico to pitch a no-hitter?
4. _____ Who was the first native of Puerto Rico to be named the MVP in the American League?
5. _____ Which native of Cuba led the American League in losses a record four consecutive years?
6. _____ Which native of Venezuela replaced Luke Appling at shortstop for the White Sox?
7. _____ Which native of Cuba won the batting title in his rookie year?
8. _____ Which native of Cuba became the first Latin to win 20 games in one year?
9. _____ Which native of Cuba four times won 20 games?
10. _____ Which native of Panama once hit .429 in a World Series with the Yankees?

52. SOUTH OF THE BORDER: TODAY I

Match the ten players in the two columns below with their respective descriptions beneath.

Raul Mondesi   Tony Fernandez
Julio Franco   Jose Canseco
Roberto Alomar   Andres Galarraga
Benito Santiago   Edgar Martinez
Juan Gonzalez   Ozzie Guillen

1. _____ Which native of Puerto Rico has won three Gold Gloves in the National League?
2. _____ Which native of the Dominican Republic is the all-time fielding percentage leader at his position?
3. _____ Which native of the Dominican Republic led all major league outfielders with 16 assist in 1994?
4. _____ Which native of Venezuela won the Rookie of the Year Award in 1985?
5. _____ Who is the native of Venezuela who won the 1993 batting title in the National League?
6. _____ Who is the native of the Dominican Republic who won the 1991 batting crown in the American League?
7. _____ Who won the 1992 and 1995 batting titles in the American League? (Though he was born in New York, he grew up in Puerto Rico.)
8. _____ Who is the native of Cuba who won home run titles in 1988 and 1992?
9. _____ Who is the native of Puerto Rico who won back-to-back home run titles?
10. _____ Who is the native of Puerto Rico who hit .300 from 1992 to 1994 and won Gold Gloves from 1991 to 1994?

53. SOUTH OF THE BORDER: TODAY II

Match the ten players in the two columns below with their respective descriptions beneath.

Danny Tartabull   Dennis Martinez
Devon White   Chili Davis
Juan Guzman   Ruben Sierra
Bernie Williams   Sammy Sosa
Jose Rijo   Carlos Baerga

1. _____ Who is the native of Puerto Rico who hit 20 home runs and drove home 100 runs in back-to-back seasons?

2. _____ Who is the native of Puerto Rico who, going into the 1995 season, had averaged 100 RBIs per year?

3. _____ Who is the native of Jamaica who has won six Gold Glove awards?

4. _____ Which native of Miami—his father Jose was born in Cuba—led the American League with a .593 slugging percentage in 1991?

5. _____ Which native of the Dominican Republic won all three of his post-season games in 1990?

6. _____ Which native of the Dominican Republic got six hits in one game in 1993?

7. _____ Who is the native of Nicaragua who pitched a perfect game against the Los Angeles Dodgers in 1991?

8. _____ Who is the native of the Dominican Republic who was 16–5 with the 1992 Blue Jays?

9. _____ Who is the native of Jamaica who has hit switch-hit home runs in one game eight times?

10. _____ Which native of Puerto Rico shares major league records for strikeouts (5) in a nine-inning game, doubles (2) in one inning, and long hits (2) in one inning?

Chapter Twelve

THE HOT CORNER

54. ONE-TOWN MEN

Which ten of the following 20 players performed for the same club throughout their major league careers: Luke Appling, Brooks Robinson, Bill Terry, Stan Hack, Ralph Kiner, Lefty Grove, Joe Cronin, Walter Johnson, Grover Alexander, Mel Ott, Gil Hodges, Johnny Podres, Lew Burdette, Al Kaline, Ted Kluszewski, Ernie Banks, Cecil Travis, Pee Wee Reese, Eddie Mathews, and Dallas Green.

1. _____
2. _____
3. _____
4. _____
5. _____
6. _____
7. _____
8. _____
9. _____
10. _____

55. THE FIRST INNING

There have been 22 new major league franchises since 1953. Can you recall their first respective managers? The following list may give you a clue: Darrell Johnson, Ted Williams, Gene Mauch, Bob Kennedy, Harry Craft, Rene Lachemann, Harry Lavagetto, Roy Hartsfield, Lou Boudreau, Charlie Grimm, Bill Rigney, Mickey Vernon, Casey Stengel, Joe Gordon, Preston Gomez, Dave Bristol, Joe Schultz, Bobby Bragan, Walt Alston, Jimmy Dykes, and Don Baylor.

1. _____ (1953) Milwaukee Braves
2. _____ (1954) Baltimore Orioles
3. _____ (1955) Kansas City Athletics
4. _____ (1958) San Francisco Giants
5. _____ (1958) Los Angeles Dodgers
6. _____ (1961) Minnesota Twins
7. _____ (1961) Washington Senators
8. _____ (1961) Los Angeles Angels
9. _____ (1962) Houston Astros
10. _____ (1962) New York Mets
11. _____ (1966) Atlanta Braves
12. _____ (1968) Oakland A's
13. _____ (1969) Kansas City Royals
14. _____ (1969) Seattle Pilots
15. _____ (1969) Montreal Expos
16. _____ (1969) San Diego Padres
17. _____ (1970) Milwaukee Brewers
18. _____ (1972) Texas Rangers
19. _____ (1977) Seattle Mariners
20. _____ (1977) Toronto Blue Jays
21. _____ (1993) Colorado Rockies
22. _____ (1993) Florida Marlins

56. THE LAST INNING

There have been ten major league franchises that have switched cities. Can you name the last respective managers of the original franchises? The following ten names should give you a start: Walt Alston, Harry Lavagetto, Charlie Grimm, Ted Williams, Joe Schultz, Marty Marion, Luke Appling, Eddie Joost, Bobby Bragan, and Bill Rigney.

1. _____ (1952) Boston Braves
2. _____ (1953) St. Louis Browns
3. _____ (1954) Philadelphia Athletics
4. _____ (1957) New York Giants
5. _____ (1957) Brooklyn Dodgers
6. _____ (1960) Washington Senators
7. _____ (1965) Milwaukee Braves
8. _____ (1967) Kansas City A's
9. _____ (1969) Seattle Pilots
10. _____ (1971) Washington Senators

57. MAJOR LEAGUE OWNERS

Some names of major league owners (past and present) are synonymous with the franchises they direct(ed). See how many of the following you can associate.

1. _____ Connie Mack
2. _____ Horace Stoneham
3. _____ Dan Topping
4. _____ Walter O'Malley
5. _____ Charles Comiskey
6. _____ Sam Breadon
7. _____ Tom Yawkey
8. _____ Lou Perini
9. _____ Bob Carpenter
10. _____ Bill Veeck
11. _____ Walter O. Briggs
12. _____ Clark Griffith
13. _____ Bob Short
14. _____ William Crosley
15. _____ Charles Finley
16. _____ Phillip K. Wrigley
17. _____ Mrs. Joan Payson
18. _____ Arthur Krock
19. _____ Calvin Griffith
20. _____ Gene Autry

a. Reds
b. Indians
c. Dodgers
d. Twins
e. Athletics (Philadelphia)
f. Tigers
g. Cubs
h. Giants
i. Padres
j. Yankees
k. Braves
l. Mets
m. Rangers
n. Phillies
o. Cardinals
p. White Sox
q. Athletics (Oakland)
r. Angels
s. Senators
t. Red Sox

58. THE MISSING LINK

Can you supply the third starting outfielder for the respective teams from the list of players that follow: Tom Brunansky, Carl Furillo, Dick Sisler, Yogi Berra, Ron Gant, Frank Robinson, Terry Moore, Joe Rudi, Sid Gordon, Greg Luzinski, Jackie Jensen, Al Simmons, Earle Combs, Vic Wertz, Don Mueller, Joe Carter, Ted Williams, Jimmy Wynn, Reggie Smith, Roger Maris, Al Kaline, Charlie Keller, Dave Henderson, Cesar Cedeno, Harry Heilmann, Duffy Lewis, Casey Stengel, Lou Piniella, Matty Alou, and Pete Reiser.

1. Mickey Mantle, Roger Maris, and _____ (Yankees, 1961)
2. Joe DiMaggio, Tommy Henrich, and _____ (Yankees, 1941)
3. Stan Musial, Enos Slaughter, and _____ (Cardinals, 1942)
4. Tris Speaker, Harry Hooper, and _____ (Red Sox, 1916)
5. Babe Ruth, Bob Meusel, and _____ (Yankees, 1927)
6. Andy Pafko, Duke Snider, and _____ (Dodgers, 1952)
7. Dom DiMaggio, Al Zarilla, and _____ (Red Sox, 1950)
8. Bobby Bonds, Elliott Maddox, and _____ (Yankees, 1975)
9. Whitey Lockman, Willie Mays, and _____ (Giants, 1954)
10. Roberto Clemente, Willie Stargell, and _____ (Pirates, 1966)
11. Richie Ashburn, Del Ennis, and _____ (Phillies, 1950)
12. Lou Brock, Curt Flood, and _____ (Cardinals, 1968)
13. Ted Williams, Jimmy Piersall, and _____ (Red Sox, 1954)

14. Hoot Evers, Johnny Groth, and _____
    (Tigers, 1950)
15. Willard Marshall, Bobby Thomson, and _____
    _____ (Giants, 1947)
16. Dixie Walker, Joe Medwick, and _____
    (Dodgers, 1941)
17. Mule Haas, Bing Miller, and _____
    (Athletics, 1931)
18. Ty Cobb, Heinie Manush, and _____
    (Tigers, 1923)
19. Ross Youngs, Irish Meusel, and _____
    (Giants, 1922)
20. Paul Blair, Don Buford, and _____
    (Orioles, 1970)
21. Carl Yastrzemski, Tony Conigliaro, and _____
    _____ (Red Sox, 1970)
22. Willie Horton, Jim Northrup, and _____
    (Tigers, 1969)
23. Jim North, Reggie Jackson, and _____
    (Athletics, 1973)
24. Bob Watson, Jimmy Wynn, and _____
    (Astros, 1973)
25. Bill Buckner, Willie Crawford, and _____
    (Dodgers, 1974)
26. Bake McBride, Garry Maddox, and _____
    (Phillies, 1980)
27. Dan Gladden, Kirby Puckett, and _____
    (Twins, 1987)
28. Jose Canseco, Rickey Henderson, and _____
    _____ (A's, 1990)
29. Candy Maldonado, Devon White, and _____
    _____ (Blue Jays, 1992)
30. Dave Justice, Otis Nixon, and _____
    (Braves, 1992)

59. WHO PLAYED THIRD?

There have been many outstanding double-play combinations in the history of the major leagues. Thirty of the more recognizable ones, since 1940, are listed. Can you recall the third baseman who played in the same infield with them?

1. _____ Mark Belanger to Davey Johnson to Boog Powell (Orioles, 1970)
2. _____ Bert Campaneris to Dick Green to Gene Tenace (A's, 1974)
3. _____ Larry Bowa to Dave Cash to Willie Montanez (Phillies, 1974)
4. _____ Bill Russell to Dave Lopes to Steve Garvey (Dodgers, 1974)
5. _____ Phil Rizzuto to Joe Gordon to Johnny Sturm (Yankees, 1941)
6. _____ Joe Cronin to Bobby Doerr to Jimmie Foxx (Red Sox, 1941).
7. _____ Pee Wee Reese to Billy Herman to Dolph Camilli (Dodgers, 1941)
8. _____ Marty Marion to Red Schoendienst to Stan Musial (Cardinals, 1946)
9. _____ Lou Boudreau to Joe Gordon to Eddie Robinson (Indians, 1948)
10. _____ Eddie Joost to Pete Suder to Ferris Fain (A's, 1949)
11. _____ Vern Stephens to Bobby Doerr to Billy Goodman (Red Sox, 1949)
12. _____ Pee Wee Reese to Jackie Robinson to Gil Hodges (Dodgers, 1952)
13. _____ Granny Hamner to Mike Goliat to Eddie Waitkus (Phillies, 1950)
14. _____ Al Dark to Ed Stanky to Whitey Lockman (Giants, 1951)
15. _____ Phil Rizzuto to Billy Martin to Joe Collins (Yankees, 1952)
16. _____ Ray Boone to Bob Avila to Luke Easter (Indians, 1952)

17. _____ Roy McMillan to Johnny Temple to Ted Kluszewski (Reds, 1954)
18. _____ Johnny Logan to Red Schoendienst to Joe Adcock (Braves, 1958)
19. _____ Dick Groat to Bill Mazeroski to Dick Stuart (Pirates, 1960)
20. _____ Tony Kubek to Bobby Richardson to Bill Skowron (Yankees, 1961)
21. _____ Luis Aparicio to Nellie Fox to Roy Sievers (White Sox, 1961)
22. _____ Dick Groat to Julian Javier to Bill White (Cardinals, 1964)
23. _____ Don Kessinger to Gene Beckert to Ernie Banks (Cubs, 1965)
24. _____ Billy Myers to Lonny Frey to Frank McCormick (Reds, 1940)
25. _____ Pete Runnels to Cass Michaels to Mickey Vernon (Senators, 1951)
26. _____ Greg Gagne to Steve Lombardozzi to Kent Hrbek (Twins, 1987)
27. _____ Walt Weiss to Glenn Hubbard to Mark McGwire (A's, 1988)
28. _____ Shawon Dunston to Ryne Sandburg to Mark Grace (Cubs, 1989)
29. _____ Rafael Belliard to Mark Lemke to Sid Bream (Braves, 1992)
30. _____ Manny Lee to Roberto Alomar to John Olerud (Blue Jays, 1992)

60. BROTHER COMBINATIONS

Provide the first name of the other brother who played in the major leagues.

1. _____ , Joe, Dom DiMaggio
2. _____ , Rick Ferrell
3. _____ , Walker Cooper
4. _____ , Larry Sherry
5. _____ , Jesse Barnes
6. _____ , Jerome Dean
7. _____ , Gaylord Perry
8. _____ , Phil Niekro
9. _____ , Stan Coveleski
10. _____ , Henry Mathewson
11. _____ , Matty, Felipe Alou
12. _____ , Johnny O'Brien
13. _____ , Joe Torre
14. _____ , Tony Conigliaro
15. _____ , Clete, Cloyd Boyer
16. _____ , Bob Meusel
17. _____ , George Dickey
18. _____ , Henry Aaron
19. _____ , Paul Waner
20. _____ , Jose, Tommy Cruz
21. _____ , Harry Walker
22. _____ , Dick Sisler
23. _____ , Marv Throneberry
24. _____ , Tom, Tim, Joe, Frank Delahanty
25. _____ , Hal Keller
26. _____ , Sandy Alomar
27. _____ , Cal Ripken
28. _____ , Jose Canseco
29. _____ , Melido, Pascual Perez
30. _____ , Ramon Martinez

61. NO HANDICAP

During the annals of major league baseball, there have been many players who had to overcome adversity in order to fulfill their lifetime ambitions. Eight of them follow: Jim Eisenreich, Jim Abbott, John Olerud, Mordecai Brown, Pete Gray, Red Ruffing, William Hoy, and John Hiller. Match them with the physical impairments that they had.

1. _____ Missing toes
2. _____ Deaf and dumb
3. _____ Missing fingers
4. _____ Missing arm (regular player)
5. _____ Missing arm (pitcher)
6. _____ Aneurism operation
7. _____ Heart condition
8. _____ Tourette's syndrome

62. BASEBALL TRAGEDIES

Match the following players who died tragically—either during or shortly after their playing careers—with the year in which they passed away: Roberto Clemente, Lyman Bostock, Kenny Hubbs, Harry Agganis, Don Wilson, Jim Umbricht, Lou Gehrig, Thurman Munson, Danny Frisella, Ray Chapman, and Ed Delahanty.

1. _____ (1903)   7. _____ (1972)
2. _____ (1920)   8. _____ (1975)
3. _____ (1941)   9. _____ (1977)
4. _____ (1955)   10. _____ (1978)
5. _____ (1964)   11. _____ (1979)
6. _____ (1964)

63. NO UNTOUCHABLES

It's pretty hard to believe that the top three hitters who ever lived—Ty Cobb, Rogers Hornsby, and Joe Jackson—were traded from one team to another. That's been the case of many great players, though. Twenty-five players who ended up their careers with .300 or better lifetime averages are listed with the team with which they first made their name. Name the team to which they were either traded or sold.

1. _____ Ty Cobb (Tigers)
2. _____ Rogers Hornsby (Cardinals)
3. _____ Joe Jackson (Indians)
4. _____ Tris Speaker (Red Sox)
5. _____ Babe Ruth (Red Sox)
6. _____ George Sisler (Browns)
7. _____ Al Simmons (A's)
8. _____ Paul Waner (Pirates)
9. _____ Eddie Collins (A's)
10. _____ Jimmie Foxx (A's)
11. _____ Joe Medwick (Cardinals)
12. _____ Chuck Klein (Phillies)
13. _____ Frank Frisch (Giants)
14. _____ Hank Greenberg (Tigers)
15. _____ Johnny Mize (Cardinals)
16. _____ Mickey Cochrane (A's)
17. _____ Richie Ashburn (Phillies)
18. _____ George Kell (Tigers)
19. _____ Dixie Walker (Dodgers)
20. _____ Ernie Lombardi (Reds)
21. _____ Harvey Kuenn (Tigers)
22. _____ Hank Aaron (Braves)
23. _____ Willie Mays (Giants)
24. _____ Joe Cronin (Senators)
25. _____ Enos Slaughter (Cardinals)

64. WHEN DID THEY COME UP?

1930s–1940s

See if you can match the players that follow with the year in which they first broke into the majors (if you are within one year of the actual season, before or after, count it as a correct answer): Tom Henrich, Warren Spahn, Red Schoendienst, Joe DiMaggio, Eddie Yost, George Kell, Joe Gordon, Stan Musial, Ted Williams, and Dom DiMaggio.

1. _____ (1936)	6. _____ (1941)
2. _____ (1937)	7. _____ (1942)
3. _____ (1938)	8. _____ (1943)
4. _____ (1939)	9. _____ (1944)
5. _____ (1940)	10. _____ (1945)

1940s–1950s

We're in the post-war era now. See how you do with the following ten players (if you are within one year of the actual season, before or after, count it as a correct answer): Whitey Ford, Willie Mays, Yogi Berra, Rocky Colavito, Jackie Robinson, Hank Aaron, Al Kaline, Richie Ashburn, Jerry Coleman, and Eddie Mathews.

1. _____ (1946)	6. _____ (1951)
2. _____ (1947)	7. _____ (1952)
3. _____ (1948)	8. _____ (1953)
4. _____ (1949)	9. _____ (1954)
5. _____ (1950)	10. _____ (1955)

1950s–1960s

We're moving into your wheelhouse now. Take a good cut at the following players (if you are within one year of the actual season, before or after, count it as a correct answer): Mel Stottlemyre, Roger Maris, Ed Kranepool, Frank Robinson, Maury Wills, Pete Rose, Catfish Hunter, Carl Yastrzemski, Juan Marichal, and Ron Fairly.

1. _____ (1956)		6. _____ (1961)
2. _____ (1957)		7. _____ (1962)
3. _____ (1958)		8. _____ (1963)
4. _____ (1959)		9. _____ (1964)
5. _____ (1960)		10. _____ (1965)

1960s–1970s

We're now in the present era. It's a home run contest. The pitches are coming right down the middle. See how you can do with the following offerings (if you are within one year of the actual season, before or after, count it as a correct answer): Fred Lynn, Cesar Cedeno, George Scott, Jim Rice, Rod Carew, Mike Schmidt, Dave Parker, Bobby Bonds, Chris Speier, and Thurman Munson.

1. _____ (1966)		6. _____ (1971)
2. _____ (1967)		7. _____ (1972)
3. _____ (1968)		8. _____ (1973)
4. _____ (1969)		9. _____ (1974)
5. _____ (1970)		10. _____ (1975)

1970s–1990s

We're with your contemporaries now. You ought to be able to read the pitches a good distance from the plate. See how you can do with the following serves (if you are within one year of the actual season, before or after, count it as a correct answer): Rick Sutcliffe, Jose Canseco, Harold Baines, Cal Ripken, Billy Hatcher, Eddie Murray, Will Clark, Carlos Baerga, Joe Carter, Paul Molitor, Ron Gant, Ken Griffey, Rickey Henderson, Craig Biggio, and Wade Boggs.

1. _____ (1976)	9. _____ (1984)
2. _____ (1977)	10. _____ (1985)
3. _____ (1978)	11. _____ (1986)
4. _____ (1979)	12. _____ (1987)
5. _____ (1980)	13. _____ (1988)
6. _____ (1981)	14. _____ (1989)
7. _____ (1982)	15. _____ (1990)
8. _____ (1983)	

Two Strikes Against Him

Ray Chapman, had he not been hit by an errant pitch by the Yankees' Carl Mays, might have ended up in the Hall of Fame.

A .278 lifetime hitter, the 29-year-old shortstop was just coming into his own right as a batsman, averaging over .300 in three of his last four years. And he was an accomplished base runner, stealing 233 career bases, including 52 in 1917, the most bases that any Indian had ever pilfered in one season until Miguel Dilone swiped 61 in 1980. Kenny Lofton stole 70 bases in 1993 to set the present record.

But the deuces were stacked against him on August 16, 1920. The number-two batter in the lineup that day, he stroked two hits—both of them doubles—scored two runs and stole two bases. Defensively, he made two assists, two putouts, and two errors. In fact, he was hit with two pitches by Mays. The second one killed him.

His replacement in the lineup, had Chapman not been killed by that ill-fated pitch, might not have ended up in the Hall of Fame. For he very well could have been relegated to years on the bench behind a blossoming star. But Chapman's back-up did go on to play 14 years in the big leagues. He averaged .312 lifetime and batted .300 ten times, including nine times in his first ten years in the majors. The one time that he failed to bat .300, he missed by just one point. But perhaps the most incredible story about this Hall of Famer was his ability to make contact. He averaged only eight strikeouts per season for 14 years. In his last nine seasons he whiffed just five times per year. And in both 1930 and 1932 he fanned only three times, the all-time low for a full-time player.

Who was this one-time Indian-Yankee star who got his best break on the day that Chapman got the worst break of any major league player?

(Answer appears on page 344.)

Chapter Thirteen

TOUCHING ALL THE BASES

65. OPENING DAY HIGHLIGHTS

Match the players in the left-hand column with the accomplishments they achieved on opening day(s) in the right-hand column.

1. _____ Bob Feller
2. _____ Brooks Robinson
3. _____ Frank Robinson
4. _____ Nelson Fox
5. _____ Jim Greengrass
6. _____ George Bell
7. _____ Karl Rhodes
8. _____ Tom Seaver
9. _____ Walter Johnson
10. _____ Billy Martin*

a. He pitched nine wins and seven shutouts.
b. He pitched a no-hitter.
c. He got two hits in one inning.
d. He started 16 games.
e. He suited up for opening day 23 consecutive times.
f. He was the only American Leaguer to hit three home runs.
g. He was the last player to get four doubles.
h. He was the only National Leaguer to hit three home runs.
i. He hit eight home runs.
j. He was the last player to get five hits.

*Russ Morman of the 1986 White Sox and Chad Kreuter of the 1988 Rangers have since tied his record.

66. WHOM DID THEY PRECEDE?

See if you can determine whom the following players preceded at their positions in the field.

1. _____ Bill White (Giants)
   a. Nippy Jones   c. Joe Torre
   b. Steve Bilko   d. Orlando Cepeda
2. _____ Tony Lazzeri (Yankees)
   a. George Stirnweiss c. Joe Gordon
   b. Frankie Crosetti   d. Jerry Priddy
3. _____ Leo Durocher (Dodgers)
   a. Arky Vaughan   c. Billy Herman
   b. Pee Wee Reese   d. Frenchy Bordagaray
4. _____ Eddie Mathews (Braves)
   a. Clete Boyer   c. Frank Bolling
   b. Dennis Menke   d. Roy McMillan
5. _____ Bobby Thomson (Giants)
   a. Clint Hartung   c. Willie Mays
   b. Whitey Lockman   d. Monte Irvin*
6. _____ Harry Walker (Phillies)
   a. Richie Ashburn   c. Dick Sisler
   b. Del Ennis   d. Bill Nicholson
7. _____ Joe DiMaggio (Yankees)
   a. Cliff Mapes   c. Johnny Lindell
   b. Mickey Mantle   d. Irv Noren
8. _____ Dom DiMaggio (Red Sox)
   a. Jackie Jensen   c. Tommy Umphlett
   b. Gene Stephens   d. Jimmy Piersall
9. _____ Yogi Berra (Yankees)
   a. Elston Howard   c. Jake Gibbs
   b. John Blanchard   d. Jesse Gonder
10. _____ Del Crandall (Braves)
   a. Joe Torre   c. Stan Lopata
   b. Del Rice   d. Bob Uecker

*Position: Center field.

132

67. WHOM DID THEY SUCCEED?

See if you can figure out whom the following players succeeded at their positions on the field.

1. _____ Babe Dahlgren (Yankees)
   a. Nick Etten   c. Wally Pipp
   b. George McQuinn   d. Lou Gehrig
2. _____ Jackie Robinson (Dodgers)
   a. Eddie Miksis   c. Cookie Lavagetto
   b. Eddie Stanky   d. Don Zimmer*
3. _____ Chico Carrasquel (White Sox)
   a. Luke Appling   c. Don Kolloway
   b. Cass Michaels   d. Willie Miranda
4. _____ Brooks Robinson (Orioles)
   a. Vern Stephens   c. George Kell
   b. Billy Hunter   d. Billy Goodman
5. _____ George Selkirk (Yankees)
   a. Ben Chapman   c. Bob Meusel
   b. Earle Combs   d. Babe Ruth
6. _____ Carl Yastrzemski (Red Sox)
   a. Ted Williams   c. Sam Mele
   b. Clyde Vollmer   d. Al Zarilla
7. _____ Lou Brock (Cardinals)
   a. Enos Slaughter   c. Stan Musial
   b. Wally Moon   d. Joe Cunningham
8. _____ Roger Maris (Yankees)
   a. Tommy Henrich   c. Norm Siebern
   b. Hank Bauer   d. Harry Simpson
9. _____ John Roseboro (Dodgers)
   a. Roy Campanella   c. Joe Pignatano
   b. Bruce Edwards   d. Rube Walker
10. _____ Wes Westrum (Giants)
    a. Ernie Lombardi   c. Walker Cooper
    b. Sal Yvars   d. Ray Mueller

*Position: Second base.

68. CHIPS OFF THE OLD BLOCK

The players who are listed below had fathers who preceded them to the major leagues. Name the source of the offspring.

1. _____ Dick Sisler
2. _____ Tom Tresh
3. _____ Mike Hegan
4. _____ Buddy Bell
5. _____ Doug Camilli
6. _____ Hal Lanier
7. _____ Bob Boone
8. _____ Bump Wills
9. _____ Roy Smalley
10. _____ Steve Trout

69. CURRENT CHIPS OFF THE OLD BLOCK

The present-day players who are listed below had fathers who preceded them to the major leagues. Name the source of the offspring.

1. _____ Roberto and Sandy Alomar
2. _____ Ed Sprague
3. _____ Todd Stottlemyre
4. _____ Barry Bonds
5. _____ Bret Boone
6. _____ Brian McRae
7. _____ Ken Griffey
8. _____ Robb Nen
9. _____ Moises Alou
10. _____ Todd Hundley

70. THE GAS HOUSE GANG

In the 1930s the St. Louis Cardinals had a colorful group of players who were known as the Gas House Gang. Match the Gas Housers with the nicknames that they acquired.

1. _____ James Collins   a. Ducky
2. _____ Frankie Frisch   b. Spud
3. _____ Leo Durocher   c. Wild
4. _____ Johnny Martin   d. Rip
5. _____ Joe Medwick   e. Dizzy
6. _____ Enos Slaughter   f. The Fordham Flash
7. _____ Virgil Davis   g. Daffy
8. _____ Jerome Dean   h. The Lip
9. _____ Paul Dean   i. Pepper
10. _____ Bill Hallahan   j. Country

71. THE YEAR OF _____

Fit the phrases listed below to the years to which they apply

The Whiz Kids
The Amazin' Ones
The Hitless Wonders
Gionfriddo's Gem
Feller's Pick-off (?)
Sandy's Snatch
Maz's Sudden Shot
The Gas House Gang
Larsen's Perfect Game
The M&M Boys
Pesky's Pause
Home Run Baker
Murderers' Row

The Babe Calls His Shot
The Go-Go Sox
The Black Sox
The Wild Hoss of the Osage
Merkle's Boner
Mays's Miracle Catch
Ernie's Snooze
Billy the Kid
Alex's Biggest Strikeout
The Miracle Braves
Mickey's Passed Ball
The Miracle of Coogan's
  Bluff

1. _____ (1906)
2. _____ (1908)
3. _____ (1911)
4. _____ (1914)
5. _____ (1919)
6. _____ (1926)
7. _____ (1927)
8. _____ (1931)
9. _____ (1932)
10. _____ (1934)
11. _____ (1939)
12. _____ (1941)
13. _____ (1946)
14. _____ (1947)
15. _____ (1948)
16. _____ (1950)
17. _____ (1951)
18. _____ (1953)
19. _____ (1954)
20. _____ (1955)
21. _____ (1956)
22. _____ (1959)
23. _____ (1960)
24. _____ (1961)
25. _____ (1969)

72. THE MEN AT THE MIKE

Most teams have an announcer who becomes known in is bailiwick as the "voice" of the club. Some of the announcers who are listed in the left-hand column have called the play-by-play with more than one team. Two, in particular, are known as the "voice" of two teams. Those teams are duly designated in the right-hand column. Match the "voice" with the respective team(s).

1. _____ Mel Allen   a. Pirates
2. _____ Red Barber   b. Browns
3. _____ Russ Hodges   c. White Sox
4. _____ Lindsey Nelson   d. A's (Oakland)
5. _____ Curt Gowdy   e. Reds
6. _____ By Saam   f. Giants
7. _____ Bob Prince   g. Yankees
8. _____ Vince Scully   h. Tigers
9. _____ Waite Hoyt   i. Dodgers (Brooklyn)
10. _____ Chuck Thompson   j. Red Sox
11. _____ Dizzy Dean   k. Cardinals/Cubs
12. _____ Jack Brickhouse   l. Orioles
13. _____ Ernie Harwell   m. Dodgers (Los Angeles)
14. _____ Harry Carey   n. Mets
15. _____ Monte Clark   o. Senators/Twins
16. _____ Bob Wolff   p. Phillies

73. PEN NAMES

In the following pairs of names, see if you can distinguish the major league player from the major league writer. Which one was the artist on the diamond?

1. Grantland Rice—Del Rice
2. Dan Parker—Wes Parker
3. Fred Winchell—Walter Winchell
4. Woody Woodward—Stanley Woodward
5. Frank Sullivan—Ed Sullivan
6. Gary Schumacher—Hal Schumacher
7. Dick Williams—Joe Williams
8. Tom Meany—Pat Meany
9. Art Fowler—Gene Fowler
10. Frank Graham—Jack Graham
11. Quentin Reynolds—Carl Reynolds
12. Frank Adams—Babe Adams
13. Bill Dailey—Arthur Dailey
14. Don Gross—Milton Gross
15. Babe Young—Dick Young
16. Red Smith—Hal Smith
17. Babe Twombly—Wells Twombly
18. Earl Lawson—Roxie Lawson
19. Ray Murray—Jim Murray
20. Johnny Powers—Jimmy Powers

74. MATCHING MOGULS

Match the present-day major league moguls in the left-hand column with the big-league teams that they direct in the right-hand column.

1. _____ Peter Angelos	a.	Toronto
2. _____ John Harrington	b.	Atlanta
3. _____ Michael Ilitch	c.	Colorado
4. _____ George Steinbrenner	d.	Florida
5. _____ P.N.T. Widdrington	e.	Baltimore
6. _____ Jerry Reinsdorf	f.	Texas
7. _____ Richard Jacobs	g.	Seattle
8. _____ David Glass	h.	Boston
9. _____ Bud Selig	i.	California
10. _____ Carl Pohlad	j.	San Francisco
11. _____ Gene Autry	k.	San Diego
12. _____ Walter Haas	l.	Chicago Cubs
13. _____ John Ellis	m.	Chicago White Sox
14. _____ George Bush, Edward Rose	n.	St. Louis
	o.	Pittsburgh
15. _____ Ted Turner	p.	Cincinnati
16. _____ H. Wayne Huizenga	q.	Cleveland
17. _____ Claude Brochu	r.	Philadelphia
18. _____ Nelson Doubleday	s.	Oakland
19. _____ William Giles	t.	Detroit
20. _____ Stanton Cook	u.	Houston
21. _____ Marge Schott	v.	New York Yankees
22. _____ Drayton McLane	w.	New York Mets
23. _____ Mark Sauer	x.	Kansas City
24. _____ August A. Busch	y.	Los Angeles
25. _____ Jerry McMorris	z.	Montreal
26. _____ Peter O'Malley	aa.	Milwaukee
27. _____ John Moores	bb.	Minnesota
28. _____ Peter Magowan		

75. A STAR IS BORN

Match the players listed with the cities in which they were born.

1. _____ Hank Aaron	a. Omaha, Neb.
2. _____ Johnny Bench	b. Martinez, Calif.
3. _____ Tommy Davis	c. Hertford, N.C.
4. _____ Al Kaline	d. Mobile, Ala.
5. _____ Brooks Robinson	e. Beaumont, Tex.
6. _____ Frank Robinson	f. Oklahoma City,
7. _____ Pete Rose	Oklahoma
8. _____ Bob Gibson	g. Little Rock, Ark.
9. _____ Jim Hunter	h. Cincinnati, Ohio
10. _____ Frank McGraw	i. Brooklyn, N.Y.
	j. Baltimore, Md.

76. THE NATIONAL PASTIME

Baseball truly is the national pastime. Today's players come from every state in the United States except four. They come from large cities, small hamlets, and rural intersects. In the following five quizzes they come to you in groups of ten. One of the quizzes contains one state that has not produced a present-day major league player; one of them contains three states that have not produced a present-day major league player. See how well you can match up the players in the left-hand columns with their respective places of birth.

Alabama to Georgia

1. _____ Jimmy Key	a. Columbus, GA
2. _____ Curt Schilling	b. Little Rock, AR
3. _____ Tom Pagnozzi	c. Huntsville, AL
4. _____ Kevin McReynolds	d. Seaford, DE
5. _____ Eddie Murray	e. Anchorage, AK
6. _____ James Mouton	f. Sanford, FL
7. _____ Mo Vaughn	g. Los Angeles, CA
8. _____ Delino DeShields	h. Tucson, AZ
9. _____ Tim Raines	i. Norwalk, CT
0. _____ Frank Thomas	j. Denver, CO

Hawaii to Maryland

_____ Ron Darling	a. Cedar Rapids, IA
_____ Rickey Henderson	b. Havre de Grace, MD
_____ Don Mattingly	c. Honolulu, HI
_____ Calvin Eldred	d. South Portland, ME
_____ Darren Daulton	e. Louisville, KY
_____ Mike Greenwell	f. Arkansas City, KS
_____ Albert Belle	g. Chicago, IL
_____ Bill Swift	h. Boise, ID
_____ Cal Ripken	i. Shreveport, LA
	j. Evansville, IN

Massachusetts to New Jersey

1. _____ Tom Glavine
2. _____ Kirk Gibson
3. _____ Paul Molitor
4. _____ Ellis Burks
5. _____ David Cone
6. _____ Jeff Ballard
7. _____ Wade Boggs
8. _____ Shawn Boskie
9. _____ Phil Plantier
10. _____ Eric Karros

a. Kansas City, MO
b. Vicksburg, MS
c. Omaha, NE
d. Hackensack, NJ
e. St. Paul, MN
f. Manchester, NH
g. Billings, MT
h. Pontiac, MI
i. Hawthorne, NV
j. Concord, MA

New Mexico to South Carolina

1. _____ Roy Ward
2. _____ Lou Whitaker
3. _____ Mark Grace
4. _____ Rick Helling
5. _____ Roger Clemens
6. _____ Joe Carter
7. _____ Dan Carlson
8. _____ Ken Griffey
9. _____ Ken Ryan
10. _____ Reggie Sanders

a. Dayton, OH
b. Pawtucket, RI
c. Parkview, NM
d. Portland, OR
e. Oklahoma City, OK
f. Florence, SC
g. Brooklyn, NY
h. Donora, PA
i. Winston-Salem, NC
j. Devils Lake, ND

South Dakota to Wyoming

1. _____ Bryan Harvey
2. _____ Chuck Knoblauch
3. _____ Bobby Witt
4. _____ John Olerud
5. _____ John Kruk
6. _____ Zane Smith
7. _____ Tom Browning

a. Houston, TX
b. Charleston, WV
c. Casper, WY
d. Bethel, VT
e. Chattanooga, TN
f. Rapid City, SD
g. Madison, WI
h. Bellows Falls, UT
i. Seattle, WA
j. Arlington, VA

77. THE INTERNATIONAL PASTIME

Not all the major leaguers in the history of baseball have been born on the mainland of the United States. Many of them have come from foreign states, countries, islands, territories, and provinces. See if you can match the players with their place of birth.

1. _____ Sandy Alomar	a. Otsuki, Japan
2. _____ Cesar Cedeno	b. Swansea, Wales
3. _____ Bert Campaneris	c. Gatun, Panama
4. _____ Rod Carew	d. Salinas, Puerto Rico
5. _____ Dave Concepcion	e. Chartham, (Ontario)
6. _____ Irish McIlveen	Canada
7. _____ Jorge Orta	f. Ozanna, Poland
8. _____ Ferguson Jenkins	g. Mantanzas, Cuba
9. _____ Bobby Thomson	h. Honolulu, Hawaii
10. _____ Moe Drabowsky	i. Mazatlan, Mexico
11. _____ Elmer Valo	j. Santo Domingo,
12. _____ Masanori Murakami	Dominican Republic
13. _____ Reno Bertoia	k. Nassau, Bahamas
14. _____ Elrod Hendricks	l. Kos, Greece
15. _____ Andre Rogers	m. Glasgow, Scotland
16. _____ Mike Lum	n. Ribnik,
17. _____ Al Campanis	Czechoslovakia
18. _____ Jimmy Austin	o. St. Vito, Udine, Italy
	p. Aragua, Venezuela
	q. St. Thomas,
	Virgin Islands
	r. Belfast, Ireland

78. BIG-LEAGUE BLOOPERS

Match the players who are listed below with the bloopers they committed on big-league diamonds.

Fred Merkle	Pee Wee Reese
Fred Snodgrass	Phil Rizzuto
Mickey Owen	Darrell Evans
Babe Ruth	Herb Washington
Babe Herman	Jimmy Piersall
Jose Canseco	Marv Throneberry
Kevin Kennedy	Hank Gowdy
Clyde Sukeforth	Dave Winfield
Casey Stengel	Jay Howell
Ted Williams	Mickey Mantle
Jack McDowell	Lonnie Smith
Lou Piniella	Steve Lyons
Joe DiMaggio	

1. _____ His passed ball with two outs in the ninth inning of the fourth game of the 1941 World Series made the difference between the Brooklyn Dodgers being even in the fall classic (2–2) against the Yankees and being down (3–1) to the Bombers.
2. _____ He was ejected from a NLCS when he was found to have pine tar in his glove.
3. _____ He was fined $5,000 when he spat at the fans.
4. _____ He was fined $10,000 after he gave the crowd an uncomplimentary finger.
5. _____ A designated runner, he was picked off first base by Mike Marshall of the Los Angeles Dodgers in the 1974 World Series.
6. _____ His failure to touch second base in a key game against the Cubs in 1908 led to the Giants' loss of a pennant they should have won.
7. _____ He was thrown out trying to steal for the last out of a World Series.

8. _____ One night in Detroit in 1950 he lost track of the number of outs and started to run toward his dugout after he gloved the second out of the inning.

9. _____ In the 1991 World Series against the Twins he lost track of the number of outs, and that cost the Braves the opportunity of winning their first fall classic.

10. _____ On opening day in 1976 he committed his fourth error of the game in the third inning. (The season got much better for this good glove and bat man.)

11. _____ One day he hit an apparent triple, but he got called out because he missed *both* first and second base.

12. _____ This New York Giant catcher cost his team a World Series because he tripped over his mask in a key play of the seventh game.

13. _____ He tripled into a double play.

14. _____ While fixing the belt of his pants on the first-base bag, he and the fans became astonished to see them slip to his ankles.

15. _____ He had the humiliating experience of seeing and feeling a batted ball bounce off his head for a home run.

16. _____ He called on Jose Canseco to pitch, a faux pas that led to elbow surgery for the home run champ of the previous year.

17. _____ He had a ball kicked out of his glove by Eddie Stanky in a key play of the 1950 World Series.

18. _____ This manager called for Johnny Kucks from the bull pen. Instead the bull pen coach, who heard wrong, sent him Virgil Trucks. Trucks got the batter to hit into a game-ending double play.

19. _____ He got embarrassed when Dick Groat of the Cardinals picked him off second base in the fourth game of the 1964 World Series on the hidden-ball trick.

20. _____ He ran around the bases backward after he hit his 100th career homer. He planned it in advance. (It's against the rules to do it today.)

145

21. _____ This bull pen coach made the decision to send in Ralph Branca rather than Carl Erskine in the 1951 sudden-death playoff game between the winning New York Giants and the Brooklyn Dodgers.

22. _____ A rookie, he stepped off third base to retrieve a thrown bat by Dixie Walker after a swinging strike and found himself called out when he was tagged by the third baseman for his Samaritan gesture.

23. _____ This present-day manager didn't obey signs from coaches; consequently, one night he got thrown out at second, third, and home.

24. _____ In the 1912 World Series he made the "$30,000 Muff," which cost the New York Giants another world title that they should have won.

25. _____ In between innings at Toronto's home park, he threw a warm-up ball at a wounded sea gull, which had rested on the grass, and killed it.

Where Are the Iron Men?

What's happened to the complete game in World Series play?

Why, in the first World Series (1903) that was ever played, a Pirate strongman pitched five complete games. That's right, it's still a record. But, in that same series, a rubber arm for the Red Sox pitched four complete games. That's the second highest number of complete games that has ever been pitched in one series.

As recently as 1956, though, five different Yankee pitchers threw complete games in consecutive contests. They were Whitey Ford, Tom Sturdivant, Don Larsen, Bob Turley, and Johnny Kucks, respectively. That's a record, too.

They must not make them the way they used to, though. Take the National League, for example. In the 1970s, 61 World Series games were played. But National League pitchers threw only five complete games. (And one of the pitchers hurled full games twice.) That's a complete-game average of 8.2 percent.

During the 1970s, 29 different pitchers in the National League started a game. Some of them did it a number of times. But only four of those 29 pitchers managed to complete a game. That's a pitcher-completion average of 13.8 percent.

National League pitchers began the decade by failing to get a complete game out of the first seven starters. In 1971 two different pitchers completed three games. But from 1972 to Game Two of the 1977 series, Senior Circuit hurlers failed to complete a game in 31 attempts. Two different pitchers completed games for the National League representative in 1977, but Chub Feeney's league got on another streak: in the next 18 games the National League did not get a route-going performance from one of its starters.

If you can name two of the four complete-game pitchers, you're already doing better than the National League hurlers of the 1970s did. If you can name three of them, you can take your turn with Ford, Kucks, *et al.* If you can come up with four of the pitchers, Bill Dinneen of the 1903 Red Sox will have to move over in order to make room for you. And if you can spiel off all four pitchers, including the one pitcher who did it twice, you and Deacon Phillippe of the 1903 Pirates are in a class by yourselves.

(Answer appears on page 344.)

Chapter Fourteen

THE MANAGERS

79. QUICK QUIZZING THE MANAGERS

I.

From the names listed in the right-hand column, list in order: (1) the youngest manager ever to begin a season, (2) the youngest manager ever to finish a season, (3) the youngest manager ever to win a pennant, (4) the oldest manager ever to debut as manager, and (5) the oldest manager ever to win a pennant for the first time.

1. _____ Roger Peckinpaugh
2. _____ Tom Sheehan
3. _____ Burt Shotton
4. _____ Joe Cronin
5. _____ Lou Boudreau

II.

Match the successful managers listed on the right-hand side with the number of pennants and World Series (combined total) they won. The total is contained in parentheses on the left-hand side.

1. _____ (17)   Walter Alston
2. _____ (16)   Casey Stengel
3. _____ (14)   John McGraw
4. _____ (13)   Joe McCarthy
5. _____ (11)   Connie Mack

III.

The men listed on the left-hand side were all playing managers who won at least one pennant. Yet each was traded—while still a player on that team—to another one which, in every case but one, the player continued to manage. Match the playing manager with the trade in which he was connected.

1. _____ Joe Cronin   a. Indians—Red Sox
2. _____ Rogers Hornsby   b. Senators—Tigers
3. _____ Lou Boudreau   c. Cardinals—Giants
4. _____ Bucky Harris   d. Cubs—Yankees
5. _____ Frank Chance   e. Senators—Red Sox

IV.

Match the managers in the right-hand column with their respective all-time winning percentages in the left-hand column.

1. _____ (.614)   Billy Southworth
2. _____ (.593)   Frank Chance
3. _____ (.593)   John McGraw
4. _____ (.589)   Joe McCarthy
5. _____ (.582)   Al Lopez

V.

Match the successful modern managers listed on the right-hand side with the number of pennants and World Series (combined total) they won. The total is contained in parentheses on the left-hand side.

1. _____ (8)   Tommy Lasorda
2. _____ (6)   Sparky Anderson
3. _____ (4)   Davey Johnson
4. _____ (4)   Tom Kelly
5. _____ (2)   Cito Gaston

80. DID THEY OR DIDN'T THEY . . . MANAGE?

When we look back, we sometimes find it hard to sort out fact from fiction in baseball. See if you can zero in on the 20 players who became managers from the following list of 40.

Joe Adcock	Red Rolfe
Bobby Brown	Roy Smalley
Joe Gordon	Duke Snider
Ken Keltner	Ben Chapman
Enos Slaughter	Jim Landis
Kerby Farrell	Jim Lemon
Bill Dickey	Jerry Lynch
Bucky Walters	Freddie Fitzsimmons
Bobby Wine	Irv Noren
Eddie Pellagrini	Wally Post
Walker Cooper	Bob Elliott
Nippy Jones	Eddie Lopat
Phil Cavarretta	Jerry Priddy
Christy Mathewson	Gene Hermanski
Sid Hudson	Babe Ruth
Bob Friend	Johnny Pesky
Bobby Thomson	Jim Hegan
Luke Appling	Dick Sisler
Eddie Joost	Mel McGaha
Mickey Vernon	Eddie Stanky

1. _____
2. _____
3. _____
4. _____
5. _____
6. _____
7. _____
8. _____
9. _____
10. _____
11. _____
12. _____
13. _____
14. _____
15. _____
16. _____
17. _____
18. _____
19. _____
20. _____

81. POST-WAR WORLD SERIES WINNERS

There have been 33 managers who have led their teams to World Series victories in the post-World War II era. Sixteen of them have been National League managers; 17 of them have been American League skippers. One of them has won titles in both leagues. See how many of them you can name.

National League	American League
1. _____	1. _____
2. _____	2. _____
3. _____	3. _____
4. _____	4. _____
5. _____	5. _____
6. _____	6. _____
7. _____	7. _____
8. _____	8. _____
9. _____	9. _____
10. _____	10. _____
11. _____	11. _____
12. _____	12. _____
13. _____	13. _____
14. _____	14. _____
15. _____	15. _____
16. _____	16. _____
	17. _____

82. BACK-TO-BACK PENNANT WINNERS

There have been 16 major league managers in the post-World War II era who have led their teams to at least two consecutive pennants. Two of them have done it twice. See if you can place the name with the period.

1. _____ (1949–53)
2. _____ (1952–53)
3. _____ (1955–56)
4. _____ (1955–58)*
5. _____ (1957–58)
6. _____ (1961–63)
7. _____ (1965–66)*
8. _____ (1967–68)
9. _____ (1969–71)
10. _____ (1972–73)
11. _____ (1975–76)
12. _____ (1976–77)
13. _____ (1977–78)
14. _____ (1988–90)
15. _____ (1991–92)
16. _____ (1992–93)

*The second time.

83. YOU'RE HIRED TO BE FIRED

In the left-hand column are listed men who managed 18 different major league clubs. Below them is noted the team that they managed (many of them guided more than one) and the year in which they were succeeded by a manager who started the season with his team. This eliminates interim managers who finished up a season while their owners were looking for full-time field leaders. Some of the managers who are listed were fired, some resigned, and two died. Match them with their successors who are listed in the right-hand column.

1. _____ Joe McCarthy
   (Yanks, 1947)

2. _____ Yogi Berra
   (Yanks, 1965)

3. _____ John McGraw
   (Giants, 1933)

4. _____ Mel Ott
   (Giants, 1949)*

5. _____ Leo Durocher
   (Dodgers, 1949)*

6. _____ Charlie Dressen
   (Dodgers, 1954)

7. _____ Billy Southworth
   (Cards, 1946)

8. _____ Johnny Keane
   (Cards, 1965)

9. _____ Eddie Sawyer
   (Phils, 1961)

10. _____ Danny Murtaugh
    (Pirates, 1965)

11. _____ Fred Hutchinson
    (Reds, 1965)

a. Burt Shotton
b. Bill Terry
c. Leo Durocher
d. Dick Sisler
e. Bucky Harris
f. Bobby Bragan
g. Johnny Keane
h. Eddie Dyer
i. Walt Alston
j. Gene Mauch
k. Whitey Lockman
l. Harry Walker
m. Red Schoendienst
n. Earl Weaver
o. Al Lopez
p. Al Dark
q. Kerby Farrell
r. Joe McCarthy
s. Rogers Hornsby
t. Billy Martin
u. Joe Torre
v. Tony Perez

*These managers were involved in two shake-ups by team organizations shortly into the season.

154

12. _____ Leo Durocher
(Cubs, 1973)
13. _____ Birdie Tebbetts
(Braves, 1963)
14. _____ Al Lopez
(Indians, 1957)
15. _____ Mayo Smith
(Tigers, 1971)
16. _____ Dick Williams
(A's, 1974)
17. _____ Zack Taylor
(Browns, 1952)
18. _____ Marty Marion
(White Sox, 1957)
19. _____ Joe Cronin
(Red Sox, 1948)
20. _____ Hank Bauer
(Orioles, 1969)
21. _____ Dick Howser
(Royals, 1987)
22. _____ Whitey Herzog
(Cards, 1991)
23. _____ Davey Johnson
(Mets, 1991)
24. _____ Lou Piniella
(Reds, 1993)
25. _____ Pete Rose
(Reds, 1990)

w. Lou Piniella
x. Billy Gardner
y. Bud Harrelson

84. MANAGERS IN SEARCH OF A PENNANT

Name the ten managers from the following 20 who never led a team to the pennant: Red Rolfe, Steve O'Neill, Eddie Stanky, Bill Rigney, Al Dark, Birdie Tebbetts, Fred Hutchinson, Al Lopez, Mike Higgins, Bobby Bragan, Danny Murtaugh, Harry Walker, Mel Ott, Sam Mele, Hank Bauer, Fred Haney, Johnny Keane, Gene Mauch, Dick Williams, and Paul Richards.

1. _____
2. _____
3. _____
4. _____
5. _____
6. _____
7. _____
8. _____
9. _____
10. _____

85. MANAGERIAL HALF TRUTHS

Mark "T" or "F" for "True" or "False" before each statement.

1. _____ Joe Cronin was the last Red Sox manager to direct the Bosox to a World Series victory.
2. _____ Joe Cronin was the last Senator manager to win a pennant.
3. _____ Lou Boudreau was the last Indian manager to win a World Series.
4. _____ Bill Carrigan (1915–16) has been the only Red Sox manager to direct Boston to back-to-back world championships.
5. _____ Del Baker was the first bench manager to guide the Tigers to a pennant (1940).
6. _____ Mickey Cochrane has been the only Tiger manager to guide the Bengals to back-to-back pennants.
7. _____ Bill Rigney was the last Giant manager to lead his charges to a pennant.
8. _____ Bill Dickey never managed the Yankees.
9. _____ Chuck Dressen was the last manager to win back-to-back pennants (1952–53) with the Dodgers.
10. _____ Walter Alston has been the only manager to lead the Dodgers to the world championship.
11. _____ Leo Durocher's tenure as manager of the Dodgers was longer than his reign as boss of the Giants.
12. _____ Charlie Grimm never managed a World Series winner.
13. _____ Frank Chance was the only manager of the Cubs who has won a world championship.
14. _____ Eddie Dyer, Johnny Keane, and Red Schoendienst have led the Cardinals to world titles in the post-World War II era.
15. _____ Frankie Frisch was a retired player when the Cardinals won the pennant and World Series in 1934.
16. _____ Al Lopez won pennants with two different clubs.

17. _____ Fred Haney directed the Braves to their first world title in 1957.

18. _____ Bucky Harris was the only Senator manager to lead his team to two pennants.

19. _____ Bucky Harris was the youngest manager to lead his team to a world title.

20. _____ Gil Hodges had a losing record as a major league manager.

21. _____ Rogers Hornsby never managed in the American League.

22. _____ Ralph Houk won pennants in his first three years as manager of the Yankees.

23. _____ Miller Huggins won more World Series than he lost.

24. _____ Fred Hutchinson never managed a pennant winner.

25. _____ Hughie Jennings of the Tigers (1907–09) was the only manager to lose three consecutive World Series.

26. _____ Fielder Jones of the White Sox was the winning manager in the only intercity World Series in Chicago.

27. _____ Johnny Keane was the last Cardinal manager to lead the Redbirds to the world title.

28. _____ Al Lopez, in his first nine years of managing (1951–59), never brought his teams home worse than second.

29. _____ Connie Mack's teams won nine pennants, but they appeared in only eight World Series.

30. _____ Gene Mauch managed the last pennant winner for the Phillies.

31. _____ Joe McCarthy had a better World Series winning percentage with the Yankees than Casey Stengel.

32. _____ John McGraw lost more World Series than any other team leader.

33. _____ Bill McKechnie was the only Red manager to lead his team to two consecutive pennants.

34. _____ Walter Alston was the only National League manager to lead his team to more than one pennant in the 1960s.

35. _____ Walter Alston's managerial opponent in the 1965 World Series was Sam Mele.

36. _____ Danny Murtaugh was the only Pirate manager to lead his team to the world title.

37. _____ Steve O'Neill was the last Tiger manager to lead the Bengals to the world championship.

38. _____ Wilbert Robinson won more pennants with the Dodgers than Leo Durocher.

39. _____ Billy Martin led two different teams to pennants.

40. _____ Red Schoendienst won more consecutive pennants as manager of the Cardinals than any other Redbird leader.

41. _____ Luke Sewell was the only Brown manager to lead his team to a pennant.

42. _____ Bill Virdon managed the Yankees.

43. _____ Mayo Smith's 1968 Tigers were the first team to defeat the Cardinals in the World Series since Joe McCarthy's 1943 Yankees.

44. _____ Billy Southworth won pennants with two different National League teams.

45. _____ Tris Speaker never managed a World Series winner.

46. _____ Earl Weaver has a winning record in World Series play.

47. _____ Bill Terry's managerial opponent in the 1933 Series (Giants–Senators) was Bucky Harris.

48. _____ Hank Bauer led a team to a World Series sweep.

49. _____ Rogers Hornsby won more games than he lost in World Series play.

50. _____ Luke Appling, Ted Lyons, and Jimmy Dykes all managed the White Sox.

51. _____ Cito Gaston's 1992–93 Blue Jays were the first club since the 1977–78 Yankees to win back-to-back World Series.

52. _____ Billy Martin managed those 1977–78 Yankees to back-to-back world titles.

53. _____ Tom Kelly has managed two World Series winners in two tries.

54. _____ Kelly's game-winning percentage in World Series is better than Gaston's.
55. _____ Tony La Russa was the last manager to lose back-to-back fall classics.
56. _____ Bobby Cox was the last skipper to win three consecutive pennants.
57. _____ Tony La Russa has a winning record (series and games) in World Series play.
58. _____ He has been the only manager in World Series history to be involved in reverse sweeps in back-to-back years.
59. _____ Tommy Lasorda is the National League manager who defeated him in four consecutive games.
60. _____ Whitey Herzog won a pennant with the Royals.
61. _____ Davey Johnson has won more than one pennant.
62. _____ Jim Fregosi managed in the American League.
63. _____ Bobby Cox also managed in the American League.
64. _____ Jim Leyland has won a pennant.
65. _____ Roger Craig won a pennant with the San Francisco Giants.

The Trivia Tandem

Sometimes we have a tendency to remember events which happened long ago better than those which occurred "only yesterday."

Take the case of Joe DiMaggio and Pete Rose, for example. Both of them manufactured the longest batting streaks in the history of their respective leagues. In 1941 DiMaggio hit safely in 56 consecutive games, which is the major league record; in 1978 Rose batted cleanly in 44 consecutive games, which is the modern-day National League record.

On the nights on which their respective streaks came to a close, they were handcuffed by a starting and a relieving pitcher. Much has been written about the duo of Indian pitchers who halted DiMaggio's streak. Jim Bagby, the son of a former 31-game season winner for the Indians, was the starter; Al Smith, who won 12 of 25 decisions that year, came on in relief.

So far little has been written about the two Brave pitchers who helped to stop Rose's streak. Undoubtedly, in time, they will become a more important trivia tandem. One of them was a rookie at the time; the other one was a journeyman relief pitcher.

I'll be surprised if you can name both of them. Can you?
(Answer appears on page 344.)

Chapter Fifteen

THE ALL-STAR GAME

86. ALL-STAR GAME STANDOUTS

Match the players who are listed below with the All-Star Game records that they set.*

Phil Cavarretta	Tom Glavine
Roberto Clemente	Terry Moore
Whitey Ford	Ted Williams
Yogi Berra	Stan Musial
Willie Mays	Pete Rose
Satchel Paige	Dave Winfield
Nelson Fox	Rod Carew
Charlie Gehringer	Brooks Robinson
Joe DiMaggio	Pie Traynor
Tony Oliva	Goose Gossage
Willie Jones	Atlee Hammaker
Hank Aaron	Joe Morgan
Ozzie Smith	George Brett
Dwight Gooden	Jim Palmer
Mickey Mantle	Steve Garvey
Lefty Gomez	Don Drysdale

1. _____ He, like Willie Mays, played on 17 winning teams.
2. _____ He played on 15 losing teams.
3. _____ He pinch-hit ten times.
4. _____ He has been the youngest player.

*One of the players can be used twice.

5. _____ He was the oldest participant.
6. _____ He played five different positions in total games.
7. _____ He batted .500 in total games.
8. _____ He had the most career total at-bats (10) without a hit.
9. _____ He had the most at-bats in a game (7) without a hit.
10. _____ He scored four runs in one game.
11. _____ He, like Dave Winfield, hit safely in seven consecutive games in the American League.
12. _____ He hit safely in seven consecutive games in the National League.
13. _____ He, like Charlie Gehringer and Ted Williams, reached base safely five times in one game.
14. _____ He hit seven doubles in total games.
15. _____ He hit two triples in one game.
16. _____ He struck out four times in one game.
17. _____ He hit three sacrifice flies in total games.
18. _____ He, like Pete Rose, hit into three double plays.
19. _____ He was the only player to steal home.
20. _____ He got caught stealing twice in one game.
21. _____ He finished six games.
22. _____ He pitched 19⅓ innings in total games.
23. _____ He pitched six innings in one game.
24. _____ He allowed 13 runs in total games.
25. _____ He allowed seven runs in one inning.
26. _____ He allowed seven hits in one inning.
27. _____ He granted three home runs in one game.
28. _____ He played ten games at first base.
29. _____ He played 13 games at second base.
30. _____ He played 12 games at shortstop.
31. _____ He played 18 games at third base.
32. _____ He played 14 games at catcher.
33. _____ He stole six bases in total games.

87. WHO'S WHO?

Identify the player who starred in a particular year.

1. _____ (1933) Who hit the event's first home run?
2. _____ (1934) Who struck out Babe Ruth, Lou Gehrig, Jimmie Foxx, Al Simmons, and Joe Cronin consecutively?
3. _____ (1934) Who was the National Leaguer who homered for the second consecutive year? (In World Series play he didn't hit a home run in 197 official at-bats.)
4. _____ (1935) Who three-hit the National League over a record six innings?
5. _____ (1937) Who was the American League pitcher who won his third decision in five years?
6. _____ (1937) Who was the National Leaguer, the Triple Crown winner that year, who paced the Senior Circuit to victory with four hits?
7. _____ (1937) Who was the Hall of Famer whose injury in this year's game abruptly short-circuited a great career?
8. _____ (1937) Who was the Hall of Famer whose line drive broke the preceding pitcher's toe?
9. _____ (1941) Who was the player whose three-run homer with two outs in the bottom of the ninth lifted the American League to a 7–5 victory?
10. _____ (1941) Who was the first player to hit two home runs in one game?
11. _____ (1942) Who was the National Leaguer who hit the game's first pinch-hit home run?
12. _____ (1943) Who was the National League pitcher who tied Carl Hubbell's mark of six strikeouts in one game?
13. _____ (1943) Who was the DiMaggio who hit a single, a triple, and a home run?

14. _____ (1944) Who was the National League first baseman who became the first player to reach base five times in one game?

15. _____ (1946) Who was the player whose four hits, including two home runs, and five RBIs led the American League to a 12–0 win?

16. _____ (1946) Who was the pitcher who gave up his first and only eephus ball home run?

17. _____ (1948) Who was the pitcher whose two-run single turned the game in the American League's favor?

18. _____ (1949) Who were the first four blacks to play in the All-Star Game?

19. _____

20. _____

21. _____

22. _____ (1950) Who was the National League second baseman whose 14th-inning home run gave the Senior Circuit a 2–1 victory?

23. _____ (1950) Who was the Hall of Famer who broke his elbow making a great catch off the left-field wall?

24. _____ (1952) Who was the Cub outfielder whose two-run home run gave the National League a 3–2 win in a five-inning game that was shortened by rain?

25. _____ (1953) Who was the great black pitcher who appeared in his only All-Star Game?

26. _____ (1954) Who was the American League third baseman whose two home runs and five RBIs tied a record?

27. _____ (1955) Who was the Hall of Famer whose home run in the bottom of the 12th gave the National League a sudden-death victory?

28. _____ (1956) Who was the third baseman whose great fielding plays and three hits sparked the National League?

29. _____ (1959) Who was the four-time home run champ whose run-tying single got the National League even in the eighth inning?

30. _____ (1959) Who was the four-time home run champ who followed the above with a game-winning triple?

31. _____ (1960) Who was the famous center fielder who got three hits in each of that year's two games?

32. _____ (1963) Who was the player whose 24th All-Star appearance set a record?

33. _____ (1964) Who was the player whose three-run homer in the bottom of the ninth gave the National League a dramatic come-from-behind 7–4 win?

34. _____ (1966) Who was the infield speedster whose tenth-inning single gave the National League a 2–1 win?

35. _____ (1967) Who was the big first baseman whose 15th-inning homer gave the National League a victory in the All-Star Game's longest contest?

36. _____ (1967) Who was the Cub pitcher whose six strikeouts tied the mark set by Hubbell and equaled by Vander Meer?

37. _____ (1969) Who was the National League first baseman who became the fourth player to hit two home runs in one game?

38. _____ (1971) Who hit the tape-measure home run on top of the roof at Tigers Stadium?

39. _____ (1971) Who became the first player to homer for both leagues?

40. _____ (1974) Who was the player, not even listed on the All-Star ballot, who was the game's star?

41. _____ (1975) Who was the long-ball-hitting left-fielder who hit a three-run pinch-hit homer?

42. _____ (1978) Who was the National League first baseman whose single tied the score in the third and whose triple proved to be the game-winner?

43. _____ (1979) Who was the Met outfielder who hit a pinch-hit home run in the eighth to tie the game, and walked with the bases loaded in the ninth to win the game?

44. _____ (1981) Who was the eight-time home run champ whose two-run homer in the eighth inning gave the National League a one-run victory?

45. _____ (1982) Who was the Red player whose two-run homer paced the National League to its 11th straight victory, 4–1, in the first game played outside the United States, in Montreal?

46. _____ (1983) Who hit the midsummer classic's only grand slam en route to the American League's 13–3 win in the 50th anniversary game?

47. _____ (1984) Who tied Carl Hubbell's record of five consecutive strikeouts via the National League's 3–1 win?

48. _____ (1985) Who was the 1974 MVP during the regular season whose two-run single propelled the National League to a 6–1 win?

49. _____ (1986) Who is the second baseman whose two-run homer ignited the American League's 3–2 win?

50. _____ (1987) Who, hitless in six prior contests, tripled home the only two runs of the contest in the 13th inning?

51. _____ (1988) Who is the catcher whose home run and sacrifice fly led the American League to a 2–1 win?

52. _____ (1989) Who became the oldest winner, 5–3, in the first game played with the designated hitter? He was 42.

53. _____ (1990) Who was the player—he was the 1991 batting title winner—whose double scored the only two runs of the game for a 2–0 American League win?

54. _____ (1991) Who was the player—he was the MVP during the regular season—whose three-run homer catapulted Tony La Russa to his third consecutive win, 4–2?

55. _____ (1992) Who is the American League West star who led the American League to a 13–6 win with three hits, including a home run?

56. _____ (1994) Who produced the game-winning double in the tenth inning of his first All-Star Game?

The Black Sox

The 1919–20 Chicago White Sox, referred to in history books as the infamous Black Sox, had a staggering array of talent.

In the season before they were declared ineligible to play professional baseball—for allegedly conspiring to fix the 1919 World Series—Joe Jackson batted .382, Happy Felsch hit .338, and Buck Weaver averaged .333. Moundsmen Claude "Lefty" Williams and Ed Cicotte won 22 and 21 games, respectively, Chick Gandil and Swede Risberg were solid starters, and Fred McMullin was a valuable utility man. It's little wonder that the White Sox, who were the best team in baseball at the time, did not win another pennant, after 1919, for another 40 years. Their roster was razed.

If it were not for the scandal, Jackson, Weaver, and Cicotte would be comfortably enshrined at the Baseball Hall of Fame in Cooperstown, N.Y. Felsch and Williams might be, too.

The notoriety of the trial of the disqualified players, however, detracted from the honorable records of the Sox stalwarts who transcended the alleged temptation and remained unsullied by the scandal.

History books have paid more attention to the barred players than they have to the untainted stars who managed to win their niche in Cooperstown. There were three such players. If you can name two of them, you deserve a special niche of your own.

(Answer appears on page 344.)

Chapter Sixteen

THE CHAMPIONSHIP SERIES

88. FROM BANDO TO WASHINGTON

Match the following players with the Championship Series records they set: Richie Hebner, Pete Rose, Jay Johnstone, Reggie Jackson, Claudell Washington, George Brett, Jim Palmer, Devon White, Phil Niekro, Fred Lynn, Paul Blair, Mike Cuellar, Jerry Martin, Will Clark, Paul Popovich, Paul Molitor, Bob Robertson, Bill North, Sal Bando, and Gary Gaetti.

1. _____ He was the youngest non-pitcher to play in the CS.
2. _____ He got 13 hits in one series.
3. _____ He went hitless in 31 consecutive at-bats.
4. _____ He appeared in ten series.
5. _____ He was the pinch-hitter who batted for six total bases in one series.
6. _____ He played on seven losing teams.
7. _____ He played in seven series with one team.
8. _____ He was the oldest non-pitcher to play.
9. _____ He hit .392 in total series.
10. _____ He hit .778 in a three-game series.
11. _____ He hit .650 in a five-game series.
12. _____ He hit a home run in his first CS at-bat.

13. _____ He had a .728 total series slugging average.
14. _____ He slugged the ball for a 1.250 average in one series.
15. _____ He had five hits in one game.
16. _____ He got three consecutive pinch-hit safeties.
17. _____ He and Steve Garvey got six consecutive hits.
18. _____ He was the only pitcher to hit a grand slam.
19. _____ He had the biggest time span (1969–82) between series appearances.
20. _____ He was the only player to decide a 1–0 game in the American League's favor with a home run.

89. FROM BAYLOR TO WYNN

Match the following players with the Championship Series records that they set: Steve Garvey, Frank Thomas, Will Clark, Bob Robertson, Don Baylor, Joe Morgan, Darryl Strawberry, Cesar Geronimo, Pedro Guerrero, Tony Taylor, Rickey Henderson, Reggie Jackson, Hal McRae, Bert Blyleven, Phil Niekro, Jim Hunter, Dennis Eckersley, Jim Palmer, and Dave Stewart. One of the players may be used twice.

1. _____ He sports an 8–0 record.
2. _____ He and Dave Stewart started ten games.
3. _____ He finished 13 games.
4. _____ He pitched five complete games.
5. _____ He has been the youngest pitcher to appear.
6. _____ He has been the oldest pitcher to appear.
7. _____ He went down swinging seven consecutive times.
8. _____ He and Rusty Staub hit home runs in consecutive innings.
9. _____ He drove home 21 runs in total series.
10. _____ He collected ten RBI in one series.
11. _____ He grounded into five double plays in total series.
12. _____ He grounded into three double plays in one game.
13. _____ He stole 16 bases in total series.
14. _____ He struck out 12 times in one series.
15. _____ He walked ten times in one series.
16. _____ He walked 23 times in total series.
17. _____ He was caught stealing six times in total series.

18. _____ He has been the only player to steal home.
19. _____ He hit four home runs in two consecutive games.
20. _____ He hit for 14 total bases in one game.

90. FROM ANDERSON TO WYNN

Match the following players with the Championship Series records that they either set or tied: Dennis Eckersley, Ron Gant, Jerry Reuss, Steve Avery, Dave McNally, Jim Hunter, Eric Show, Steve Carlton, Mike Cuellar, Jim Palmer, Wes Gardner, Nolan Ryan, Juan Guzman, Earl Weaver, Sparky Anderson, Billy Martin, Steve Garvey, George Brett, Pete Rose, and Roger Clemens. One of the players may be used more than once.

1. _____ He managed four different clubs in series play.
2. _____ He managed in six American League series.
3. _____ He managed five winning teams.
4. _____ He allowed four walks in one inning, nine walks in one game, and 13 walks in one series.
5. _____ He struck out eight batters in one game in relief.
6. _____ He and Nolan Ryan struck out 46 batters in total series.
7. _____ He struck out 20 batters in one series.
8. _____ He and Tommy John hit three batters in one game.
9. _____ He recorded ten saves in total series.
10. _____ He issued 28 walks in total series.
11. _____ He recorded four saves in one series.
12. _____ He allowed five home runs in one series.
13. _____ He lost seven consecutive games.
14. _____ He got touched for 19 hits in one series.
15. _____ He allowed 12 home runs in total series.

16. _____ He pitched 11 consecutive hitless innings in one game.
17. _____ He pitched 22⅓ consecutive scoreless innings in total series.
18. _____ He scored 22 runs in total series.
19. _____ He sprayed 45 hits in total series.
20. _____ He and five other players drove home four runs in one inning.

91. FROM BANDO TO YASTRZEMSKI

All of the players who are listed below hit .400 or better for an American League team in a Championship Series. Ten of them hit .500 or better. See if you can zero in on the ten .500 hitters. One of them did it twice.

Spike Owen
Bob Boone
Wally Joyner
Brooks Robinson
Eddie Murray
Kirk Gibson
Carl Yastrzemski
Fred Lynn
Reggie Jackson
Larry Milbourne
Rod Carew
Paul Blair
Sal Bando
Bob Watson
Cliff Johnson
Cecil Cooper
Cal Ripken

Frank White
Devon White
Carlton Fisk
Graig Nettles
Thurman Munson
Boog Powell
Amos Otis
Chris Chambliss*
Brooks Robinson*
Charlie Moore
Mickey Rivers
Tony Oliva
Jerry Mumphrey
Rick Burleson
George Brett
Hal McRae
Reggie Jackson*

1. _____
2. _____
3. _____
4. _____
5. _____
6. _____
7. _____
8. _____
9. _____
0. _____

They hit .400 or better twice.

92. FROM BAKER TO ZISK

All of the players who are listed below hit .400 or better for a National League team in a Championship Series. Eight of them hit .500 or better. See if you can zero in on the eight .500 hitters.

Darrell Porter
Jose Cruz
Bob Boone
Dusty Baker
Mike Schmidt
Jay Johnstone
Bill Russell
Steve Garvey
Phil Garner
Bob Tolan
Tony Perez
Art Shamsky
Orlando Cepeda
Dave Concepcion
Pete Rose
Ozzie Smith
Dave Concepcion*

Willie Stargell**
Pete Rose
Derrel Thomas
Bob Robertson
Terry Puhl
Gary Carter
Ozzie Smith*
Pete Rose**
Willie Stargell**
Richie Zisk
Cleon Jones
Willie McCovey
Dave Cash
Tito Landrum
Gary Matthews
Will Clark

1. _____
2. _____
3. _____
4. _____
5. _____
6. _____
7. _____
8. _____

**They hit .400 or better three times.
*They hit .400 or better twice.

176

93. FROM AARON TO STAUB

Match the following players with the number of Championship Series home runs that they've hit: Jeff Leonard, Rickey Henderson, Lenny Dykstra, Kirby Puckett, Greg Luzinski, Rich Hebner, Boog Powell, Pete Rose, Jim Rice, George Brett, Gary Matthews, Willie Stargell, Tony Perez, Steve Garvey, Reggie Jackson, Ron Cey, Graig Nettles, Johnny Bench, Al Oliver, Hank Aaron, Sal Bando, Bill Madlock, Rusty Staub, Bob Robertson, George Foster, Jose Canseco, Kirk Gibson, Jay Bell, Dave Justice, and John Olerud.

1. _____ (9)		16. _____ (4)
2. _____ (8)		17. _____ (3)
3. _____ (6)		18. _____ (3)
4. _____ (5)		19. _____ (3)
5. _____ (5)		20. _____ (3)
6. _____ (5)		21. _____ (3)
7. _____ (5)		22. _____ (3)
8. _____ (5)		23. _____ (3)
9. _____ (4)		24. _____ (3)
10. _____ (4)		25. _____ (3)
11. _____ (4)		26. _____ (3)
12. _____ (4)		27. _____ (3)
13. _____ (4)		28. _____ (2)
14. _____ (4)		29. _____ (2)
15. _____ (4)		30. _____ (2)

94. CHAMPIONSHIP SERIES GAME WINNERS

National League

There have been many dramatic hits in Championship Series play. Some of them are referred to below. See if you can identify the players who provided the drama.

1. _____ Who was the Red in Game One of 1970 whose 10th-inning single, which was followed by Lee May's two-run double, broke up a scoreless pitching duel between winner Gary Nolan and Doc Ellis?
2. _____ Who was the Red in Game Three of 1970 whose single in the eighth inning enabled Cincinnati to break a 2–2 tie and sweep the Bucs?
3. _____ Who was the Pirate in Game Three of 1971 whose eighth-inning homer off Juan Marichal snapped a 1–1 tie and gave Bob Johnson a 2–1 win?
4. _____ Who was the Pirate in Game Three of 1972 who homered for the first Pittsburgh run and drove in the tie-breaking counter in the eighth inning to give his team a 3–2 win?
5. _____ Who was the Red in Game One of 1973 whose ninth-inning homer off Tom Seaver gave Cincinnati a 2–1 come-from-behind victory?
6. _____ Who was the Red in Game Four of 1973 whose 12th-inning home run off Met pitcher Harry Parker gave Cincinnati a 2–1 win?
7. _____ Who was the Dodger in Game Three of 1977 whose ninth-inning single capped a three-run rally that lifted Los Angeles over the Phillies, 6–5?
8. _____ Who was the Dodger in Game Four of 1978 whose tenth-inning single, following Garry Maddox' muff of a fly ball, scored Ron Cey with the winning run to give the Dodgers the National League Championship?

9. _____ Who was the Pirate in Game One of 1979 whose three-run homer in the 11th gave Pittsburgh a 5–2 win over the Reds?

10. _____ Who was the Pirate in Game Two of 1979 whose tenth-inning single gave Pittsburgh a 3–2 win?

11. _____ Who was the Phillie in Game Five of 1980 whose tenth-inning double downed Houston, 8–7, and gave Philadelphia its first pennant since 1950?

12. _____ Who was the Expo in Game Three of 1981 whose three-run homer gave Montreal a 4–1 win over the Dodgers?

13. _____ Who was the Dodger in Game Five of 1981 whose homer with two outs in the ninth inning gave Los Angeles a 2–1 win over Montreal and the National League pennant?

14. _____ Who was the Cardinal in Game Two of 1982 whose ninth-inning single gave St. Louis a 4–3 win over Atlanta?

15. _____ Who was the Phillie in Game One of 1983 whose home run gave Steve Carlton a 1–0 win over Jerry Reuss and the Dodgers?

16. _____ Who was the Padre in Game Four of 1984 whose two-run homer in the bottom of the ninth inning gave San Diego a 7–5 win over the Cubs?

17. _____ Who was the Astro in Game One of 1986 whose home run gave Mike Scott a 1–0 victory over Dwight Gooden and the Mets?

18. _____ Who was the Met in Game Three of 1986 whose two-run homer in the ninth inning lifted New York over Houston, 6–5?

19. _____ Who was the Astro in Game Four of 1986 whose two-run homer made the difference in Houston's 3–1 win over the Mets?

20. _____ Who was the Met in Game Five of 1986 whose 12th-inning single gave New York a 2–1 win over Houston?

21. _____ Who homered in his fourth consecutive game—it was a two-run shot—to give the San Francisco Giants a 4–2 win in Game Three of 1987?

22. _____ Who hit a two-run homer in the seventh inning of Game Three in 1989 to give the San Francisco Giants a 5–4 win over the Cubs?

23. _____ Who was the Phillie whose tenth-inning home run off Mark Wohlers of the Braves gave Philadelphia a 4–3 win over Atlanta in Game Five of 1993?

American League

1. _____ Who was the Oriole in Game One of 1969 whose two-out suicide squeeze bunt in the 12th inning gave Baltimore a 4–3 win over Minnesota?

2. _____ Who was the Oriole in Game Two of 1969 whose pinch-hit single in the bottom of the 11th inning gave Dave McNally a 1–0 win over Minnesota?

3. _____ Who was the Oriole in Game One of 1971 whose two-run double in the seventh inning ignited Baltimore to a 5–3 win over Oakland?

4. _____ Who was the A in Game Five of 1972 whose only hit of the series drove home George Hendrick with the winning run of the game, 2–1, and the series.

5. _____ Who was the A in Game Three of 1973 whose home run in the bottom of the 11th inning gave Ken Holtzman a 2–1 win over Mike Cuellar of the Orioles?

6. _____ Who was the Oriole in Game Four of 1973 whose eighth-inning homer gave Baltimore a come-from-behind 5–4 victory over the A's?

7. _____ Who was the A in Game Three of 1974 whose home run provided Vida Blue the edge in a 1–0 win over Jim Palmer of the Orioles?

8. _____ Who was the A in Game Four of 1974 whose double scored the deciding run in the game, 2–1, and the series 3–1?

9. _____ Who was the Yankee in Game Five of 1976 whose sudden-death homer in the ninth gave the Yankees their first pennant since 1964?

10. _____ Who was the Yankee in Game Three of 1978 whose two-run homer in the eighth inning gave New York a 6–5 win over Kansas City?

11. _____ Who was the Yankee in Game Four of 1978 whose sixth-inning homer gave New York a 2–1 win and the American League pennant?

12. _____ Who was the Oriole in Game One of 1979 whose three-run pinch-hit home run gave Baltimore a 6–3 win over California?

13. _____ Who was the Angel whose looping double in the bottom of the ninth gave California a 4–3 win?

14. _____ Who was the Royal in Game Three of 1980 whose three-run homer powered Kansas City to its first pennant?

15. _____ Who was the Brewer in Game Three of 1982 whose two-run homer proved to be the margin of difference, 5–3, over the Angels?

16. _____ Who was the Brewer in Game Five of 1982 who singled in the tying and winning runs to give Milwaukee its first American League pennant?

17. _____ Who was the Oriole in Game Four of 1983 whose tenth-inning home run was the catalyst in Baltimore's pennant-winning game?

18. _____ Who was the Tiger in Game Two of 1984 whose two-run double in the eleventh inning sparked Detroit to a 5–3 victory?

19. _____ Who was the Angel in Game Four of 1986 whose ninth-inning hit into the left field corner gave California a 4–3 victory and a 3–1 lead in games?

20. _____ Who was the Red Sox player in Game Five of 1986 whose two-run homer in the top of the ninth gave Boston a 6–5 victory and prevented California manager Gene Mauch from winning his first pennant?

21. _____ Who was the Tiger whose two-run homer in the eighth gave the Bengals a come-from-behind 7–6 victory in Game Three of 1987?

22. _____ Who was the former Yankee whose pinch-hit home run in the tenth inning of Game Three in 1991 gave the Twins a 3–2 win and 2–1 lead in games?

23. _____ Who was the A whose lead-off homer in the top of the ninth inning off Jack Morris gave Oakland a 4–3 win over Toronto in Game One of 1992?

24. _____ Whose two-run homer off Dennis Eckersley of the A's in the ninth inning of Game Four of 1992 tied the score, 6–6? Pat Borders' sacrifice fly in the 11th won the game for the Blue Jays, 7–6.

The Shoe Polish Plays

Everything is not always black and white in baseball. But in the following two instances it was.

In the fourth game of the 1957 World Series, with the Yankees leading the host Braves by the score of 5–4 in the tenth inning, a pinch-hitter came to the plate for Warren Spahn. A pitch from Tommy Byrne to the pinch-hitter was called a ball. But the substitute batter, who claimed that the ball had hit him, retrieved it and showed the enlightened Augie Donatelli a smudge of black shoe polish on the spheroid. Bob Grim relieved Byrne and was greeted with a game-tying double by Johnny Logan and a game-winning homer by Eddie Matthews. So the shoe polish call was a pivotal one.

In the fifth-and-final game of the 1969 World Series, a similar play took place. In the sixth inning one of the host Mets was hit on the foot with a pitch by Dave McNally. Umpire Lou DiMuro called the pitch a ball. The batter protested. Upon inspection of the ball, DiMuro gave the hitter first base: he detected shoe polish on the ball. The shoe polish call once again proved to be pivotal. At the time the Mets were losing 3–0. But Donn Clendenon followed with a two-run homer, and the Mets were back in the game. Al Weis homered in the seventh to tie the game. The Mets went on to score the decisive two runs of a 5–3 series-clinching victory in the eighth on doubles by two Met outfielders and errors by two Oriole infielders.

Both of the players who figured prominently in the shoe polish plays had the same last name. That should give you a solid clue. Who are the two?

(Answer appears on page 344.)

Chapter Seventeen

THE WORLD SERIES

95. WORLD SERIES STANDOUTS

I.

Match the following players with the World Series records that they set: Lou Gehrig, Hank Bauer, Pee Wee Reese and Elston Howard, Yogi Berra, Willie Wilson, Casey Stengel, Pepper Martin, Billy Hatcher, Bobby Richardson, and Mickey Mantle.

1. _____ He was on the winning club ten times.
2. _____ He was on the losing team six times.
3. _____ He was a series manager ten times.
4. _____ He hit .750, the all-time high, in one series.
5. _____ He had a career average of .418.
6. _____ He collected 12 RBI in one series.
7. _____ He hit safely in 17 consecutive games.
8. _____ He hit four home runs in four games.
9. _____ He struck out 12 times in one series.
10. _____ He struck out 54 times in series play.

II.

Match the following pitchers with the World Series records they set: Bill Bevens, Whitey Ford, Harry Brecheen, Babe Ruth, Darold Knowles, Don Larsen, Christy Mathewson, Carl Mays, Bob Gibson, and Jim Palmer.

1. _____ He pitched 33⅔ consecutive scoreless innings.
2. _____ He pitched seven games in one series.
3. _____ He pitched three shutouts in one series.
4. _____ He struck out 17 batters in one game.
5. _____ He issued 10 walks in one game.
6. _____ He did not allow a single walk in 26 innings of pitching in one series.
7. _____ He gave up a total of four hits in two consecutive games.
8. _____ He was the youngest pitcher who threw a shutout.
9. _____ He was the first post-World War II pitcher who won three games.
10. _____ He pitched the longest game, 14 innings, which he won.

III.

Match the following teams that have won consecutive World Series with the proper time spans (teams may be used more than once): Yankees, Cubs, Athletics, Giants, Red Sox, Blue Jays, and Reds.

1. _____ (1907–08)   8. _____ (1949–53)
2. _____ (1910–11)   9. _____ (1961–62)
3. _____ (1915–16)   10. _____ (1972–74)
4. _____ (1921–22)   11. _____ (1975–76)
5. _____ (1927–28)   12. _____ (1977–78)
6. _____ (1929–30)   13. _____ (1992–93)
7. _____ (1936–39)

IV.

Match the following World Series defensive standouts with the years in which they excelled: Dick Green, Kirby Puckett, Tommie Agee, Willie Mays, Al Gionfriddo, Brooks Robinson, Billy Cox, Bill Virdon, Mickey Mantle, Eddie Mathews, Graig Nettles, and Sandy Amoros.

1. _____ (1947)		7. _____ (1960)
2. _____ (1952)		8. _____ (1969)
3. _____ (1954)		9. _____ (1970)
4. _____ (1955)		10. _____ (1974)
5. _____ (1956)		11. _____ (1981)
6. _____ (1957)		12. _____ (1991)

V.

Match the following World Series starting pitchers with the years in which they stood in the sun: Jimmy Key, Sandy Koufax, Lew Burdette, Mickey Lolich, Harry Brecheen, Jack Morris, Johnny Podres, Jose Rijo, Bob Gibson, Whitey Ford, Bret Saberhagen, Bob Turley, Jim Hunter, Don Larsen, and Dave Stewart.

1. _____ (1946)		10. _____ (1972)
2. _____ (1955)		11. _____ (1984 and 1991)
3. _____ (1956)		
4. _____ (1957)		
5. _____ (1958)		12. _____ (1985)
6. _____ (1960)		13. _____ (1989)
7. _____ (1963)		14. _____ (1990)
8. _____ (1967)		15. _____ (1992)
9. _____ (1968)		

96. WORLD SERIES PLAYERS

From the players listed below, pick out the ones who have played in the World Series.

Richie Ashburn
Ernie Banks
Ted Williams
Al Kaline
Luke Appling
Mickey Vernon
Chili Davis
Dean Chance
Ralph Kiner
Richie Allen
Harvey Kuenn
George Kell
Herb Score
Johnny Logan
Ted Kluszewski
Ted Lyons
Mike Greenwell
Ferris Fain
Gaylord Perry
Vada Pinson

Felipe Alou
Jesus Alou
Tony Pena
Gus Bell
Willard Marshall
Walker Cooper
Ray Sadecki
Bob Allison
Steve Howe
Eddie Yost
Ferguson Jenkins
Satchel Paige
Johnny Callison
Buddy Kerr
Bill White
Jeff Heath
Milt Pappas
Frank Torre
Terry Mulholland

97. TWO-TEAM WORLD SERIES PLAYERS

From the performers listed below, pick out the ones who played in the World Series with two different teams.

Mariano Duncan
Juan Marichal
Denny McLain
Gino Cimoli
Lenny Dykstra
Tommy Holmes
Willie Horton
Bill Skowron
Roger Maris
Al Dark
Kirk Gibson
Mickey Cochrane
Julian Javier
Rusty Staub
Jim Lonborg
Reggie Smith
Joe Gordon
Curt Simmons
Tommy Davis
Johnny Sain

Enos Slaughter
Brian Harper
Ron Fairly
Orlando Cepeda
Maury Wills
Rickey Henderson
Moe Drabowsky
Joe Cronin
Luis Aparicio
Jack Morris
Dick Groat
Ron Perranoski
Claude Osteen
Frank Robinson
Willie Davis
Camilo Pascual
Tony Oliva
Mike Garcia
Ken Boyer
Curt Flood

98. MOUND CLASSICS

Below you will find the matchups and years in which pitchers have engaged in 1–0 mound duels since 1946. Name the pitcher who won their duels.

1. _____ Bob Feller vs. Johnny Sain (1948)
2. _____ Don Newcombe vs. Allie Reynolds (1949)
3. _____ Preacher Roe vs. Vic Raschi (1949)
4. _____ Vic Raschi vs. Jim Konstanty (1950)
5. _____ Bob Turley vs. Clem Labine (1956)
6. _____ Whitey Ford vs. Lew Burdette (1957)
7. _____ Bob Shaw, Billy Pierce, and Dick Donovan vs. Sandy Koufax (1959)
8. _____ Ralph Terry vs. Jack Sanford (1962)
9. _____ Jim Bouton vs. Don Drysdale (1963)
10. _____ Claude Osteen vs. Wally Bunker (1966)
11. _____ Don Drysdale vs. Dave McNally (1966)
12. _____ Jack Billingham and Clay Carroll vs. John Odom (1972)
13. _____ Bruce Hurst vs. Ron Darling (1986)
14. _____ John Smoltz vs. Jack Morris (1991)
15. _____ Dennis Martinez vs. Tom Glavine (1995)

99. SEVENTH-GAME WINNERS

From the following pairs of seventh-game starting pitchers since the end of World War II, pick the 13 moundsmen who have been credited with wins. One of the 13 pitchers picked up two seventh-game victories.

1. _____ (1946) Boo Ferriss (Red Sox) vs. Murry Dickson (Cardinals)
2. _____ (1947) Hal Gregg (Dodgers) vs. Frank Shea (Yankees)
3. _____ (1952) Ed Lopat (Yankees) vs. Joe Black (Dodgers)
4. _____ (1953) Carl Erskine (Dodgers) vs. Whitey Ford (Yankees)
5. _____ (1955) Johnny Podres (Dodgers) vs. Tommy Byrne (Yankees)
6. _____ (1956) Johnny Kucks (Yankees) vs. Don Newcombe (Dodgers)
7. _____ (1957) Lew Burdette (Braves) vs. Don Larsen (Yankees)
8. _____ (1958) Don Larsen (Yankees) vs. Lew Burdette (Braves)
9. _____ (1960) Bob Turley (Yankees) vs. Vernon Law (Pirates)
10. _____ (1962) Ralph Terry (Yankees) vs. Jack Sanford (Giants)
11. _____ (1964) Mel Stottlemyre (Yankees) vs. Bob Gibson (Cards)
12. _____ (1967) Bob Gibson (Cards) vs. Jim Lonborg (Red Sox)
13. _____ (1968) Mickey Lolich (Tigers) vs. Bob Gibson (Cards)
14. _____ (1971) Steve Blass (Pirates) vs. Dave McNally (Orioles)
15. _____ (1972) John Odom (A's) vs. Jack Billingham (Reds)
16. _____ (1973) Jon Matlack (Mets) vs. Ken Holtzman (A's)

17. _____ (1975) Don Gullett (Reds) vs. Bill Lee (Red Sox)
18. _____ (1979) Jim Bibby (Pirates) vs. Scott McGregor (Orioles)
19. _____ (1982) Pete Vuckovich (Brewers) vs. Joaquin Andujar (Cards)
20. _____ (1985) John Tudor (Cards) vs. Bret Saberhagen (Royals)
21. _____ (1986) Bruce Hurst (Red Sox) vs. Ron Darling (Mets)
22. _____ (1987) Joe Magrane (Cards) vs. Frank Viola (Twins)
23. _____ (1992) John Smoltz (Braves) vs. Jack Morris (Blue Jays)

100. WORLD SERIES SHORTS

Three-Game Winners

The last five pitchers who won three games in a World Series were Lew Burdette, Stan Coveleski, Harry Brecheen, Mickey Lolich, and Bob Gibson. Put them in their proper order.

1. _____ (1920)
2. _____ (1946)
3. _____ (1957)
4. _____ (1967)
5. _____ (1968)

Home Run Hitters

Match the following players with the number of series homers they hit: Duke Snider, Mickey Mantle, Babe Ruth, Lou Gehrig, and Yogi Berra.

1. _____ (18)
2. _____ (15)
3. _____ (12)
4. _____ (11)
5. _____ (10)

Individual Records

Match the following players with the World Series records they set: Whitey Ford, Christy Mathewson, Lefty Gomez, Lefty Grove, and Bob Gibson.

1. _____ Fewest number of chances accepted (0), series (26 innings)
2. _____ Most career wins (10)
3. _____ Most strikeouts per nine innings (10.22)

4. _____ Most career shutouts (4)
5. _____ Best career-winning percentage (1.000), six decisions

Career Records

Match the following players with the career World Series records they set: Yogi Berra, Bobby Richardson, Frank Isbell, Thurman Munson, Eddie Collins and Lou Brock.

1. _____ Tied for stolen base leadership (14)
2. _____ Most games (75)
3. _____ Most consecutive hits (7), career
4. _____ Most two-base hits (4), one game
5. _____ Most consecutive games played (30)

101. FOUR HOMERS IN ONE SERIES

Reggie Jackson, of course, hit five home runs in the 1977 World Series. But there have been seven players who hit four home runs in a series. One of them did it twice. Out of the following players pick the ones who accomplished the feat: Mickey Mantle, Willie Mays, Lou Gehrig, Gene Tenace, Roy Campanella, Joe DiMaggio, Babe Ruth, Duke Snider, Johnny Bench, Hank Bauer, Willie Aikens, and Lenny Dykstra. Also, see if you can put them in their proper time spans. And remember, one of them did it twice.

1. _____ (1926)   5. _____ (1958)
2. _____ (1928)   6. _____ (1972)
3. _____ (1952)   7. _____ (1980)
4. _____ (1955)   8. _____ (1993)

102. WORLD SERIES CHRONOLOGY

There have been 91 World Series. The autumn classic began in 1903 and has been played every year with the exception of 1905, when the New York Giants refused to play the Red Sox, winners of the first series, and 1994, when the season wasn't finished because of the players' strike. I'm gong to give you one question for each series, presented in sequence. Let's see how you know the World Series—from start to finish.

1. _____ Who hit the first home run?
2. _____ Who has been the only pitcher to spin three shutouts in the same series?
3. _____ Who struck out a record 12 batters in the intercity series between the White Sox and Cubs in 1906?
4. _____ Who was the other member of the Tinker to Evers to Chance infield who hit .471 in 1907?
5. _____ Who was the Cub pitcher, in addition to Three Finger Brown, who won two games in 1908?
6. _____ Who has been the only rookie pitcher to win three games in one series?
7. _____ Who managed to win all three of his decisions in 1910 despite the fact that he yielded 23 hits and 14 free passes?
8. _____ Who hit home runs in consecutive games for the Athletics in 1911?
9. _____ Who won three games for the Red Sox in 1912?
10. _____ Who was the only substitute whom the Athletics used in 1913?
11. _____ Who was the member of the Tinker to Evers to Chance infield who hit .438 for the winning Braves in 1914?
12. _____ Who was the Red Sox pitcher who won two games and batted .500 in 1915?
13. _____ Who strung together the most consecutive scoreless innings in one game?

14. _____ Who was the White Sox pitcher who won three games in 1917?

15. _____ Who was the Cub second baseman who became the last out of the third game in 1918 when he unsuccessfully tried to steal home?

16. _____ Who was the untainted member of the 1919 Black Sox who won both of his decisions?

17. _____ Who hit the first grand slam?

18. _____ Who did not allow an earned run in 27 innings of pitching, but lost the final game of 1921 on an error?

19. _____ Who was the first pitcher to win the final game of two consecutive series?

20. _____ Who was the first player to hit three home runs in the same series?

21. _____ Who hit the bad-hop single that gave the Senators their first and only world championship?

22. _____ Who was the first pitcher to win the seventh game of one world series (1924) and lose the seventh game of the following post-season get-together?

23. _____ Who, in addition to Grover Alexander, won two games for the Cardinals in 1926?

24. _____ Who hit the only two home runs of the 1927 classic?

25. _____ Who was deprived of a "quick-pitch" strikeout of Babe Ruth in 1928?

26. _____ Who was the Athletic outfielder who, in addition to Jimmie Foxx and Mule Haas, hit two home runs in 1929?

27. _____ Who was the 46-year-old pitcher who appeared in the 1930 series?

28. _____ Who "peppered" 12 hits and swiped five bases in 1931?

29. _____ Who was the Yankee player who, in addition to Babe Ruth and Lou Gehrig, hit two home runs in one game in 1932?

30. _____ Who hit the home run in the tenth inning that won the 1933 finale?

31. _____ Who, in 1934, played on his second world championship team with one club in the 1930s after performing on two world title clubs with another team in the 1920s?

32. _____ Who was the veteran outfielder whose single in 1935 gave the Tigers their first world championship?

33. _____ Who was the Giant pitcher who stopped the Yankees' 12-game win streak in 1936?

34. _____ Who was the 20-game winner for the Giants in 1937 who lost both of his series decisions?

35. _____ Who won two games during the Yankees' four-game sweep in 1938?

36. _____ Who won his fourth and final game (1939) without a defeat in series play?

37. _____ Who won both of his decisions, weaved a 1.50 ERA, and hit a home run in 1940?

38. _____ Who was the Dodger pitcher in 1941 who broke the Yankees' ten-game winning streak?

39. _____ Who hit a two-run homer in the final game of 1942 to give the Cardinals the world title?

40. _____ Who allowed only one run in 18 innings of pitching as the Yankees scored a turnabout five-game win over the Cardinals in 1943?

41. _____ Who was the Cardinal pitcher who lost a two-hitter to the Browns in 1944?

42. _____ Who was the starting pitcher who did not retire a single Tiger batter in Game Seven of 1945?

43. _____ Who scored the decisive run of 1946 by racing from first to home on a single?

44. _____ Who was the Dodger pitcher who finished a record six games against the Yankees in 1947?

45. _____ Who was the Indian pitcher who suffered both of his team's reversals in 1948?

46. _____ Who hit the ninth-inning home run that scored the only run in a classic duel between Allie Reynolds and Don Newcombe in the 1949 opener?

47. _____ Who was the 21-year-old rookie pitcher who won the final game in 1950?

48. _____ Who made the sliding catch that ended the 1951 series on a victorious note for the Yankees?

49. _____ Who was the Yankee part-time player who hit a record three home runs in three consecutive games in 1952?

50. _____ Who was the Dodger pitcher who struck out a record 14 batters in one game?

51. _____ Who was the Indian slugger who hit the 450-foot fly ball that Willie Mays ran down in Game One of 1954?

52. _____ Who was the Dodger slugger who drove home both runs in Johnny Podres' 2–0 win over Tommy Byrne in Game Seven of 1955?

53. _____ Who was the 40-year-old outfielder whose three-run game-winning homer (Game Three) turned the series around for the Yankees in 1956?

54. _____ Who was the Brave pitcher of 1957 who won three games?

55. _____ Who won two of the last three games—and saved the other one—in 1958?

56. _____ Who was the former Rose Bowl performer who set a record by hitting two pinch-hit homers for the Dodgers in 1959?

57. _____ Who was the Pirate pitcher who saved three games in a winning cause in 1960?

58. _____ Who was the Yankee pitcher who won two games for the second consecutive year in 1961?

59. _____ Who was the former Yankee celebrity who defeated the Pinstripers in his only decision in 1962?

60. _____ Who was the Yankee pinch-hitter whom Sandy Koufax fanned for his record 15th strikeout in 1963?

61. _____ Who was the last runner to steal home?

62. _____ Who (in addition to Sandy Koufax, who threw two shutouts) pitched a whitewash for the Dodgers in 1965?

63. _____ Who was the only Oriole pitcher who did not complete a game in 1966?

64. _____ Who was the only Cardinal pitcher to throw three consecutive complete-game wins in a series?

65. _____ Who picked two runners off first base in the sixth inning of the final game in 1968?

66. _____ Who was the light-hitting infielder for the Mets who batted .455 in 1969?

67. _____ Who was the Oriole player who excelled on offense and defense in 1970?

68. _____ Who was the Pirate player who extended his batting streak to 14 games in 1971?

69. _____ Who was the Oakland starter who picked up his second win of the series in relief in Game Seven of 1972?

70. _____ Who outpitched Jon Matlack in both the first and last game of 1973?

71. _____ Who, in addition to Catfish Hunter, won two games for the A's in 1974?

72. _____ Who was the Red Slugger who hit three home runs in 1975?

73. _____ Who was the Red Slugger who batted .533 during his team's sweep of the Yankees in 1976?

74. _____ Who was the Yankee batter who extended his consecutive-game hitting streak to ten in 1977?

75. _____ Who was the Yankee fill-in infielder who batted .438 in 1978?

76. _____ Who, in addition to Willie Stargell, collected 12 hits for the Pirates in 1979?

77. _____ Who was the Phillie pitcher who won Game Five and saved Game Six in 1980?

78. _____ Who, in addition to Pedro Guerrero, hit an eighth-inning home run in Game Five of 1981 to give Jerry Reuss and the Dodgers a 2–1 win?

79. _____ Who was the Brewer who got 12 hits in 1982?

80. _____ Who was the Oriole slugger who came out of a slump to hit two home runs in the series-clinching game of 1983?

81. _____ Who was the Tiger who hit two home runs in the series-clinching game of 1984?

82. _____ Who was the second-year Royal pitcher who was 2–0 in 1985?

83. _____ Who was the 1986 MVP whom the winning team didn't sign for 1987?

84. _____ Who was the pitcher who won the first and seventh games for the Twins in 1987?

85. _____ Who closed out a great 1988 season when he won both of his fall classic decisions, posted a 1.00 ERA, and won the MVP Award of the World Series?

86. _____ Who batted .474 and stole three bases during the earthquake-interrupted series that was won by the A's in four games?

87. _____ Who allowed only one run in 17 innings of pitching as the 1990 Reds routed the A's in four games?

88. _____ Who won both Game One and Game Seven, a 1–0 classic, as the Twins nipped the Braves in ten innings?

89. _____ Who was the 1992 player whose two-run double in the 11th inning lifted the Blue Jays to a 4–3 win in Game Six, and their first world title?

90. _____ Who was the player whose three-run homer in the bottom of the ninth inning of Game Six spearheaded the Blue Jays to their second consecutive world title in 1993?

91. _____ Who was the pitcher whose 1–0 shutout gave the Atlanta Braves their first world title?

103. WORLD SERIES MULTIPLE CHOICE

1. _____ Who was eligible to play in 37 games but appeared in only one?
   a. Gus Niarhos   c. Charlie Silvera
   b. Jake Gibbs   d. Stan Lopata

2. _____ Who was eligible to play in 23 games but didn't appear in one of them?
   a. Dick Williams   c. Bruce Edwards
   b. Arndt Jorgens   d. Mike Hegan

3. _____ Who played on four world championship teams his first four years in the majors?
   a. Jackie Robinson   c. Charlie Keller
   b. Reggie Jackson   d. Joe DiMaggio

4. _____ Who was the infielder who played in his first and in his second series 14 years apart?
   a. Billy Herman   c. Rabbit Maranville
   b. Stan Hack   d. Johnny Evers

5. _____ Who was the pitcher who played in his first and in his last series 17 years apart?
   a. Walter Johnson   c. Grover Alexander
   b. Jim Kaat   d. Eppa Rixey

6. _____ Who was the outfielder who played in his first and in his last series 22 years apart?
   a. Sam Crawford   c. Willie Mays
   b. Al Kaline   d. Mickey Mantle

7. _____ Who was the pitcher who played in his first and in his last series 18 years apart?
   a. Burleigh Grimes   c. Joe Bush
   b. Christy Mathewson   d. Herb Pennock

8. _____ Who was the pitcher who played the most years in the majors before appearing in his first series?
   a. Joe Niekro   c. Ted Lyons
   b. Steve Carlton   d. Early Wynn

9. _____ Who was the oldest regular-day player to appear in the series?
   a. Enos Slaughter   c. Johnny Mize
   b. Johnny Hopp   d. Pete Rose

10. _____ Who pinch-hit in ten games?
   a. Bobby Brown   c. Dusty Rhodes
   b. Johnny Blanchard   d. Gino Cimoli
11. _____ Who pinch-ran in nine games?
   a. Herb Washington   c. Bill North
   b. Allan Lewis   d. Sam Jethroe
12. _____ Who twice got four hits in a game?
   a. Pete Rose   c. Robin Yount
   b. Lou Brock   d. Paul Molitor
13. _____ Who went hitless in 31 consecutive at-bats?
   a. Mark Belanger   c. Julian Javier
   b. Marv Owen   d. Dal Maxvill
14. _____ Who hit ten doubles in total series?
   a. Mickey Mantle   c. Frank Frisch and Yogi
   b. Joe Medwick   Berra
                           d. Pee Wee Reese
15. _____ Who hit six doubles in one series?
   a. Pete Fox   c. Frank Isbell
   b. Nellie Fox   d. Pete Rose
16. _____ Who was the rookie who hit three home runs in his first series?
   a. Tony Kubek   c. Amos Otis
   b. Willie Aikens   d. Charlie Keller
17. _____ Who twice hit four home runs in a series?
   a. Hank Bauer   c. Gene Tenace
   b. Duke Snider   d. Roberto Clemente
18. _____ Who hit seven home runs in two consecutive series?
   a. Babe Ruth   c. Lou Gehrig
   b. Reggie Jackson   d. Mickey Mantle
19. _____ Who hit nine home runs in three consecutive series?
   a. Mickey Mantle   c. Reggie Jackson
   b. Roger Maris   d. Babe Ruth
20. _____ Who got the most long hits in one game?
   a. Reggie Jackson   c. Yogi Berra
   b. Frank Isbell   d. Babe Ruth
21. _____ Who drove home six runs in one game?
   a. Bobby Richardson   c. Gil Hodges
   b. Monte Irvin   d. Hank Aaron

22. _____ Who was hit by pitches three times in one series?
   a. Minnie Minoso   c. Don Baylor
   b. Ron Hunt   d. Max Carey

23. _____ Who grounded into five double plays in one series?
   a. Willie Mays   c. Joe DiMaggio
   b. Irv Noren   d. Gil McDougald

24. _____ Who was caught stealing nine times in total series?
   a. Ty Cobb   c. Frank Schulte
   b. Pee Wee Reese   d. Willie Randolph

25. _____ Who pitched consecutive games in consecutive series?
   a. Deacon Phillippe   c. Lefty Grove
   b. George Earnshaw   d. Ed Reulbach

26. _____ Who was the relief pitcher who appeared in 16 games in total series?
   a. Johnny Murphy   c. Rollie Fingers
   b. Wilcy Moore   d. Hugh Casey

27. _____ Who was the relief pitcher who appeared in six different series?
   a. Joe Page   c. Elroy Face
   b. Bob Kuzava   d. Johnny Murphy

28. _____ Who won seven consecutive games?
   a. Bob Gibson   c. Lefty Gomez
   b. Red Ruffing   d. Herb Pennock

29. _____ Who twice pitched four consecutive opening games?
   a. Allie Reynolds   c. Red Ruffing
   b. Whitey Ford   d. Carl Hubbell

30. _____ Who was the pitcher who was on the losing end of three shutouts, including two 1–0 scores?
   a. Vic Raschi   c. Bob Turley
   b. Preacher Roe   d. Eddie Plank

31. _____ Who pitched a 12-inning game without issuing a base on balls?
   a. Whitey Ford   c. Dizzy Dean
   b. Schoolboy Rowe   d. Tommy Bridges

32. _____ Who, in a nine-inning game, struck out 11 batters but lost, 1–0?
   a. Don Newcombe   c. Tom Seaver
   b. Bob Turley   d. Bob Feller

33. _____ Who, in a ten-inning game, struck out 11 batters but lost, 1–0?
   a. Carl Hubbell   c. Ewell Blackwell
   b. Bob Turley   d. Lefty Grove

34. _____ Who, in a 12-inning game, struck out 12 batters but lost?
   a. Rube Waddell   c. Chief Bender
   b. Christy Mathewson   d. Walter Johnson

35. _____ Who was the first baseman who didn't make an error in 31 consecutive games?
   a. Gil Hodges   c. Bill Terry
   b. Bill Skowron   d. Hank Greenberg

36. _____ Who played in seven series at second base?
   a. Frank Frisch   c. Jackie Robinson
   b. Joe Gordon   d. Eddie Stanky.

37. _____ Who was the second baseman who didn't make an error in 23 consecutive games?
   a. Junior Gilliam   c. Tony Lazzeri
   b. Red Schoendienst   d. Billy Martin

38. _____ Who played in six series at third base?
   a. Pepper Martin   c. Billy Cox
   b. Red Rolfe   d. Sal Bando

39. _____ Who was the third baseman who didn't make an error in 22 consecutive games?
   a. Graig Nettles   c. Pete Rose
   b. Ron Cey   d. Brooks Robinson

40. _____ Who was the shortstop who didn't make an error in 21 consecutive games?
   a. Leo Durocher   c. Pee Wee Reese
   b. Marty Marion   d. Phil Rizzuto

41. _____ Who played in 12 series as an outfielder?
   a. Casey Stengel   c. Babe Ruth
   b. Joe DiMaggio   d. Mickey Mantle

42. _____ Who was the catcher who didn't make an error in 30 consecutive games?
   a. Roy Campanella   c. Walker Cooper
   b. Yogi Berra   d. Bill Dickey

43. _____ Who was the pitcher who didn't make an error in 18 consecutive games?
   a. Carl Hubbell   c. Don Drysdale
   b. Sandy Koufax   d. Whitey Ford
44. _____ Who was the youngest manager of a series winner?
   a. Lou Boudreau   c. Joe Cronin
   b. Bucky Harris   d. Mickey Cochrane
45. _____ Who was the youngest manager of a series club?
   a. Joe Cronin   c. Frank Frisch
   b. Roger Peckinpaugh d. Lou Boudreau
46. _____ Who was the manager who lost 28 series games?
   a. Connie Mack   c. John McGraw
   b. Leo Durocher   d. Bill Terry
47. _____ Who was the manager who won 37 series games?
   a. Casey Stengel   c. Walter Alston
   b. Joe McCarthy   d. Connie Mack
48. _____ Who managed in the series with three different teams from the same league?
   a. Sparky Anderson   c. Bill McKechnie
   b. Dick Williams   d. Alvin Dark
49. _____ Who appeared in 15 series as a coach?
   a. Jimmy Dykes   c. Frank Crosetti
   b. Art Fletcher   d. Chuck Dressen
50. _____ Who appeared in 18 series as an umpire?
   a. Shag Crawford   c. Tom Connolly
   b. Bill Klem   d. Bill McKinley

104. WORLD SERIES CLUES
WHO'S WHO

1. _____ Who pitched a record ten complete games in World Series play?
   a. He won five and lost five.
   b. He pitched 27 consecutive scoreless innings in one series.

2. _____ Who was the Yankee pitcher from the 1930s and 1940s who won seven of nine decisions in series action?
   a. He twice led the American League in losses.
   b. He won 20 or more games four straight years.

3. _____ Who was the Yankee pitcher from the 1920s and 1930s who won five of five decisions in series play?
   a. He got three saves, too.
   b. He won 240 career games.

4. _____ Who was the Yankee pitcher from the 1940s and 1950s who won seven of nine decisions in World Series play?
   a. He picked up four saves, too.
   b. In 1953, his last series, he saved Game Six and he won Game Seven in relief.

5. _____ Who picked up a record six series saves?
   a. He picked them up in three consecutive series.
   b. In those three series he pitched in a total of 16 games.

6. _____ Who struck out a record 11 batters in relief in one series game?
   a. He did it for the Orioles ...
   b. ... against the Dodgers.

7. _____ Who hit a double and a triple in the same inning of a series game?
   a. He did it for the 1921 Giants.
   b. He hit .300 in nine of his ten seasons.

8. _____ Who was the player who ripped five consecutive extra-base hits in series action?
   a. He got 25 hits in two consecutive series.
   b. He stole seven bases in each of those series, too.

9. _____ Who was the player for the Giants who got all three of his team's hits in a 1923 series game against the Yankees?
   a. He batted .310 lifetime, one point higher than his brother.
   b. He and his brother played against each other in three World Series.

10. _____ Who got a record five hits in one series game?
   a. He got 11 hits in the entire series.
   b. He did it in 1982.

11. _____ Who was the pitcher who allowed three home runs in the same inning?
   a. He pitched for the 1967 Cards.
   b. Two years later he was out of baseball.

12. _____ Who was the outfielder who started two double plays in the same series game?
   a. He did it for the 1919 Reds.
   b. A Hall of Famer, he hit .323 lifetime.

13. _____ Who was the youngest player ever to appear in a series?
   a. He was 18.
   b. In that series he got four hits in one game against Walter Johnson.

14. _____ Who played in 50 games and never hit a homer?
   a. He appeared for the Giants and the Cards.
   b. He hit two home runs in All-Star games.

15. _____ Who, in addition to Bob Gibson, has been the only pitcher to hit two home runs in series play?
   a. He won four of six series decisions ...
   b. ... for the Orioles.

16. _____ Who hit three home runs in each of back-to-back series?
   a. He played for the 1924–25 Senators.
   b. He batted .316 lifetime and .287 in five series with the Senators and the Tigers.

17. _____ Who threw out ten runners in one series?
   a. He did it for the 1919 White Sox.
   b. He's in the Hall of Fame.

18. _____ Who pitched the longest complete-game loss in series history?
   a. In two series he had an 0.89 ERA.
   b. His initials are S.S.

19. _____ Who hit two home runs in one game and two triples in another?
   a. He did it in the first series for the winning Red Sox.
   b. Two years later he played with the winning White Sox.

20. _____ Who was the player who was fired after a series because he struck out nine times?
   a. The series took place in 1909.
   b. He played for the Pirates, who defeated the Tigers.

21. _____ Who was the three-game winner for the White Sox who tried to steal third with the base already occupied?
   a. He did it in 1917.
   b. He won 254 major league games.

22. _____ Who retired the last 21 batters of a game in order?
   a. He did it in 1926.
   b. He was 39 at the time.

23. _____ Who, in the 1920s, struck out ten batters in a relief appearance?
   a. His brother pitched on the same team.
   b. They won 214 major league games between them.

24. _____ Who was traded after he player-managed his team to the world title?
   a. He won batting titles with two different teams.
   b. He was a second baseman.

25. _____ Who made the "$30,000 Muff?"
   a. He did it while playing with the 1912 Giants.
   b. Later in that inning, he made one of the greatest catches in series history.

26. _____ Who has been the only Tiger manager in 87 years to lead his team into the series in back-to-back years?
   a. He was a .320 lifetime hitter.
   b. He played in five series in seven years.

27. _____ Who was the Cardinal pitcher who lost a two-hitter?
a. George McQuinn's two-run homer was the key hit.
b. He bounced back to win Game Five, 2–0.

28. _____ Who has been the only Red manager to win back-to-back world titles?
a. He played just one season in the majors ...
b. ... with the 1959 Phillies.

29. _____ Who was the youngest pitcher ever to hurl in the series?
a. He was 19 at the time.
b. He has a famous baseball brother, now retired.

30. _____ Who missed the opening assignment of a series because it fell on a Jewish religious holiday?
a. He had a .655 lifetime winning percentage.
b. He had an .097 lifetime batting average.

31. _____ Who hit for the highest series average (.391) in 20 or more games?
a. He got a record-tying 13 hits in one series.
b. He played on two world title teams in the 1960s.

32. _____ Who got a record six consecutive hits in the 1924 World Series?
a. He hit seven home runs in three series.
b. He got the series-winning hit for the Tigers in 1935.

33. _____ Who got seven consecutive hits in back-to-back series?
a. He was a catcher.
b. He was a Rookie of the Year and an MVP.

34. _____ Who batted in six runs in one series as a pinch-hitter?
a. He did it in the 1950s.
b. He helped his team to a four-game sweep.

35. _____ Who was the National Leaguer who hit the most homers in series play?
a. He hit 11.
b. He twice hit four homers in a series.

36. _____ Who pitched a one-hitter for the Cubs in 1906?
a. He won 181 games.
b. He was called "Big Ed."

37. _____ Who was the American League player who hit safely in 15 of the 16 games in which he played?
   a. He hit better than .300 and drove home 100 or more runs in three consecutive years.
   b. He once hit .529 in a series.

38. _____ Who was the infielder in the 1920s who cost two different teams world titles because of errors in seventh games?
   a. He managed the Yankees before he cost them the 1921 title.
   b. He was the MVP in one of those years (1925).

39. _____ Who won three pennants and two world titles in his first three years of managing?
   a. He was a catcher who hit .272 lifetime.
   b. He moved into the front office after his three straight successes.

40. _____ Who has been the only pitcher, in addition to Don Drysdale, to both win and lose 1–0 decisions in series play?
   a. He beat Jim Konstanty.
   b. He lost to Preacher Roe.

41. _____ Who was the most recent pitcher to win the final game of back-to-back series?
   a. The years were 1952–53.
   b. He starred as a starter and as a reliever.

42. _____ Who was the Yankee pitcher who picked up saves in the final game of back-to-back series?
   a. The years were 1951–52.
   b. They called him "Sarge."

43. _____ Who lost a record two 1–0 games?
   a. He did it in 1905 and 1914.
   b. He won over 300 career games.

44. _____ Who picked off two runners in the sixth inning of the seventh game in 1968?
   a. He picked off Lou Brock and Curt Flood.
   b. He won three games in that series.

45. _____ Who was the first pitcher to win the seventh game of one series and lose the seventh game of the following series?
   a. He won the seventh game in 1924.
   b. He was 1–2 the year that his team won and 2–1 the season that his club lost.

46. _____ Who was the first pitcher to win the final game of two consecutive series?
   a. He did it in 1921 and 1922.
   b. He split eight decisions in series play for the Giants.

47. _____ Who pitched a one-hitter for the Cubs in 1945?
   a. He won 162 games.
   b. Rudy York got the hit.

48. _____ Who was the player who, after getting 11 hits in the 1951 World Series, was pinch-hit for three times in the 1954 classic?
   a. He got four hits and stole home in Game One of 1951.
   b. Dusty Rhodes pinch-hit for him.

49. _____ Who was the catcher whose passed ball cost his team a big victory in 1941?
   a. The pitcher was Hugh Casey.
   b. He later jumped to the Mexican Leagues.

50. _____ Who tagged Don Newcombe for three homers and eight RBIs in the same series?
   a. He did it in 1956.
   b. Two of the shots were two-run blasts in the final game.

51. _____ Who was the pitcher who threw a one-hitter for the Yankees in 1947?
   a. He lost.
   b. He never started another major league game.

52. _____ Who was the only pitcher, in addition to Carl Hubbell, to beat the Yankees in the 1930s?
   a. He did it for the Giants in 1936.
   b. He was called "Prince Hal."

53. _____ Who was the Yankee pitcher who struck out a record five times in one World Series game?
   a. In 1928 he had a league-high 24 wins.
   b. He later became an umpire.

54. _____ Who batted into five outs in two consecutive at-bats in a World Series game?
   a. He hit into a triple play the first time.
   b. He hit into a double play the second time.

55. _____ Who pitched a one-hitter for the Red Sox in 1967?
a. Julian Javier got the hit.
b. A skiing accident didn't help his future.

56. _____ Who, in the 1920s, won the sixth and seventh games of a series?
a. He did it for the 1925 Pirates.
b. He twice won 20 games for the Pirates.

57. _____ Who was the .257 regular-season hitter in 1953 who batted .500 in the series and delivered a record 12 hits for a six-game clash?
a. He batted .257 lifetime, too.
b. In five series, however, he hit .333.

58. _____ Who set a record when he struck out the first five batters to face him in a starting assignment?
a. He was the MVP in 1942.
b. He won more than 20 games three years in a row.

59. _____ Who was the Oriole short-inning man who did not allow a run in three consecutive series?
a. He won ten games in relief in 1970.
b. Despite an 0.00 ERA, he lost his only decision in post-season play.

60. _____ Who was the National League pitcher who allowed only one run in 25⅓ innings of pitching in series play?
a. He did it in the 1970s . . .
b. . . . for the Reds.

61. _____ Who was the Pirate star who was benched by manager Donie Bush in the 1927 series?
a. He hit .321 over 18 years.
b. He got the series-winning hit in 1925 for the Pirates.

62. _____ Who was the 40-year-old player who hit a game-winning home run in 1956?
a. He played on two world championship clubs in St. Louis.
b. He played on two world championship clubs in New York.

63. _____ Who hit the single that scored Enos Slaughter from first base for the winning run in the 1946 series?
a. He won a batting title.
b. His brother won one, too.

64. _____ Who became the first player to hit two home runs in two different games in the same series?
a. He hit .400 in the 1980 World Series.
b. He was named after Willie Mays.

65. _____ Who, on his special night, got four hits, including a home run?
a. The year was 1973.
b. He ended up his career as a deluxe pinch-hitter.

66. _____ Who was the only pitcher to hit a grand slam in the series?
a. He won 20 or more games four years in a row.
b. He hit two home runs in World Series play.

67. _____ Who, in Game Three of 1969, made two sensational catches—on balls hit by Elrod Hendricks and Paul Blair—that rank with the classic catches of series past?
a. He also homered in that game.
b. He came to the Mets from the White Sox.

68. _____ Who was the Tiger left fielder whose perfect throw cut down Lou Brock, trying to score, in the key play of Game Five in 1968?
a. He played 18 years in the majors.
b. He hit 325 career homers.

69. _____ Who was the Yankee first baseman who lost a crucial throw from third baseman Clete Boyer because of the glare of the shirt-sleeves in the third-base boxes?
a. He replaced Bill Skowron.
b. The following year, he hit a grand slam home run against the Cardinals.

70. _____ Who was the Cardinal outfielder who, first, lost Jim Northrup's fly ball in the sun and, second, slipped as the ball sailed by him for the game-winning triple in Game Seven of 1968?
a. He was a great defensive outfielder.
b. He tested baseball's reserve clause.

71. _____ Who pitched back-to-back complete games twice in the same series?
a. He won three games and lost two.
b. He pitched five complete games.

72. _____ Who was the three-game winner who allowed seven hits in one inning?
   a. He won 34 games that year.
   b. He was the roommate of Tris Speaker's during all of his 14 years in the majors.

73. _____ Who won five games and posted a .333 batting average in series play?
   a. He once won 31 games in a season.
   b. They called him "Colby Jack."

74. _____ Who was the player who hit two home runs in the 1924 series, despite the fact that he hit only 9 in 12 major league seasons?
   a. He was a young manager.
   b. He ended up an old manager.

75. _____ Who retired the first 22 batters in order?
   a. He was 5–0 in series play.
   b. He pitched in series 18 years apart.

76. _____ Who was the first player to hit a pinch-hit home run in series play?
   a. He hit a total of 12 homers in series play.
   b. He, like Frankie Frisch, hit ten doubles.

The Shutout Series

If you don't believe that there was a dead ball era, you should glance at the statistics of the 1905–07 World Series, and then zero in on the records of the first of those classics.

In 16 games during the 1905–07 time span, there was not one home run hit in post-season play. To say that the pitchers dominated the hitters is to underscore the obvious.

Take the 1905 series, for example. The victorious Giants allowed the formidable Athletics just three runs in 45 innings of play. And none of the runs was earned. Christy Mathewson, the ace of John McGraw's staff, pitched a record three shutouts against Connie Mack's vaunted heroes. "Big Six" was so completely in control that he allowed just 14 hits and a walk in 27 innings of pitching.

Joe McGinnity, also of the Giants, was almost as good as his celebrated teammate. He pitched a shutout, allowed only ten hits in 17 innings of pitching—a 22-game winner hurled one inning of relief in the "Iron Man's" first outing—and posted an 0.00 ERA. But his record was not perfect—he split his two decisions. In Game Two he was victimized by his defense, which allowed three unearned runs, and by his pitching opponent, who threw a four-hit shutout. (All five games ended in shutouts.)

Who was that Giant relief pitcher who later hurled a no-hitter for nine innings in the opening game of 1909—he lost the game in 13 innings, 3–0—and who was the Athletic shutout pitcher who went on to set a record by pitching nine consecutive complete games in World Series play?

(Answer appears on page 344.)

Chapter Eighteen

MAJOR LEAGUE CLUBS

CHICAGO CUBS

Infielders

True or False.

1. _____ Frank Chance, Charlie Grimm, and Phil Cavarretta ended their careers with lifetime batting averages in the .290s.
2. _____ Rogers Hornsby hit a club-high .380 in 1929.
3. _____ Ernie Banks played more games at shortstop than he did at first base.
4. _____ Heinie Zimmerman was the third baseman in the Tinker-to-Evers-to-Chance infield.
5. _____ Billy Herman compiled a lifetime average of .300 or better.
6. _____ Bill Madlock was the only Cub to win two batting titles.

Outfielders

Fill in the blanks.

7. _____ Who was the Bruin who won four home run crowns?
8. _____ Who was the club's Triple Crown winner in 1994?
9. _____ Who won back-to-back home run titles in 1943–44?

10. _____ Who was the .320 lifetime hitter—he played two and one-half seasons with the Cubs—who ended his career with 300 home runs?

11. _____ Who was the Cub outfielder who played in 1,117 consecutive games to set a then-National League record?

12. _____ Who was the one-time Cub—he batted .285 lifetime with 213 career home runs—who played in World Series with the Cubs, Dodgers, and Braves?

Catchers

Matching.

13. _____ Johnny Kling	a.	He managed the Cubs
14. _____ Gabby Hartnett		and the Tigers.
15. _____ Bob Scheffing	b.	He managed the Braves.
	c.	He player-managed the Cubs to a pennant.

Pitchers

Multiple Choice.

16. _____ Who was the pitcher against whom Babe Ruth "called his shot" in the 1932 World Series?
   a. Charlie Root   c. Hippo Vaughn
   b. Pat Malone   d. Guy Bush.

17. _____ Who holds the club record with 20 consecutive converted saves?
   a. Bruce Sutter   c. Mike Morgan
   b. Randy Myers   d. Steve Trout

18. _____ Who was the losing pitcher—Fred Toney of the Reds was the winner—in the only nine-inning double no-hit game in major league history?
   a. Grover Alexander   c. Larry French
   b. Hank Borowy   d. Hippo Vaughn

19. _____ A winner of 162 major league games, he picked up a victory and a save in the 1945 World Series.
   a. Hank Borowy   c. Claude Passeau
   b. Lon Warneke   d. Charlie Root

20. _____ Who was the three-time 20-game winner who later became an umpire?
   a. Pat Malone   c. Lon Warneke
   b. Guy Bush   d. Bill Lee

21. _____ Who was the Cub pitcher who won 20 or more games in each of his first six full seasons in the majors?
   a. Ferguson Jenkins   c. Mordecai Brown
   b. Ed Reulbach   d. Johnny Schmitz

22. _____ Name the five-time 20-game winner who turned in the best single-season ERA (1.04) in National League history.
   a. Ferguson Jenkins   c. Bob Rush
   b. Grover Alexander   d. Mordecai Brown

23. _____ A 21-game winner for the Yankees and the Cubs in 1945, he split four World Series decisions that year.
   a. Lon Warneke   c. Hank Borowy
   b. Claude Passeau   d. Johnny Schmitz

24. _____ This 300-plus winner led the league in 1920, with the Cubs, in wins (27) and ERA (1.91).
   a. Mordecai Brown   c. Guy Bush
   b. Grover Alexander   d. Charlie Root

25. _____ The only National League pitcher to lead the loop in winning percentage for three consecutive seasons, he was the only pitcher to throw shutouts in both ends of a doubleheader.
   a. Grover Alexander   c. Pat Malone
   b. Ed Reulbach   d. Larry French

MONTREAL EXPOS

Infielders

Matching.

1. _____ Ron Fairly
2. _____ Dave Cash
3. _____ Ron Hunt
4. _____ Maury Wills
5. _____ Bob Bailey
6. _____ Larry Parrish

a. In 1971 he was hit by pitches a record 50 times.
b. A one-time Expo infielder, he hit well over 200 home runs.
c. He came up with the Pirates; he bowed out with the Red Sox. In between, he averaged 21 homers a year over a five-year span for the Expos.
d. In the three years before he joined the Expos, he led the league in at-bats with an average of 685 per season.
e. In his only season with the Expos, he led the team in stolen bases.
f. This veteran of 21 years—and four World Series—averaged 15 home runs a year in his five seasons with the Expos.

Outfielders

Multiple Choice.

7. _____ Who hit a single-season high .339?
   a. Ken Singleton
   b. Moises Alou
   c. Mack Jones
   d. Manny Mota

8. _____ Name the Expo who drove home 123 runs in one season.
   a. Boots Day   c. Rusty Staub
   b. Tim Wallach   d. Larry Parrish
9. _____ Who was the outfielder with the strong arm who averaged 24 home runs a year from 1977–79?
   a. Ellis Valentine   c. Andre Dawson
   b. Warren Cromartie   d. Rico Carty
10. _____ Who led the league in stolen bases from 1991 to 1992 and picked up Gold Gloves in 1993 and 1994?
   a. Marquis Grissom   c. Larry Walker
   b. Moises Alou   d. Wil Cordero
11. _____ Who was the Expo who set a record when he pinch-hit safely 25 times in 1977?
   a. Jerry White   c. Sam Mejias
   b. Warren Cromartie   d. Jose Morales
12. _____ Who, in 1971, hit a then-club-high .311, drove home 97 runs, and moved to the Mets in 1972?
   a. Manny Mota   c. Rusty Staub
   b. Rico Carty   d. Tommy Davis

Catchers

True or False.
13. _____ Barry Foote was the first-string catcher for the Expos before Gary Carter took over full-time in 1977.
14. _____ Tim McCarver played at least two full seasons with Montreal.
15. _____ Gary Carter tied a record with five home runs in two consecutive games.

Pitchers

Fill in the blanks.
16. _____ Who won the most games (20) in one season for Montreal?
17. _____ Who was the pitcher who struck out the most batters (251) in one season for the Expos?

18. _____ Name the starting pitcher whom the Expos traded to the Reds for Tony Perez.

19. _____ Who was the only relief pitcher, in addition to Goose Gossage, to register at least 20 saves a season from 1982–86?

20. _____ Who was the relief pitcher who led the loop in appearances for two consecutive years before he set records for games by a fireman with the Dodgers and the Twins?

21. _____ Who was the Rookie of the Year in 1970?

22. _____ Who pitched two no-hitters for the Expos?

23. _____ Who no-hit the Giants in 1981?

24. _____ Who was the 158-game winner who two times led the National League in losses?

25. _____ Who, along with Ken Singleton, was traded to the Orioles, where he won 20 games in his only year with Baltimore, for Dave McNally and Rich Coggins?

NEW YORK METS

Infielders

True or False.
1. _____ Gil Hodges ended his career with the Mets.
2. _____ Ron Hunt hit a key home run for the Mets in the final game of the 1969 World Series.
3. _____ Bud Harrelson hit .250 or over lifetime.
4. _____ Wayne Garrett came to the Mets in the deal for Nolan Ryan.
5. _____ Ed Kranepool was a lifetime Met.
6. _____ Donn Clendenon hit three home runs in the 1969 World Series.

Outfielders

Fill in the blanks.
7. _____ Who set a club record with at least one RBI in nine consecutive games?
8. _____ Who stroked a club-high 39 homers in a season?
9. _____ Who hit a team-high .340 one year?
10. _____ Who was the former "Whiz Kid"—he hit .308 lifetime—who ended his career with the Mets?
11. _____ Who is the outfielder who led the majors in assists (22) in 1991 and the Orioles in batting (.289) in 1992?
12. _____ Who hit two home runs to defeat Steve Carlton in a game in which the Card lefty struck out a then-record 19 batters?

Catchers

Matching.

13. _____ Yogi Berra   a. He was born in St. Louis.
14. _____ Jerry Grote   b. He was born in San Antonio.
15. _____ John Stearns   c. He was born in San Francisco.

Pitchers

Multiple Choice.

16. _____ Who holds the club record for season wins (25) and strikeouts (289)?
    a. Jerry Koosman   c. Tom Seaver
    b. Nolan Ryan   d. Jon Matlack.

17. _____ Who was the pitcher who gave up Roberto Clemente's 3,000th—and final—hit?
    a. Jon Matlack   c. Danny Frisella
    b. Tug McGraw   d. Gary Gentry

18. _____ Who was the pitcher who coined the expression "You gotta believe"?
    a. Tom Seaver   c. Tug McGraw
    b. Bob Apodaca   d. Jerry Koosman

19. _____ Which one of the following pitchers won four of his 363 wins with the Mets?
    a. Mickey Lolich   c. Juan Marichal
    b. Warren Spahn   d. Early Wynn

20. _____ The pitcher who threw the historic 61st home run pitch to Roger Maris in 1961, he later lost 20 games for the 1964 Mets.
    a. Tracy Stallard   c. Dick Schwall
    b. Bill Monbouquette   d. Mike Fornieles

21. _____ Who became the first pitcher to go 3-0 in a championship series?
    a. Tug McGraw   c. Nolan Ryan
    b. Jesse Orosco   d. Dwight Gooden

22. _____ Who set a club record when he failed to allow a free pass in 47⅓ consecutive innings?
    a. Dwight Gooden   c. David Cone
    b. Bret Saberhagen   d. Jerry Koosman

23. _____ Twice a 20-game loser for the Mets, he split four World Series decisions with three different teams.
a. Jack Fisher   c. Al Jackson
b. Roger Craig   d. Pedro Ramos

24. _____ Which one of the following pitchers is 3-0 in World Series play?
a. Jon Matlack   c. Gary Gentry
b. Tom Seaver   d. Jerry Koosman

25. _____ Who became the first pitcher to fan 200 batters in his first three seasons in the majors?
a. Dwight Gooden   c. Tom Seaver
b. Nolan Ryan   d. Jerry Koosman

PHILADELPHIA PHILLIES

Infielders

True or False.

1. _____ John Kruk hit .300 for the Phillies in three straight seasons.
2. _____ Dave Cash registered more official at-bats (699) in one season than any other National League player.
3. _____ Larry Bowa hit .300 in a season.
4. _____ Mike Schmidt led the National League in home runs a loop-high eight times.
5. _____ Emil Verban was the "Whiz Kid" second baseman in 1950.
6. _____ Willie Jones hit more home runs in a season than Dick Allen did.

Outfielders

Fill in the blanks.

7. _____ Who set a league record when he paced the loop in both at-bats and walks in the same season?
8. _____ Who was the Phillie slugger who two times led the National League in home runs three years in a row?
9. _____ Who didn't win the RBI title despite the fact that he drove home 170 runs?
10. _____ Name the Phillie who hit a league-leading .398 one year?
11. _____ Whose tenth-inning home run on the last day of the 1950 season won the pennant for the Phillies?
12. _____ A .308 lifetime hitter, he won two batting titles with the Phillies in the 1950s.

Catchers

Matching.

13. _____ Curt Davis
14. _____ Andy Seminick
15. _____ Tim McCarver

a. He was Steve Carlton's favorite receiver.
b. He was the "Whiz Kids' " receiver.
c. He hit .333 career-wise for the Phillies, .308 overall.

Pitchers

Multiple Choice.

16. _____ Who was the pitcher who won a record 28 games in his rookie year?
    a. Grover Alexander
    b. Harry Coveleski
    c. Eppa Rixey
    d. Bucky Walters

17. _____ Name the 500-plus home run hitter who ended his career with the Phillies as a pitcher.
    a. Babe Ruth
    b. Ernie Banks
    c. Eddie Mathews
    d. Jimmie Foxx

18. _____ "The Giant Killer," he defeated New York five times in one week.
    a. Cal McLish
    b. Chris Short
    c. Harry Coveleski
    d. Art Mahaffey

19. _____ Who was the first relief pitcher to win the MVP Award?
    a. Mike Marshall
    b. Jim Konstanty
    c. Tug McGraw
    d. Joe Black

20. _____ Excluding Warren Spahn and Steve Carlton, he won more games than any other National League left-hander.
    a. Eppa Rixey
    b. Curt Simmons
    c. Chris Short
    d. Jim Kaat

21. _____ Who was the Phillie pitcher who threw a career-record 502 home runs?
    a. Steve Carlton
    b. Bucky Walters
    c. Jim Bunning
    d. Robin Roberts

22. _____ An American League transplant, he notched the 250th win of his 283-win career with the Phils.
   a. Jim Bunning
   b. Mickey Lolich
   c. Jim Kaat
   d. Jim Lonborg

23. _____ Who was the pitcher who threw a perfect game for the Phils?
   a. Jim Bunning
   b. Schoolboy Rowe
   c. Jim Lonborg
   d. Curt Simmons

24. _____ Who was the pitcher who led the league in wins (27) one year and losses (20) the following season?
   a. Grover Alexander
   b. Steve Carlton
   c. Jim Lonborg
   d. Curt Simmons

25. _____ Which one of the following pitchers was a Cy Young Award winner?
   a. Jim Lonborg
   b. Robin Roberts
   c. Jim Bunning
   d. Jim Kaat

PITTSBURGH PIRATES

Infielders

Fill in the blanks.

1. _____ Who was the first baseman who set a record when he drilled home runs in eight straight games?

2. _____ Who was the second baseman who hit two game-winning home runs in the 1960 World Series?

3. _____ Who was the Pirate shortstop who hit a club-high .385 in 1935?

4. _____ Who was the .320 lifetime hitter whom many experts consider to be the best all-around third baseman ever to play the game?

5. _____ A four-time home run champ in the American League, he finished his career in 1947 when he hit 25 home runs for the Pirates. Who was he?

6. _____ Name the infielder who won batting titles a National League-high eight times.

Outfielders

Matching.

7. _____ Tommy Leach
8. _____ Max Carey
9. _____ Paul Waner
10. _____ Jerry Lynch
11. _____ Roberto Clemente
12. _____ Lloyd Waner

a. He led the National League in stolen bases ten times.

b. A .317 lifetime hitter, he won four batting titles.

c. He set a record, since surpassed, by hitting 18 career pinch-hit homers.

d. A .333 lifetime hitter, he won three batting crowns.

e. He collected over 200 hits in each of his first three years in the majors.

f. In 1902 he won the home run crown with six home runs, the lowest figure in history.

Catchers

Multiple Choice.

13. _____ He caught in the 1909 World Series.
   a. George Gibson   c. Earl Smith
   b. Al Lopez   d. Johnny Gooch

14. _____ He caught in the 1925 and the 1927 World Series.
   a. Al Lopez   c. Earl Smith
   b. George Gibson   d. Hal Smith

15. _____ He caught in the 1960 World Series.
   a. Manny Sanguillen   c. Earl Smith
   b. Johnny Gooch   d. Smoky Burgess

True or False.

16. _____ Rip Sewell (143–97) was known primarily for his knuckleball.,

17. _____ Bob Friend had a winning major league record.

18. _____ Roy Face was the first reliever to pick up three saves in the same series.

19. _____ Vernon Law was the winning pitcher in the seventh game of the 1960 World Series.

20. _____ Murry Dickson led the National League in losses more times than any other Senior Circuit hurler.

21. _____ Steve Blass led his league in winning percentage one year.

22. _____ Deacon Phillippe had the most decisions in one World Series.

23. _____ Steve Cooke in 1993 led all major league rookie pitchers in starts, innings, and strikeouts.

24. _____ Zane Smith in 1974 hit a single off Pedro Martinez of the Expos after going hitless in his first 40 career at-bats, the third longest career-starting slump in history.

25. _____ Larry French (197–171) never won 20 games in a season.

ST. LOUIS CARDINALS

Infielders

Multiple Choice.
1. _____ Which one of the following first basemen won one home run title, two RBI crowns, and hit over .300 in nine of his first ten years in the majors?
   a. Jim Bottomley   c. Johnny Mize
   b. Rip Collins   d. Stan Musial
2. _____ Which one of the following second basemen hit .400 three times?
   a. Frankie Frisch   c. Emil Verban
   b. Red Schoendienst   d. Rogers Hornsby
3. _____ Name the shortstop who got at least 100 hits in 17 consecutive seasons.
   a. Marty Marion   c. Dal Maxvill
   b. Ozzie Smith   d. Leo Durocher
4. _____ Which one of the following players hit a grand slam home run in a World Series game?
   a. Pepper Martin   c. Ken Boyer
   b. Whitey Kurowski   d. Joe Torre
5. _____ Select the player from the following first basemen who performed for the 1934 "Gashouse Gang."
   a. Rip Collins   c. Johnny Mize
   b. Johnny Hopp   d. Stan Musial
6. _____ Who, among the following players, hit a home run that won an All-Star Game?
   a. Bill White   c. Dick Groat
   b. Red Schoendienst   d. Joe Torre

Outfielders

True or False.

7. _____ Stan Musial was the last National League player to win three consecutive batting titles.

8. _____ Joe Medwick won a Triple Crown.

9. _____ Enos Slaughter retired with a lifetime average that was under .300.

10. _____ Lou Brock broke Ty Cobb's stolen base record (96 thefts) when he stole 118 bases in 1974.

11. _____ Terry Moore played center field, between left fielder Stan Musial and right fielder Enos Slaughter, in the early 1940s.

12. _____ Chick Hafey, Joe Medwick, Harry Walker, and Curt Flood won batting titles.

Catchers

Fill in the blanks.

13. _____ Who was the catcher who threw out Babe Ruth, in an attempted steal, to end the 1926 World Series?

14. _____ Name the receiver who played in three consecutive World Series for the Cardinals.

15. _____ Who is the catcher who won three consecutive Gold Glove awards?

Matching.

16. _____ Jesse Haines
17. _____ Grover Alexander
18. _____ Burleigh Grimes
19. _____ Dizzy Dean
20. _____ Mort Cooper
21. _____ Max Lanier
22. _____ Harry Brecheen
23. _____ Bob Gibson
24. _____ Steve Carlton
25. _____ Johnny Beazley

a. Nine times he struck out more than 200 batters in a season, and he pitched 13 shutouts in one year.

b. In five full seasons with the Cardinals, he averaged 24 victories a season.

c. He picked up three wins, one of them coming in relief, in a series.

d. With another team he won 30 or more games three straight years.

e. He, like Grover Alexander, won two games against the Yankees in 1926.

f. He missed the 1947–48 seasons because he was banned from baseball for "jumping" to the Mexican Leagues in 1946.

g. He won only 31 career contests, but he copped 21 of them, in addition to two series victories, in 1942.

h. In 1942 he led the league in ERA (1.78) and shutouts (10).

i. At the age of 38, he won two World Series games for the Cardinals.

j. He struck out 19 batters in a 10-inning game, but lost.

ATLANTA BRAVES

Infielders

Multiple Choice.

1. _____ Whom did they call "The Baby Bull"?
   a. Felipe Alou   c. Tito Francona
   b. Deron Johnson   d. Orlando Cepeda

2. _____ Identify the player who hit more home runs (43) in one season than any other second baseman in the history of the game.
   a. Milt Bolling   c. Bob Aspromonte
   b. Felix Millan   d. Davey Johnson

3. _____ Who is the Brave infielder who set a club record for the best fielding percentage (.994) by a second baseman?
   a. Eddie Stanky   c. Red Schoendienst
   b. Mark Lemke   d. Glenn Hubbard

4. _____ Which one of the following third basemen played in five World Series?
   a. Clete Boyer   c. Darrell Evans
   b. Eddie Mathews   d. Dennis Menke

5. _____ Who was the Brave who hit a club-high 47 homers and a club-high 135 RBIs?
   a. Orlando Cepeda   c. Deron Johnson
   b. Eddie Mathews   d. Willie Montanez

6. _____ Who is the first baseman who once hit 30 home runs in a season for the Phillies and, in a brief stint with the Braves, hit .321 in 1976 and 20 home runs in 1977?
   a. Darrell Evans   c. Willie Montanez
   b. Darrel Chaney   d. Jerry Royster

Outfielders

True or False.

7. _____ Mike Lum was the only batter ever to pinch-hit for Hank Aaron.
8. _____ Hank Aaron hit more home runs in Atlanta than he did in Milwaukee.
9. _____ Felipe Alou was called "The Road Runner."
10. _____ Dale Murphy has been the youngest back-to-back MVP winner in National League history.
11. _____ Rico Carty put big numbers on the board (.330 batting average and 22 home runs) as a rookie.
12. _____ Ken Griffey, Sr., played on back-to-back World Series winners.

Catchers

Fill in the blanks.

13. _____ Name the catcher who hit .315 with 36 home runs and 101 RBIs in 1966.
14. _____ Who was the rookie catcher who hit 33 home runs in 1971?
15. _____ Who is the catcher who hit home runs in five consecutive games?

Pitchers

Matching.

6. _____ Tony Cloninger
7. _____ Phil Niekro
8. _____ Tom Glavine
9. _____ Greg Maddux
0. _____ Hoyt Wilhelm
1. _____ Denny McLain
2. _____ Andy Messersmith
3. _____ Rick Mahler
4. _____ David Palmer
5. _____ Joe Niekro

a. He pitched a five-inning rain-abbreviated perfect game.
b. He drove home nine runs in one game.
c. He won the Cy Young Award a record four straight seasons.
d. He led the league in wins (21) and losses (20) in the same year.
e. He won the Cy Young Award in 1991.
f. His 7–0 start in 1985 was among the best in Braves' history.
g. He played out his option and signed with the Braves in an historic free agent deal.
h. The last 30-game winner in the majors, he ended up his career in Atlanta.
i. He won 20 games in back-to-back years for another club.
j. He played with nine major league teams.

CINCINNATI REDS

Infielders

Matching.
1. _____ Ted Kluszewski
2. _____ Joe Morgan
3. _____ Barry Larkin
4. _____ Pete Rose
5. _____ Frank McCormick
6. _____ Connie Ryan

a. He succeeded Eddi
   Stanky as manager o
   the Rangers.
b. He won the MV
   Award in 1940.
c. He won back-to-bac
   MVP titles.
d. He got five hits in
   game a Nationa
   League record-tyin
   nine times.
e. He batted .300 fiv
   years in a row.
f. He averaged 43 hom
   runs a year for a four
   year span.

Outfielders

Multiple Choice.
7. _____ Who was the player who made a bigger nam
   for himself in professional football than he did in profes
   sional baseball?
   a. Harry Craft   c. Greasy Neale
   b. Ival Goodman   d. Wally Berger
8. _____ Which one of the following players has led th
   National League in RBIs?
   a. Cesar Geronimo   c. Vada Pinson
   b. George Foster   d. Ken Griffey
9. _____ In one season he hit .377, the club high.
   a. Cy Seymour   c. Edd Roush
   b. Frank Robinson   d. Curt Walker

0. _____ An ineffective pitcher for the Athletics, he switched to the outfield with the Reds and posted a .301 lifetime batting average, which included a .351 mark over a three-year period (1924–26).
   a. Rube Bressler   c. Ival Goodman
   b. Curt Walker   d. Harry Craft

1. _____ Name the .323 lifetime hitter who won two batting titles.
   a. Frank Robinson   c. Edd Roush
   b. Vada Pinson   d. Cy Seymour

2 _____ Who was the Red MVP winner who posted a .294 lifetime average and slugged 586 home runs?
   a. Edd Roush   c. Vada Pinson
   b. Wally Berger   d. Frank Robinson

Catchers

True or False.

3. _____ Johnny Bench has won more than one home run crown.

4. _____ Bubbles Hargrave was one of two catchers to win the batting title.

5. _____ Ernie Lombardi had a lifetime batting average of .300 or better.

Pitchers

Fill in the blanks.

6. _____ Who was the only pitcher to throw consecutive no-hitters?

7. _____ The youngest player ever to appear in a major league game, he led the National League in shutouts (5) in 1955.

8. _____ Who was the two-time 20-game winner who struck out more than 200 batters four years in a row?

9. _____ Name the 198-game winner who began his major league career as a third baseman.

20. _____ A one-time 27-game loser, he reeled off three straight 20-game winning seasons for the 1938–40 Reds.

21. _____ Called "The Whip," he led the league in wins (22), complete games (23), and strikeouts (193) in 1947.

22. _____ Who won both of his decisions in the 1990 sweep of the A's?

23. _____ In the 1972 World Series he, with relief aid from Clay Carroll in the ninth inning, pitched the Reds to their only 1–0 win in post-season play.

24. _____ Who was the first Little League product to pitch in the major leagues?

25. _____ Who was the Red relief specialist who notched 29 saves in 1986?

HOUSTON ASTROS

Infielders

Fill in the blanks.

1. _____ Who was the first baseman—the American League's RBI champ in 1976—who averaged 27 home runs per year during his three-year stay in Houston?

2. _____ Who was the .288 lifetime hitter who finished his career with the Astros after setting a record of appearing at the plate 600 or more times for 12 consecutive years in the American League?

3. _____ Who recently led the National League in stolen bases?

4. _____ Who was the Astro third baseman who three times hit more than 20 home runs in a season?

5. _____ Who was the former first baseman with the Astros who wrote a confessional best seller, *Joe, You Coulda Made Us Proud*?

6. _____ Who was the Houston rookie second baseman (1965) who reached double figures in doubles (22), triples (12), and home runs (14)?

Outfielders

Matching.

7. _____ Cesar Cedeno	
8. _____ Gerald Young	
9. _____ Rusty Staub	
10. _____ Jimmy Wynn	
11. _____ Jose Cruz	
12. _____ Terry Puhl	

a. He tied a record when he didn't make one error in a 157-game season.

b. He stole 61 bases, a then-club mark which stood for 11 years.

c. He broke the former stolen base mark when he swiped 65 in 1988.

d. He clubbed 37 home runs in 1967, the team mark until 1994.

e. He hit .333 in 1967, the club high until 1994.

f. Six times he batted .300 or better with the Astros.

Catchers

Multiple Choice.

13. _____ This veteran of 16 campaigns played in two World Series with both the Mets and the Dodgers, but he played his first two years in the majors with the Astros.
    a. Jerry Grote   c. John Bateman
    b. Ed Herrman   d. Johnny Edwards

14. _____ A long-ball hitter with defensive liabilities, he was traded to the Yankees during the 1977 season.
    a. Joe Ferguson   c. Ed Herrman
    b. Cliff Johnson   d. John Bateman

15. _____ Name the catcher who was traded for Larry Dierker.
    a. Cliff Johnson   c. Ed Herrman
    b. Jerry Grote   d. Joe Ferguson

Pitchers

True or False.

16. _____ Joe Niekro is the Astros' all-time single-season winner.
17. _____ Don Wilson pitched two no-hitters for the Astros.
18. _____ Mike Cuellar came up to the majors with Houston.
19. _____ Larry Dierker had a 20-win season with the Astros.
20. _____ Doug Drabek won the Cy Young Award with another team.
21. _____ Jim Bouton finished his career with the Astros.
22. _____ Nolan Ryan established a modern mark when he struck out the first eight batters in a game.
23. _____ Shane Reynolds walked an average of only 1.5 batters per game in 1994.
24. _____ Bo Belinsky pitched a no-hitter for Houston.
25. _____ Mike Scott's 306 strikeouts in 1986 is the all-time high for the Astros.

LOS ANGELES DODGERS

Infielders

Matching.

1. _____ Steve Garvey
2. _____ Charlie Neal
3. _____ Maury Wills
4. _____ Ron Cey
5. _____ Gil Hodges
6. _____ Davey Lopes

a. He drove home 100 or more runs for seven consecutive years.
b. He stole 11 bases in the World Series.
c. He hit four home runs in a Championship Series.
d. He hit .370 in the 1959 World Series.
e. He hit more than 300 home runs.
f. He won the stolen base title six consecutive years.

Outfielders

Multiple Choice.

7. _____ Who was called "The Reading Rifle"?
   a. Manny Mota
   b. Carl Furillo
   c. Dick Allen
   d. Rick Monday
8. _____ Who was the Dodger who hit two pinch-hit home runs in the 1959 World Series?
   a. Chuck Essegian
   b. Ron Fairly
   c. Jimmy Wynn
   d. Gino Cimoli
9. _____ Name the Dodger who hit 407 lifetime home runs.
   a. Duke Snider
   b. Wally Moon
   c. Frank Howard
   d. Tommy Davis
10. _____ Who hit more than 30 home runs three times?
    a. Mike Marshall
    b. Dusty Baker
    c. Pedro Guerrero
    d. Ken Landreaux
11. _____ A seven-year member of the Dodgers, he hit

better than 40 home runs three straight years for another club.

a. Frank Howard   c. Tommy Davis
b. Jimmy Wynn   d. Dick Allen

12. _____ Winner of back-to-back batting titles, he drove home a club-high 153 runs in one season.

a. Tommy Davis   c. Frank Howard
b. Duke Snider   d. Jimmy Wynn

Catchers

True or False.

13. _____ Johnny Roseboro spent his entire career with the Dodgers.

14. _____ Mike Piazza hit .318 and .319 his first two years in the majors.

15. _____ Jeff Torborg hit higher than .250 in his career.

Pitchers

Fill in the blanks.

16. _____ From 1959–65 he struck out more than 200 batters six of seven times.

17. _____ Who tied Carl Hubbell's record in the All-Star Game when he struck out five consecutive American League batters?

18. _____ Who threw the 715th home run pitch to Hank Aaron?

19. _____ Who chalked up an 11–0 record at Dodger Stadium one year?

20 _____ Who posted a record 21 consecutive seasons of more than 100 strikeouts?

21. _____ Who did the Dodgers get from the White Sox for Dick Allen?

22. _____ Name the 148-game winner who won his last four World Series decisions, including a seventh-game clincher.

23. _____ Who was the 16–3 relief pitcher who led the National League in winning percentage (.842) and games (69) in 1963 while he saved 21 contests?

24. _____ Who was the Dodger reliever who was nicknamed "The Vulture"?

25. _____ Who was the Dodger lefty, a two-time 20-game winner, who ended his career with 196 wins and 195 losses?

SAN DIEGO PADRES

Infielders

True or False.

1. _____ Nate Colbert hit more home runs in one season than any other Padre.
2. _____ Alan Wiggins stole a club-high 70 bases.
3. _____ Bip Roberts has hit .300 as many as four times in his major league career.
4. _____ Graig Nettles, in back-to-back seasons in which he played 150 or more games, failed to hit a triple.
5. _____ Steve Garvey hit more than 300 career homers.
6. _____ Gary Sheffield won a batting title with the Padres.

Outfielders

Fill in the blanks.

7. _____ Who led the league in hits in both 1984 and 1986?
8. _____ Who was selected by the Atlanta Hawks in the NBA draft, the Utah Stars in the ABA draft, and the Minnesota Vikings in the NFL draft?
9. _____ Nicknamed "Downtown," he twice hit 20 or more home runs in a season for the Padres. What's his real name?
10. _____ Who was the long-ball hitter who tied a record by playing on four different teams in the same year?
11. _____ He drove home 42 runs in 49 games in 1994.
12. _____ Who was the 1975–76 outfielder who played for the Cardinals in the 1967–68 World Series and the Reds in the 1970 and 1972 fall classics?

Catchers

Matching.

13. _____ Gene Tenace	a.	He was part of a package deal for George Hendrick.
14. _____ Fred Kendall	b.	This retired player is the son of a former major leaguer.
15. _____ Terry Kennedy	c.	He averaged 17 home runs a year for the Padres in four seasons.

Pitchers

Multiple Choice.

16. _____ He won the Cy Young Award.
    a. Randy Jones   c. Rick Wise
    b. Ed Whitson   d. John Montefusco

17. _____ He won Cy Young awards in both leagues.
    a. Rollie Fingers   c. Randy Jones
    b. LaMarr Hoyt   d. Gaylord Perry

18. _____ Identify the Padre pitcher who struck out a club-record 231 batters in one season.
    a. Butch Metzger   c. Clay Kirby
    b. Johnny Podres   d. Steven Arlen

19. _____ Who was the winner over the Yankees in the 1976 World Series who was 13–30 in his short stay with the Padres?
    a. Butch Metzger   c. Fred Norman
    b. Dave Roberts   d. Clay Kirby

20. _____ Who was the pitcher whose 12 consecutive victories at the start of his career are a record?
    a. Butch Metzger   c. Rich Folkers
    b. Pat Dobson   d. Johnny Podres

21. _____ Who is the pitcher who was suspended in 1986 for criticizing the owner's product?
    a. Ed Whitson   c. Goose Gossage
    b. Eric Show   d. Dave Dravecky

22. _____ Who was the winner of 148 career games and four World Series starts who finished his career by posting a 5–6 record with the Padres?
a. Don Larsen   c. Johnny Podres
b. Mudcat Grant   d. Jim Bouton

23. _____ Who was the Cy Young Award winner in the American League who was released by the Padres before the 1987 season?
a. Joe Niekro   c. LaMarr Hoyt
b. Goose Gossage   d. Rollie Fingers

24. _____ Who led the league in saves in back-to-back years?
a. Bob Shirley   c. Rollie Fingers
b. Tim Lollar   d. Goose Gossage

25. _____ Who was the two-game winner for the Brewers in the 1982 World Series who pitched his first three years with the Padres?
a. Rollie Fingers   c. Mike Caldwell
b. Tim Lollar   d. Joe Niekro

SAN FRANCISCO GIANTS

Infielders

Multiple Choice.

1. _____ Who was the slugger who tied Ted Williams for tenth place on the all-time home run list?
   a. Orlando Cepeda   c. Willie Montanez
   b. Willie McCovey   d. Dave Kingman

2. _____ Which one of the following players hit a grand slam in World Series play?
   a. Chuck Hiller   c. Ron Hunt
   b. Don Blasingame   d. Hal Lanier

3. _____ Which one of the following players was the first San Francisco Giant shortstop?
   a. Chris Speier   c. Jose Pagan
   b. Tito Fuentes   d. Daryl Spencer

4. _____ Which one of the following players hit as many as 43 home runs in a season?
   a. Jim Davenport   c. Matt Williams
   b. Bill Madlock   d. Darrell Evans

5. _____ Which one of the following hit .300 for three different teams?
   a. Willie McCovey   c. Darrell Evans
   b. Orlando Cepeda   d. Jose Pagan

6. _____ In three consecutive years he hit .300 in three different cities.
   a. Willie Montanez   c. Ron Hunt
   b. Jim Ray Hart   d. Tito Fuentes

Outfielders

True or False.

7. _____ Willie Kirkland hit the first home run at Candlestick Park.

8. _____ Dave Kingman struck out more times (189) in one season than any other player in the history of the game.

9. _____ Willie Mays hit more home runs in one season in New York than he did in San Francisco.

10. _____ Barry Bonds has a .300 average in 68 at-bats in League Championship play.

11. _____ Harvey Kuenn won a batting title with the Giants.

12. _____ All three Alou brothers—Matty, Felipe, and Jesus—once played in the same outfield at the same time.

Catchers

Fill in the blanks.

13. _____ Who was the Giant catcher who hit 27 home runs one year?

14. _____ Name the former Red backstop who hit 17 and 21 home runs in his two full seasons with the Giants?

15. _____ Who is the recent-day catcher who topped League receivers with a .995 fielding percentage?

Pitchers

Matching.

16. _____ John Montefusco
17. _____ Gaylord Perry
18. _____ Juan Marichal
19. _____ Stu Miller
20. _____ Jack Sanford
21. _____ Billy Loes
22. _____ Don Larsen
23. _____ Ruben Gomez
24. _____ Billy O'Dell
25. _____ Billy Pierce

a. A former Yankee, he beat the Bombers in the 1962 World Series.

b. He won a club-record 16 consecutive games in 1962.

c. He pitched the last Giant no-hitter.

d. Joe Adcock once "ran him off" the mound.

e. He pitched two of his four 20-game-win seasons with the Giants.

f. He was a uniformed witness on the days Gil Hodges, Joe Adcock, Rocky Colavito, and Willie Mays hit four home runs in a game.

g. He won 20 or more games six times in a seven-year period.

h. In 1961 he led the league's relief pitchers in wins (14), winning percentage (.737), and saves (17).

i. A 19-game winner for the pennant-winning 1962 club, he led the NL's relief pitchers in wins in 1964 and 1965.

j. Two times a 20-game winner in the American League, he helped the Giants win the 1963 pennant by posting a 16-6 record.

BALTIMORE ORIOLES

Infielders

Fill in the blanks.

1. _____ From 1960–62 this slugging first baseman hit 100 home runs, including a career-high 46 in
1961.

2. _____ Name the second baseman who hit
.280 or better for three consecutive pennant winners.

3. _____ Who was the infielder who set a club
record when he stole 57 bases in 1964?

4. _____ In 1969 he hit .500 in the league
Championship Series, and in 1970 he hit .583; in 1970
he hit .429 in the World Series, and in 1971 he hit
.318.

5. _____ Known for his consistency, he has
won both the Rookie of the Year Award and the
MVP crown.

6. _____ Three times an RBI champ, this
long-ball-hitting right-handed hitter (247 career homers)
was the first starting third baseman with the Orioles.

Outfielders

Matching.

7. _____ Bob Nieman
8. _____ Dick Williams
9. _____ Paul Blair
10. _____ Frank Robinson
11. _____ Gene Woodling
12. _____ Brady Anderson

a. A .284 lifetime hitter, "Young Reliable" played on five world championship teams.

b. In 1958 he hit .325, which remained the Orioles' all-time batting high until 1977.

c. He hit 49 home runs in one season, the club's all-time high.

d. A journeyman outfielder with a .260 lifetime average, he later managed three different teams to four pennants and two world titles.

e. In 1994 he swiped 31 bases in 32 tries for a .969 success rate, the best percentage in history for a man with at least 25 attempts.

f. Considered the best defensive outfielder in the American League during his time, he turned slugger in the 1970 World Series, ripping the Red pitching staff for a .474 average.

Catchers

Multiple Choice.

13. _____ Which one of the following Oriole receivers had a couple of on-field run-ins with Billy Martin?
    a. Hal Smith   c. John Orsino
    b. Clint Courtney   d. Dick Brown

14. _____ A .255 lifetime hitter, he later emerged as one of the premiere batting instructors in the game.
    a. Charlie Lau   c. Hal Smith
    b. Gus Triandos   d. Dick Brown

15. _____ Who was the power-hitting backstop (167 home runs) whose career began to decline when Hoyt Wilhelm brought his knuckleball to Baltimore?
    a. John Orsino   c. Gus Triandos
    b. Dick Brown   d. Hal Smith

Pitchers

True or False.

16. _____ Both Mike Cuellar and Dave McNally won 24 games, the club high, in one season.

17. _____ Jim Palmer holds the strikeout mark with 202 in a season.

18. _____ Wally Bunker was the youngest pitcher to hurl a shutout in World Series play.

19. _____ Chuck Estrada was traded to Cincinnati in the controversial deal for Frank Robinson.

20. _____ Stu Miller threw the pitch that Mickey Mantle hit for his 500th home run.

21. _____ Don Larsen won 21 games in his only season with the Orioles.

22. _____ Mike Flanagan won a Cy Young Award.

23. _____ Jim Palmer, Wally Bunker, and Dave McNally tossed shutouts against the Dodgers in the 1966 World Series.

24. _____ Hoyt Wilhelm, in a rare start, pitched a no-hitter against the Yankees in 1958.

25. _____ Ben McDonald didn't miss a single start from 1992 to 1994.

BOSTON RED SOX

Infielders

Matching.

1. _____ Billy Goodman
2. _____ Pete Runnels
3. _____ Vern Stephens
4. _____ Rico Petrocelli
5. _____ Jimmy Collins
6. _____ Wade Boggs

a. He won five batting titles.
b. A .294 lifetime hitter, he managed Boston to its first pennant and series victory.
c. A batting champ, he ended his career with a *.300* lifetime average.
d. From 1969–71 he averaged almost 33 home runs per season.
e. He won batting titles two years apart.
f. A two-time RBI champ with Boston, he won another crown before coming to the Sox.

Outfielders

Multiple Choice.

7. _____ Though this .306 lifetime hitter played only seven years in the big time, he set a major league record when he rocked 67 doubles in one season.
   a. Duffy Lewis
   b. Ben Chapman
   c. Harry Hooper
   d. Earl Webb
8. _____ He was the only player ever to pinch-hit for Ted Williams.
   a. Gene Stephens
   b. Carroll Hardy
   c. Sam Mele
   d. Al Zarilla
9. _____ He holds the club's stolen base record for one season.
   a. Dom DiMaggio
   b. Tris Speaker
   c. Tommy Harper
   d. Reggie Smith

10. _____ In the same year that he led the league in stolen bases (22), he rapped into 32 double plays, a major
league record at that time.
   a. Jackie Jensen   c. Fred Lynn
   b. Clyde Vollmer   d. Ken Harrelson
11. _____ Hollywood made a movie, *Fear Strikes Out,*
about a segment of his life.
   a. Jimmie Foxx   c. Ted Williams
   b. Hoot Evers   d. Jimmy Piersall
12. _____ He won three batting titles with a combined
mark of .315 for those years.
   a. Dale Alexander   c. Elmer Flick
   b. Carl Yastrzemski   d. Ted Williams

Catchers

True or False.
13. _____ Bill Carrigan, who hit .257 during a ten-year
career with the Red Sox, later managed Boston to back-
to-back world titles.
14. _____ Rick Ferrell handled the pitching serves of his
brother, Wes, with the Red Sox.
15. _____ Birdie Tebbetts was the starting catcher on the
great Red Sox teams of the late 1940s.

Pitchers

Fill in the blanks.
16. _____ Which Red Sox pitcher threw the
first perfect game of the modern era?
17. _____ Who won two games, including a
one-hitter, in the 1967 World Series?
18. _____ Son of a Hall of Famer, he pitched
for Boston from 1956–59. Who was he?
19. _____ Name the relief pitcher who led the
American League bull pen specialists in wins in each of
his first three years in the majors (1962–64) and who
struck out more batters than he pitched innings in each
of those seasons.

20. _____ Who was the pitcher who lost the playoff game, between the Indians and the Red Sox, that decided the 1948 pennant?

21. _____ Who set the league record for shut-outs by southpaws (9) in one season?

22. _____ Name the pitcher who won his 300th—and final—game with the Red Sox.

23. _____ A two-time 20-game loser with the Red Sox, he went on to win seven World Series games with another American League team. Who was he?

24. _____ Who was the pitcher who, including the regular season and series, won 37 games and lost six in 1912?

25. _____ Who was the pitcher who came on in relief, with a runner who had walked on first base with no one out in the first inning, and proceeded to pitch a perfect game?

CLEVELAND INDIANS

Infielders

Fill in the blanks.

1. _____ Who was the first baseman who drove home 162 runs, a club record, in one season?
2. _____ Who was the second baseman who made an unassisted triple play in the 1920 World Series?
3. _____ When Lou Boudreau was traded to the Red Sox, who took his place at shortstop?
4. _____ Name the third baseman who made two great defensive plays against Joe DiMaggio on the night "The Yankee Clipper's" 56-game batting streak was broken.
5. _____ Name the infielder who is one of the few men at his position to bat .300, hit 20 home runs, and drive home 100 runs in back-to-back seasons.
6. _____ Who was the batter who hit the ball that Willie Mays ran down in the 1954 World Series?

Outfielders

Matching.

7. _____ Elmer Flick
8. _____ Joe Jackson
9. _____ Tris Speaker
10. _____ Albert Belle
11. _____ Jeff Heath
12. _____ Larry Doby

a. He was the first black player to compete in the American League.

b. He won a batting title with a .306 average.

c. He never won a batting title, even though he hit .408 in one season and .356 lifetime.

d. He hit at least one home run in every major league park that was in use during his career.

e. He stopped Ty Cobb's string of nine consecutive batting titles when he led the league with a .386 average in 1916.

f. Recently he batted 87 points better than his previous career high mark.

Catchers

Multiple Choice.

13. _____ Who caught Bob Feller when "Rapid Robert" no-hit the Yankees, 1–0, in 1946, and provided the only run in the game with a home run?
   a. Buddy Rosar   c. Rollie Hemsley
   b. Frank Hayes   d. Jim Hegan

14. _____ Name the catcher who handled six different 20-game winners during his career with the Tribe.
   a. Steve O'Neill   c. Jim Hegan
   b. Luke Sewell   d. Johnny Romano

15. _____ Which one of the following catchers won the Rookie of Year Award?
   a. Buddy Rosar   c. Jim Hegan
   b. Ray Fosse   d. Sandy Alomar

Pitchers

True or False.

16. _____ Jim Bagby won more games in one season than any other Indian pitcher.

17. _____ Herb Score never won 20 games in a season.

18. _____ Johnny Allen won 15 of 16 decisions in 1937 to set an American League mark (.938) for winning percentage in one season.

19. _____ The two pitchers who joined forces to halt Joe DiMaggio's 56-game hitting streak were Jim Bagby and Al Smith.

20. _____ Bob Feller, Bob Lemon, Early Wynn, and Mike Garcia all won 20 or more games in the same season.

21. _____ Gene Bearden, who pitched Cleveland to a pennant and a World Series crown in 1948 when he posted a record of 20–7, never before or after registered a winning record.

22. _____ Bob Feller pitched more no-hitters than any other right-handed pitcher.

23. _____ Both Jim and Gaylord Perry turned in 20-win seasons with the Tribe.

24. _____ Wes Ferrell had more consecutive 20-win seasons than did Bob Feller, Bob Lemon, or Early Wynn.

25. _____ Early Wynn finished his career with the Indians.

DETROIT TIGERS

Infielders

Multiple Choice.

1. _____ One year he drove home 183 runs, the club high; the following season, he clubbed 58 home runs, the team high.
   a. Norm Cash
   b. Hank Greenberg
   c. Walt Dropo
   d. George Burns

2. _____ He was the last Tiger to win a batting title.
   a. George Kell
   b. Harvey Kuenn
   c. Al Kaline
   d. Norm Cash

3. _____ Which one of the following players has been one of only two players who competed in every game of a 154-game schedule without hitting into a double play?
   a. Dick McAuliffe
   b. Lu Blue
   c. Tom Tresh
   d. George Kell

4. _____ Who in 1949 became the first American League third baseman to win the batting title?
   a. Marv Owen
   b. Ray Boone
   C. Eddie Yost
   d. George Kell

5. _____ Name the league's batting leader (1959) who was traded after the season for the league's home run hitter.
   a. Charlie Gehringer
   b. Harvey Kuenn
   c. Al Kaline
   d. Norm Cash

6. _____ Who won RBI titles in his first three full seasons?
   a. Hank Greenberg
   b. Norm Cash
   c. Cecil Fielder
   d. Al Kaline

Outfielders

True or False.

7. _____ Sam Crawford was the only modern-day player to lead the National League and the American League in both triples and home runs.

8. _____ Ty Cobb and Harry Heilmann have been the only teammates to hit .400.

9. _____ Al Kaline compiled a .300 lifetime average.

10. _____ In the seventh inning of the seventh game of the 1968 World Series, Rocky Colavito got the key triple that broke up a pitching duel between Mickey Lolich and Bob Gibson and paced the Bengals to a 4–1 victory.

11. _____ Hoot Evers, Johnny Groth, and Vic Wertz, outfielders for the Tigers, all hit .300 or better in the same season.

12. _____ Ty Cobb was the youngest player to win a major league batting title.

Catchers

Fill in the blanks.

13. _____ Who set a record when he hit 18 home runs in one month?

14. _____ Who was the playing manager who compiled a lifetime batting average of .320?

15. _____ Who was the starting receiver for the Tigers' 1968 world champions?

Matching.

16. _____ Mark Fidrych
17. _____ Denny McLain
18. _____ Mickey Lolich
19. _____ Jim Bunning
20. _____ Frank Lary
21. _____ Bob Cain
22. _____ Virgil Trucks
23. _____ Hal Newhouser
24. _____ Schoolboy Rowe
25. _____ George Mullin

a. He was the pitcher who tried to keep the ball low to Bill Veeck's midget, Eddie Gaedel.

b. He tied an American League record by winning 16 consecutive decisions.

c. He was the only modern-day pitcher to lose 20 games with a pennant winner.

d. He was the only Tiger pitcher to win the Rookie of the Year Award.

e. He was known as "The Yankee Killer."

f. He won Cy Young awards in back-to-back seasons.

g. He was the only Tiger pitcher to strike out 300 or more batters in a season.

h. Two of the five games he won in one season were no-hitters.

i. He won more than 100 games in each league, and he struck out more than 1,000 batters in each loop.

j. He led the league in wins three straight years.

MILWAUKEE BREWERS

Infielders

True or False.

1. _____ George Scott led the league in homers.
2. _____ Paul Molitor hit a club-high .353 one year.
3. _____ Robin Yount ended his career with more than 3,000 hits.
4. _____ Kevin Seitzer never got 200 hits in a season.
5. _____ Cecil Cooper drove home a club-high 126 runs one year.
6. _____ Don Money never hit 20 home runs in a season for the Brewers.

Outfielders

Fill in the blanks.

7. _____ Who was the Hall of Famer who played the last two years of his 23-year record-studded career with the Brewers?
8. _____ Who is the player who hit 33 home runs in his rookie season?
9. _____ Who hit a season-high 45 homers in 1979?
10. _____ Who was the infielder-outfielder, known more for his base-stealing exploits than his power, who blasted 31 home runs in 1970, the first year of the franchise?
11. _____ Who tied Reggie Jackson for the home run lead in 1980?
12. _____ Who hit .300 from 1986 to 1989?

Catchers

Matching.

13. _____ Darrell Porter
14. _____ Ellie Rodriguez
15. _____ Charlie Moore

a. His best batting average with Milwaukee was .285.
b. His best mark with the Brewers was .254.
c. His best season with Milwaukee was .301.

Pitchers

Multiple Choice.

16. _____ Who won a club-high 22 games in 1978?
   a. Jim Slaton   c. Mike Caldwell
   b. Ken Sanders   d. Jim Lonborg
17. _____ Who leads the Brewer moundsmen with 240 strikeouts in a season?
   a. Jim Slaton   c. Bill Travers
   b. Ken Sanders   d. Ted Higuera
18. _____ Who was the former bonus baby who lost 18 games in 1970?
   a. Lew Krausse   c. Skip Lockwood
   b. Gene Brabender   d. John O'Donoghue
19. _____ Who was the Milwaukee pitcher who was killed in an Arizona dune buggy crash on January 1, 1976?
   a. Danny Frisella   c. Dan Story
   b. Milt Tracy   d. Jim Clancy
20. _____ Name the former Cy Young Award winner who was 14–12 in his only season with the Brewers?
   a. Chris Short   c. Bill Parson
   b. Jim Lonborg   d. Al Downing
21. _____ Whose 6–0 start in 1994 was one game off the club record set by Eddie Rodriguez?
   a. Bill Wegman   c. Mike Fetters
   b. Cal Eldred   d. Ricky Bones
22. _____ Who won the MVP Award?
   a. Mike Caldwell   c. Pete Vuckovich
   b. Rollie Fingers   d. Pete Ladd

23. _____ Who won the Cy Young Award?
   a. Don Sutton   c. Pete Vuckovich
   b. Mike Caldwell   d. Moose Haas
24. _____ Who in 1994 became the first Brewer starting pitcher since Teddy Higuera in 1986 to make the All-Star team?
   a. Cal Eldred   c. Mike Fetters
   b. Bill Wegman   d. Ricky Bones
25. _____ Who was the former All-Star Game pitcher who chalked up a career-high 16 saves in 1986?
   a. Mark Clear   c. Dan Plesac
   b. Juan Nieves   d. Bill Wegman

NEW YORK YANKEES

Infielders

Fill in the blanks.

1. _____ Who was the first baseman who replaced Lou Gehrig in the lineup after "The Iron Horse"
   ended his string of 2,130 consecutive games?

2. _____ Who was the second baseman whose
   twelfth hit of the 1953 World Series scored Hank Bauer
   with the winning run in the ninth inning of the sixth
   and decisive game?

3. _____ Name the shortstop who was given
   his release on Old Timers' Day in 1956.

4. _____ Who was the Yankee third baseman
   who won four home run titles with another team?

5. _____ Who won his ninth Gold Glove
   Award in 1994?

6. _____ Who was the first baseman who hit
   .293 and banged eight home runs in eight series?

Outfielders

Matching.
7. _____ Joe DiMaggio
8. _____ Hank Bauer
9. _____ Roger Maris
10. _____ Elston Howard
11. _____ Tommy Henrich
12. _____ Babe Ruth

a. He came to the Yankees in a trade with Kansas City.
b. Primarily a catcher, he also played the outfield and first base in the series.
c. He won two home run titles.
d. He was called "Old Reliable."
e. He got a second chance after a quick pitch, and hit a home run.
f. He drove home all four of his team's runs in a series win.

Catchers

Multiple Choice.
13. _____ One year he hit .362, the all-time high for catchers.
   a. Bill Dickey
   b. Yogi Berra
   c. Thurman Munson
   d. Elston Howard
14. _____ He hit two two-run home runs in the seventh game of a World Series win.
   a. Wally Schang
   b. Bill Dickey
   c. Yogi Berra
   d. Aaron Robinson
15. _____ He hit .373 in three World Series.
   a. Ralph Houk
   b. Yogi Berra
   c. Bill Dickey
   d. Thurman Munson

Pitchers

True or False.

16. _____ Bill Bevens, after he lost both a no-hitter and the game on the last pitch of a 1947 series game, never again won an outing in the major leagues.

17. _____ Don Larsen struck out Duke Snider for the last out of his perfect game in the 1956 World Series.

18. _____ Johnny Sain saved the last game in both the 1951 and the 1952 World Series.

19. _____ Whitey Ford both won and lost more games than any other pitcher in series competition.

20. _____ Red Ruffing hit more home runs than any other major league pitcher.

21. _____ Herb Pennock and Lefty Gomez won a combined total of 11 games without dropping a decision in series play.

22. _____ Allie Reynolds pitched more no-hitters than any other Yankee hurler.

23. _____ Jimmy Key won the Cy Young Award in 1994.

24. _____ Joe Page, Johnny Murphy, Luis Arroyo, and Lindy McDaniel were relief pitchers, in the presented order, for the Yankees.

25. _____ Spud Chandler and Sparky Lyle both won MVP awards.

TORONTO BLUE JAYS

Infielders

Matching.

1. _____ John Olerud
2. _____ Robby Alomar
3. _____ Tony Fernandez
4. _____ Paul Molitor
5. _____ Alfredo Griffin
6. _____ Danny Ainge

a. He played professional baseball and basketball.
b. He hit a club-high .363 one year.
c. He won his fourth Gold Glove in 1994.
d. He set a club record with 213 hits in 1986.
e. He was co-winner of the Rookie of the Year Award in 1979.
f. He hit safely in 39 consecutive games in 1987.

Outfielders

Multiple Choice.

7. _____ Who was the star acquisition in 1993 who bombed in the ALCS (.120) and World Series (.227)?
   a. Joe Carter
   b. Paul Molitor
   c. Rickey Henderson
   d. Candy Maldonado

8. _____ Who hit a club-high 47 home runs in one year?
   a. John Mayberry
   b. Ron Fairly
   c. Rico Carty
   d. George Bell

9. _____ Who drove home a club-record 134 runs one year?
   a. Rico Carty
   b. George Bell
   c. Jesse Barfield
   d. John Mayberry

10. _____ Who, in addition to playing great defense, batted .292, and drove home seven runs in the 1993 World Series?
    a. Rickey Henderson   c. Joe Carter
    b. Devon White   d. Paul Molitor
11. _____ Who stole a club-record 64 bases in 1984?
    a. Dave Collins   c. Barry Bonnell
    b. Al Woods   d. Tommy Hutton
12. _____ Who at age 39—in his only season with Toronto—batted .279, hit 19 home runs, and drove home 64 runs?
    a. Rico Carty   c. Ron Fairly
    b. Tommy Hutton   d. Bob Bailor

Catchers

True or False.
13. _____ Alan Ashby was the first full-time catcher of the Blue Jays.
14. _____ Rick Cerone, among others, was traded by the Blue Jays to the Yankees for Chris Chambliss, among others, who never played a game for Toronto.
15. _____ Ernie Whitt once hit 20 home runs in a season.

Pitchers

Fill in the blanks.
16. _____ Whose lifetime percentage dipped from .784 to .703 in 1994?
17. _____ Who is the pitcher who struck out a club-high 198 batters in one season?
18. _____ Who became the first starting left-handed pitcher to win for the Blue Jays since Paul Mirabella in 1980?
19. _____ Who, with a glittering 1.72 ERA, fell five innings short of qualifying for the American League title one year?
20. _____ Who led Toronto in saves in his first three seasons with the club.

270

21. _____ Who had 11 wins at the All-Star Game break in both 1993 and 1994?

22. _____ Who was the 1982 Cy Young Award winner who was 7–7 in his only season with the Blue Jays?

23. _____ Who had a .500 record (30–30) in his last three years in Toronto?

24. _____ Who was the one-time no-hit pitcher with the Dodgers who finished up with the Blue Jays in 1977, their maiden season?

25. _____ Who was the Blue Jays' "big" winner in their initial season?

CALIFORNIA ANGELS

Infielders

Multiple Choice.

1. _____ He batted safely in a club-record 25 consecutive games in 1982.
   - a. Rod Carew
   - b. Steve Bilko
   - c. Ted Kluszewski
   - d. Vic Power

2. _____ He played in 162 games in both 1970 and 1971.
   - a. Doug DeCinces
   - b. Jerry Adair
   - c. Bobby Knoop
   - d. Sandy Alomar

3. _____ He had a club-high 26 sacrifice hits in 1982.
   - a. Tim Foli
   - b. Jim Fregosi
   - c. Joe Koppe
   - d. Leo Cardenas

4. _____ He batted .301 and hit 30 home runs in 1982.
   - a. Rod Carew
   - b. Bobby Grich
   - c. Tim Foli
   - d. Doug DeCinces

5. _____ He ended up in a four-way tie for the home run lead in 1981.
   - a. Rod Carew
   - b. Bobby Grich
   - c. Rick Burleson
   - d. Butch Hobson

6. _____ He drove home 100 runs in his first two years in the majors.
   - a. Bobby Grich
   - b. Doug DeCinces
   - c. Wally Joyner
   - d. Jim Fregosi

Outfielders

True or False.

7. _____ Leon Wagner hit more home runs (37) in one season than any other Angel.

8. _____ Bobby Bonds stole more bases in one season than any other Angel.

9. _____ Alex Johnson hit for the highest Angel average in one season.

10. _____ Joe Rudi, Don Baylor, and Bobby Bonds were all free agents when the Angels signed them.

11. _____ Frank Robinson hit 30 home runs in one season for the Angels.

12. _____ Chili Davis won the Triple Crown for the 1994 Angels.

Catchers

Fill in the blanks.

13. _____ Name the one-time Angel catcher who is the son of a former big leaguer.

14. _____ Name the Angel receiver who was California's starting catcher for the most seasons.

15. _____ Name the Angel backstop who later managed Cleveland to three sixth-place finishes.

Matching.

16. _____ Dean Chance
17. _____ Bo Belinsky
18. _____ Don Sutton
19. _____ Andy Messersmith
20. _____ Clyde Wright
21. _____ Nolan Ryan
22. _____ Frank Tanana
23. _____ Bill Singer
24. _____ Rudy May
25. _____ Lee Smith

a. He won 22 in 1970 for the Angels; he lost 20 in 1974 for the Twins.

b. He pitched four no-hitters for the Angels.

c. He was the first Angel pitcher to win 20 games in a season.

d. He was the first Angel pitcher to throw a no-hitter.

e. After spending the majority of his first 11 years with the Angels, he started for the Yankees in the historic opening of the new stadium in 1976.

f. Before excelling for the Dodgers, he spent four years with the Angels, winning 20 games in 1971.

g. He won 20 games for the Dodgers in 1969 before he equaled that total for the Angels in 1973.

h. He started his 700th game, the second all-time high, for the Angels in 1986.

i. Twice this lefty flame-thrower struck out more than 250 batters in a season.

j. He led the majors in saves in 1994.

CHICAGO WHITE SOX

Infielders

Matching.

1. _____ Frank Thomas
2. _____ Eddie Collins
3. _____ Luke Appling
4. _____ Bill Melton
5. _____ Nelson Fox
6. _____ Ozzie Guillen

a. He played the most consecutive major league games (98) without striking out.
b. He played on four world championship teams.
c. He won the Rookie of the Year Award.
d. He was a unanimous MVP selection.
e. He was the first Pale Hose player to win a home run title.
f. One year he hit only six home runs but drove home 128 runs.

Outfielders

Multiple Choice.

7. _____ He never hit less than .300 in his entire career.
   a. Rip Radcliff   c. Bibbs Fall
   b. Wally Moses   d. Joe Jackson

8. _____ He set the then-American League record for strikeouts (175) in one season.
   a. Gus Zernial   c. Dave Nicholson
   b. Smead Jolley   d. Larry Doby

9. _____ Once part of a famous outfield, he finished his career with the White Sox, batting .302 over his last five seasons.
   a. Happy Felsch   c. Mule Haas
   b. Harry Hooper   d. Minnie Minoso

10. _____ Which one of the following outfield trios had ballhawks who each hit .300 or better in the same season?
   a. Dixie Walker, Mike Kreevich, and Rip Radcliff
   b. Mule Haas, Al Simmons, and Rip Radcliff
   c. Smead Jolley, Red Barnes, and Carl Reynolds
   d. Nemo Leibold, Happy Felsch, and Joe Jackson

11. _____ Which one of the following White Sox outfielders copped the batting crown with another team?
   a. Bob Fothergill   c. Wally Moses
   b. Taft Wright   d. Ralph Garr

12. _____ Which one of the following players was hit by more pitches than any other American League player before Don Baylor?
   a. Al Simmons   c. Johnny Mostil
   b. Minnie Minoso   d. Jim Landis

Catchers

True or False.

13. _____ Ray Schalk
14. _____ Moe Berg
15. _____ Mike Tresh

a. He became a secret agent after his baseball career.
b. He called the signals for four pitchers who won 20 or more games in the same season.
c. He was the father of a son who hit four World Series home runs.

Pitchers

Fill in the blanks.

16. _____ Who was the White Sox pitcher who threw a perfect game?

17. _____ Who holds the club record for wins (40) and strikeouts (269)?

18. _____ Name the pitcher who won 260 games in 21 years, all with the White Sox.

19. _____ Can you recall the promising young hurler who lost a leg in a 1938 hunting accident?

20. _____ A 21-game winner for the 1920 White Sox, he was a holdout for the entire 1922 season and a suspended player for the following three years. Who was he?

21. _____ Who was the Black Sox pitcher who lost all three of his decisions in the tainted 1919 World Series?

22. _____ Who is the recent-day pitcher who both won and lost 20 games in the same season?

23. _____ Who was the 200-game winner who used to hook up with Whitey Ford in some classic pitching duels in the 1950s?

24. _____ Who won three games in a World Series?

25. _____ Who was the "steady" White Sox pitcher who later played on five consecutive world championship teams with the Yankees?

KANSAS CITY ROYALS

Infielders

Multiple Choice.

1. _____ Name the first baseman who holds the season club high in home runs.
   - a. Bob Oliver
   - b. John Mayberry
   - c. Steve Balboni
   - d. Tommy Davis

2. _____ Who has been the only second baseman in American League history to win eight Gold Gloves?
   - a. Frank White
   - b. Cookie Rojas
   - c. Jackie Hernandez
   - d. Jerry Adair

3. _____ In nine seasons at shortstop for the Royals, he averaged 37 steals.
   - a. Jackie Hernandez
   - b. Freddie Patek
   - c. Bobby Knoop
   - d. U. L. Washington

4. _____ Who became the sixth player to collect 20 or more doubles, triples, and home runs in the same season?
   - a. Frank White
   - b. John Mayberry
   - c. Willie Aikens
   - d. George Brett

5. _____ Who with another team drove home 100 runs in each of his first two season?
   - a. Greg Gagne
   - b. Brian McRae
   - c. Jose Lind
   - d. Wally Joyner

6. _____ Who played on two World Series winners with another team?
   - a. Greg Gagne
   - b. Jose Lind
   - c. Wally Joyner
   - d. Brian McRae

Outfielders

True or False.

7. _____ Lou Piniella won the Rookie of the Year Award.

8. _____ Amos Otis drove home more runs (133) in one season than any other Royal player.

9. _____ Willie Wilson hits a high percentage of inside-the-park home runs.

10. _____ Hal McRae won a batting title.

11. _____ Amos Otis hit three home runs in a World Series.

12. _____ Brian McRae played the outfield for his father Hal.

Catchers

Fill in the blanks.

13. _____ Who was the recent-day catcher who led the American League with a .995 fielding percentage?

14. _____ Who had a career-high .291 batting average, 20 home runs, and 112 RBIs in 1979?

15. _____ Who stole a record 36 bases for catchers in 1982?

Pitchers

Matching.

16. _____ Steve Busby
17. _____ Mark Littell
18. _____ Larry Gura
19. _____ Dennis Leonard
20. _____ Paul Splittorff
21. _____ Bret Saberhagen
22. _____ David Cone
23. _____ Dan Quisenberry
24. _____ Jim Colborn
25. _____ Tom Gordon

a. He averaged 8.3 strike-outs per nine innings for his first seven years in the majors.

b. Pitched 2 no-hitters.

c. He struck out a club-high 244 batters in one year.

d. He was the youngest recipient of the World Series MVP Award.

e. The Yankees traded him for Fran Healy.

f. He threw the pitch that Chris Chambliss hit for the playoff-deciding home run in 1976.

g. He won two games and lost none in the three Championship Series from 1976 to 1978.

h. He logged the highest number of saves (212) 1980–1985.

i. A 20-game winner with the Brewers, he pitched a no-hitter in his only full season with the Royals.

j. A Kansas City native, he won the Cy Young Award in his ninth season (his second with the Royals).

MINNESOTA TWINS

Infielders

Matching.
1. _____ Rod Carew
2. _____ Gary Gaetti
3. _____ Zoilo Versalles
4. _____ Harmon Killebrew
5. _____ Chuck Knoblauch
6. _____ Billy Martin

a. He won six home run titles.
b. He hit two home runs on the opening day of the season.
c. Four times he got 200 hits, including a career-high 239 in 1977.
d. From 1963–65 he led the league in triples.
e. A veteran of four world championship teams, he finished his career with the Twins, a team he later managed to a division title.
f. A scrappy second baseman, he batted .312 and stole 35 bases in 1994.

Outfielders

Multiple Choice.
7. _____ From 1956–58 he led the league in strikeouts.
   a. Jimmy Hall   c. Bob Allison
   b. Don Mincher   d. Jim Lemon
8. _____ Who is the recent-day Twin who collected 223 hits in a season?
   a. Kirby Puckett   c. Mickey Hatcher
   b. Tom Brunansky   d. Gary Ward

9. _____ He hit 20 home runs in 1976, including an historic one at Yankee Stadium.
   a. Steve Braun   c. Larry Hisle
   b. Lyman Bostock   d. Dan Ford
10. _____ He made a great sliding catch against the Dodgers in the 1965 World Series.
   a. Sandy Valdespino   c. Bob Allison
   b. Ted Uhlaender   d. Bill Tuttle
11. _____ Who was the player who hit 33 circuit clouts in 1963, the all-time high for a Twin lefty before Ken Hrbek?
   a. Jimmy Hall   c. Ted Uhlaender
   b. Lenny Green   d. Tony Oliva
12. _____ Who was the Twin who batted .300 four of five times from 1990 to 1994?
   a. Alex Cole   c. Pedro Munoz
   b. Shane Mack   d. Rich Becker

Catchers

True or False.
13. _____ Butch Wynegar made the All-Star team in his rookie year.
14. _____ Johnny Roseboro had a higher lifetime batting average than Earl Battey did.
15. _____ In their most productive long-ball seasons, Roseboro hit more home runs than Battey did.

Pitchers

Fill in the blanks.
16. _____ Who was the Twin pitcher who won more games in one season than any other Minnesota hurler?
17. _____ Name the pitcher who struck out 258 batters, the club high, in one season.
18. _____ Can you recall the pitcher whom Billy Martin "punched out" in 1969?

19. _____ Which of the Perry brothers enjoyed 20-win seasons in 1969-70 for the Twins?

20. _____ Who was the first Minnesota pitcher to register back-to-back 20-win seasons?

21. _____ Who was the pitcher who won two games in the 1965 World Series?

22. _____ Name the pitcher who was a 20-game winner with the Angels before he was a 20-game winner with the Twins.

23. _____ Who was the Twin relief pitcher who starred with the Dodgers before he led the American League in saves in 1969 (31) and 1970 (34)?

24. _____ Who was the relief pitcher who bounced from club to club before he averaged 18 saves a year for the 1965–68 Twins?

25. _____ Who rolled up a 30⅓ scoreless inning string in 1991?

OAKLAND A'S

Infielders

Fill in the blanks.

1. _____ Who played in four World Series, on four championship teams, with two different teams?

2. _____ Who hit two home runs in his first major league game?

3. _____ Who, in 1986, played in 162 games for the second straight year, batted .285, and stole 33 bases?

4. _____ Who was the Oakland infielder of the 1970s who ended his career with 242 home runs?

5. _____ Who was traded to the A's when the Red Sox had to make room for the emerging Wade Boggs?

6. _____ Who two times hit 40-plus home runs in a season?

Outfielders

Matching.

7. _____ Tony Armas
8. _____ Rick Monday
9. _____ Dave Kingman
10. _____ Bill North
11. _____ Gonzalo Marquez
12. _____ Herb Washington

a. He was the A's designated runner in the 1974 World Series.
b. He tied for a home run title.
c. Three times he pinch-hit singles in the 1972 World Series.
d. The 1976 stolen base champ, he averaged 53 thefts per season in his first four years in the majors.
e. In 1986 he hit over 30 home runs for the third straight year; the following year, he was out of baseball.
f. He was the first player to be selected in the free agent draft.

Catchers

Multiple Choice.

13. _____ Who was the only player to be traded for a manager?
   a. Dave Duncan   c. Ray Fosse
   b. Gene Tenace   d. Manny Sanguillen
14. _____ Which one of the following catchers compiled the highest single-season average with the A's?
   a. Dave Duncan   c. Phil Roof
   b. Ray Fosse   d. Frank Fernandez
15. _____ Which one of the following catchers hit the most home runs in one season?
   a. Dave Duncan   c. Phil Roof
   b. Ray Fosse   d. Frank Fernandez

Pitchers

True or False.

16. _____ Dennis Eckersley went over the 300 career save mark in 1995.

17. _____ Vida Blue was the youngest player to win the MVP Award.

18. _____ Catfish Hunter won all of his four World Series decisions with the A's.

19. _____ Jay Howell recorded as many as 29 saves in a season.

20. _____ Ken Holtzman never won 20 games for the A's.

21. _____ Holtzman matched Hunter's total of four World Series wins with Oakland.

22. _____ Vida Blue won the most games in one season for the A's.

23. _____ Blue never won a World Series game.

24. _____ Rollie Fingers was the only pitcher to hurl in all seven games of a World Series.

25. _____ Fingers recorded the most saves by any pitcher in series history.

SEATTLE MARINERS

Infielders

True or False.

1. _____ Alvin Davis's 116 RBIs as a rookie in 1984 are the most ever by a Mariner.

2. _____ Harold Reynolds stole a club-high 60 bases one year.

3. _____ Julio Cruz once successfully stole bases on 32 consecutive attempts.

4. _____ Jim Presley of the 1985–87 Mariners hit 24 or more home runs for three straight seasons.

5. _____ Tino Martinez is a product of the same high school that produced Fred McGriff.

6. _____ Edgar Martinez has won one batting title.

Outfielders

Fill in the blanks.

7. _____ Who was the 1981 outfielder who batted .326. He batted .282 over an 18-year career in the majors.

8. _____ Who hit a club-high 45 home runs in 1993?

9. _____ Who, in addition to Ken Griffey, has hit 40 or more homers in a season?

10. _____ Dan Meyer (1979) and what power-hitter from 1982 amassed a club-high 21-game batting streak.

11. _____ Who was the rookie with 25 home runs whom the Mariners traded after the 1986 season?

12. _____ Who was the slugger with 325 career home runs who played all 162 games in 1979 and hit 29 circuit clouts?

Catchers

Matching.

13. _____ Jerry Narron
14. _____ Dave Valle
15. _____ Bob Kearney

a. He led American League catchers in total chances (897) in 1984.
b. He became the Yankees' starting catcher after Thurman Munson's tragic death.
c. He hit 13 home runs for the Mariners in 1993.

Pitchers

Multiple Choice.

16. _____ Who struck out a club-high 308 batters in one year?
   a. Randy Johnson   c. Pete Ladd
   b. Mike Moore   d. Mike Morgan

17. _____ Who won a club-record 19 games in 1987? (Randy Johnson tied the mark in 1993.)
   a. Mike Morgan   c. Mark Langston
   b. Bill Swift   d. Mike Moore

18. _____ Who in 1992 was 11–3 at the All-Star Game break?
   a. Bobby Ayala   c. Dave Fleming
   b. Chris Bosio   d. Greg Hibbard.

19. _____ Who converted 18 of 24 save attempts in 1994?
   a. Bobby Ayala   c. Ron Villone
   b. Greg Hibbard   d. Dave Fleming

20. _____ Who was the former Mariner pitcher who was once suspended for "doctoring" a baseball?
   a. Rick Honeycutt   c. Gaylord Perry
   b. Jim Colborn   d. Bill Caudill

21. _____ Who led the league in strikeouts (209) in 1982?
   a. Gaylord Perry   c. Dick Drago
   b. Floyd Bannister   d. Jim Colborn

22. _____ Who won his 300th game with the Mariners?
   a. Don Sutton   c. Phil Niekro
   b. Tom Seaver   d. Gaylord Perry

23. _____ Scott Bankhead set a club mark when he won nine consecutive games in 1989. Who tied that mark in 1992?
   a. Bobby Ayala   c. Randy Johnson
   b. Dave Fleming   d. Mark Langston
24. _____ Who set a club mark when he saved 33 games in 1989?
   a. Bill Caudill   c. Matt Young
   b. Ed Vande Berg   d. Mike Schooler
25. _____ Who lost a club-record 16 consecutive games in 1980?
   a. Mike Moore   c. Mike Parrott
   b. Erik Hanson   d. Ed Vande Berg

TEXAS RANGERS

Infielders

Matching.

1. _____ Will Clark
2. _____ Rafael Palmeiro
3. _____ Buddy Bell
4. _____ Bump Wills
5. _____ Larry Parrish
6. _____ Julio Franco

a. He hit a club-high .341 in 1991.
b. He stole a club-record 52 bases one year.
c. He hit .329 in his first American League season.
d. He scored 124 runs in 1993 and he ripped 49 doubles in 1991, both club marks.
e. He batted .302 for the six full seasons he played with the Rangers.
f. He had 17 game-winning RBIs in 1983 and an RBI in 11 consecutive games in 1984, both club records.

Outfielders

Multiple Choice.

7. _____ Name the player who hit a club-high 46 home runs in one season.
   a. Rico Carty   c. Juan Gonzalez
   b. Larry Parrish   d. Frank Howard
8. _____ Name the rookie who hit 30 home runs in 1986.
   a. Pete Incaviglia   c. Frank Howard
   b. Al Oliver   d. Rico Carty
9. _____ Who, like Larry Parrish, hit a club-high three grand slams in one year?
   a. Al Oliver   c. Juan Gonzalez
   b. Ruben Sierra   d. Jeff Burroughs

10. _____ Who got a team-high 210 hits in his first year with the Rangers?
  a. Rico Carty c. Larry Parrish
  b. Al Oliver d. Mickey Rivers
11. _____ Who set team marks with 14 triples in 1989 and 44 career three-baggers?
  a. Mickey Rivers c. Ruben Sierra
  b. Gary Ward d. Al Oliver
12. _____ Whose .319 average in his four years with the Rangers is a team high?
  a. Al Oliver c. Buddy Bell
  b. Mickey Rivers d. Jeff Burroughs

Catchers

True or False.
13. _____ Jim Sundberg played a record 12 years with the Rangers.
14. _____ John Ellis hit 20 or more home runs in a season with Texas.
15. _____ Darrell Porter played on two pennant-winning teams outside of Texas.

Pitchers

Fill in the blanks.
16. _____ Who won 25 games, the club's all-time high, in one season?
17. _____ Who was the former Texas moundsman who started the first game of the 1976 World Series with the Yankees?
18. _____ Who was the former Ranger pitcher who started World Series games for the Pirates and the Yankees?
19. _____ Who was the "Wild Thing" who appeared in a club-record 85 games in 1987?
20. _____ Who struck out a club-high 301 batters in one year?

21. _____ Who set career marks with 139 wins and 98 complete games?

22. _____ Who won a club-record 12 consecutive games in 1990?

23. _____ Who saved a club-record 40 games in 1993?

24. _____ Who, like Ferguson Jenkins, recorded a team-high six shutouts in one season? He won 271 career games.

25. _____ A 20-game winner with three different teams, he posted 15–14 and 15–12 records with the 1976–77 Rangers. Who is he?

A Man for All Seasons

A baseball executive who never played in the major leagues had the Midas touch when it came to getting the most out of ballplayers; undoubtedly he "touched," either directly or indirectly, every era that we've covered in this book.

In the late 1890s he discovered Honus Wagner, who later won eight batting championships for the Pirates. In 1903 and 1904 he managed the Tigers to second-division finishes. But he put together the machinery that later (1907–09) produced three straight pennants. In 1918 he took over the managerial duties of the Red Sox, and he led them to a pennant and world title. But more important, in the same year he switched Babe Ruth from a regular-turn pitcher to an everyday first baseman-outfielder.

This baseball administrator managed the Red Sox through 1920. In the interim between 1918 and 1920, he had seen a pattern beginning to take shape. Red Sox owner Harry Frazee, who was in financial trouble, was unloading pennant-winning ballplayers to the Yankees. So when Yankee owner Jake Ruppert offered him the general manager's job in New York, he moved to the Bronx.

In 1921, his first year in New York, the Yankees won their first pennant. In his additional 24 years in the Yankee G.M. job, the Bronx Bombers won 13 pennants and 10 world championships. The pride that he helped to build in the pinstripe uniform has carried over to the present time; the Yankees have gone on to win 19 additional pennants and 12 world titles.

If you can name this "man for all seasons," you most probably have "touched" all of the bases in this book. Who was he?

Answer appears on page 344)

Chapter Nineteen

THE RECORD BOOK

This chapter is divided into three parts. The first section deals only with American League records. The second section deals only with National League marks. (In some cases, where players from both leagues share a major league record, statements about each player may appear under their respective league.) The third section deals only with major league marks. Let's see how many of the record-holders you can call to mind.

105. AMERICAN LEAGUE RECORDS

1. _____ Who compiled the highest average (.422) in one season?
   a. George Sisler   c. Harry Heilmann
   b. Napoleon Lajoie   d. Ty Cobb
2. _____ Who collected 107 career pinch-hits?
   a. Dave Philley   c. Gates Brown
   b. Johnny Mize   d. Bobby Brown
3. _____ Who had one or more hits in 135 games one year?
   a. Johnny Pesky   c. Rod Carew
   b. George Brett   d. Wade Boggs
4. _____ Who was the first right-handed batter who had 200 or more hits in five consecutive years?
   a. Joe DiMaggio   c. Al Simmons
   b. Jimmie Foxx   d. Hank Greenberg

5. _____ Joe Jackson (1912) and what other player (1914) drilled 26 triples one year?
   a. Earle Combs   c. Sam Crawford
   b. George Stirnweiss   d. Ty Cobb

6. _____ Who hit for the cycle three times?
   a. Bob Meusel   c. Larry Doby
   b. Nellie Fox   d. Harvey Kuenn

7. _____ Bill Stein and what other player got seven consecutive pinch-hits?
   a. Dave Philley   c. Sam Leslie
   b. Merv Rettenmund   d. Randy Bush

8. _____ Who collected 187 singles in one season?
   a. Willie Wilson   c. Wade Boggs
   b. Ty Cobb   d. George Sisler

9. _____ Who was the right-handed batter who hit 64 doubles in one season?
   a. Hank Greenberg   c. George Burns
   b. Luke Appling   d. Vern Stephens

10. _____ Who was the right-handed batter who hit 573 career home runs?
   a. Frank Robinson   c. Hank Greenberg
   b. Harmon Killebrew   d. Jimmie Foxx

11. _____ Who hit 16 career pinch-hit home runs?
   a. Cliff Johnson   c. Johnny Mize
   b. Gates Brown   d. Merv Rettenmund

12. _____ Who hit three home runs on opening day?
   a. George Bell   c. Lou Gehrig
   b. George Kell   d. Dick Wakefield

13. _____ Who rolled up the most strikeouts by a left-handed pitcher in one season?
   a. Herb Score   c. Rube Waddell
   b. Hal Newhouser   d. Ron Guidry

14. _____ Who became the first of three American League pitchers to throw two no-hitters in one season?
   a. Bob Feller   c. Virgil Trucks
   b. Allie Reynolds   d. Nolan Ryan

15. _____ Who struck out 186 times in a season?
   a. Rob Deer   c. Dave Nicholson
   b. Pete Incaviglia   d. Reggie Jackson

16. _____ Who hit five home runs, out of five hits, in five games?
   a. Bob Meusel   c. Gus Zernial
   b. Ken Williams   d. Bill Skowron
17. _____ Who was the Twin who three times hit pinch-hit grand slams in his career?
   a. Rich Reese   c. Bob Allison
   b. Jimmy Hall   d. Jim Lemon
18. _____ Who totaled 400 bases five times in his career?
   a. Jimmie Foxx   c. Lou Gehrig
   b. Babe Ruth   d. Joe DiMaggio
19. _____ Who had five long hits in one game?
   a. Ted Williams   c. Lou Boudreau
   b. Jim Rice   d. Fred Lynn
20. _____ Who was the right-handed batter who drove home 183 runs in one season?
   a. Hank Greenberg   c. Joe DiMaggio
   b. Al Simmons   d. Frank Howard
21. _____ Who was the catcher who drove home 133 runs one year?
   a. Yogi Berra   c. Carlton Fisk
   b. Gus Triandos   d. Bill Dickey
22. _____ Who drove home at least one run in 13 consecutive games?
   a. Cass Michaels   c. Dale Mitchell
   b. George Kell   d. Taft Wright
23. _____ Who drove home 11 runs in one game?
   a. Earl Averill   c. Tony Lazzeri
   b. Hal Trosky   d. Ben Chapman
24. _____ Who, like Billy Rogell, walked seven consecutive times?
   a. Eddie Yost   c. Jimmy Dykes
   b. Jose Canseco   d. Lou Gehrig
25. _____ Who drew 33 intentional walks one year?
   a. Jimmie Foxx   c. Harmon Killebrew
   b. Ted Williams   d. Roger Maris
26. _____ Who hit 17 sacrifice flies in 1971?
   a. Roy White   c. Reggie Jackson
   b. Frank Robinson   d. Brooks Robinson

27. _____ Who is the pitcher who started 34 games one year but didn't finish one of them?
   a. Frank Tanana   c. Kirk McCaskill
   b. Wilbur Wood   d. Ed Whitson

28. _____ Who was the pitcher who finished up a game with 17 innings of relief?
   a. Schoolboy Rowe   c. Ed Walsh
   b. Ed Rommel   d. George Pipgras

29. _____ Who won 24 games in his rookie season?
   a. Bob Grim   c. Carl Mays
   b. Edgar Summers   d. Urban Shocker

30. _____ Who was the Indian pitcher who won 17 consecutive games?
   a. Bob Feller   c. Bob Lemon
   b. Early Wynn   d. Johnny Allen

31. _____ Who was the Oriole pitcher who won 17 consecutive games?
   a. Mike Cuellar   c. Jim Palmer
   b. Mike Flanagan   d. Dave McNally

32. _____ Who was the starting pitcher who won nine consecutive games at the start of his career?
   a. Whitey Ford   c. Ellis Kinder
   b. Ned Garver   d. Hal Newhouser

33. _____ Who was the Yankee pitcher who won 23 consecutive games from the Athletics?
   a. Bob Shawkey   c. Waite Hoyt
   b. Joe Bush   d. Carl Mays

34. _____ Who was the Yankee relief pitcher who won 12 consecutive games one season?
   a. Joe Page   c. Luis Arroyo
   b. Bob Grim   d. Ron Davis

35. _____ Who was the Yankee pitcher who won 12 consecutive games in his rookie season?
   a. Atley Donald   c. Bump Hadley
   b. Spud Chandler   d. Monte Pearson

36. _____ Who won 15 consecutive games at the end of one season?
   a. Schoolboy Rowe   c. Alvin Crowder
   b. Ted Lyons   d. Tommy Bridges

37. _____ Who was the switch-hitter who got 100 hits from both sides of the plate one year?
    a. Mickey Mantle   c. Willie Wilson
    b. Eddie Murray   d. Tommy Tresh

38. _____ Who was the Athletic pitcher who lost 19 consecutive games one year?
    a. Carl Scheib   c. John Nabors
    b. Lou Brissie   d. Alex Kellner

39. _____ Who got hit by a pitch 35 times in the same season?
    a. Minnie Minoso   c. Don Baylor
    b. Frank Crosetti   d. Phil Rizzuto

40. _____ Who led the league in lowest ERA four consecutive years?
    a. Mickey Lolich   c. Whitey Ford
    b. Hal Newhouser   d. Lefty Grove

41. _____ Who pitched five consecutive shutouts?
    a. Jack Chesbro   c. Cy Young
    b. Ed Walsh   d. Doc White

42. _____ Who pitched an 18-inning 1–0 shutout?
    a. George Earnshaw   c. Lefty Grove
    b. Walter Johnson   d. Stan Coveleski

43. _____ Who relieved 807 times during his career?
    a. Sparky Lyle   c. Dave Righetti
    b. Dennis Eckersley   d. Goose Gossage

44. _____ Who allowed 422 career homers?
    a. Mike Torrez   c. Frank Tanana
    b. Bert Blyleven   d. Jim Hunter

45. _____ Who was the left-handed pitcher who struck out 2,679 batters during his American League career?
    a. Mickey Lolich   c. Billy Pierce
    b. Herb Score   d. Ron Guidry

46. _____ Who was the rookie left-hander who struck out 245 batters?
    a. Whitey Ford   c. Hal Newhouser
    b. Herb Score   d. Bob Feller

47. _____ Who played 150 or more games in each of 12 consecutive years?
    a. Lou Gehrig   c. Joe Cronin
    b. Everett Scott   d. Cal Ripken

48. _____ Who struck out 18 batters in one game but lost?
   a. Nolan Ryan   c. Bob Turley
   b. Bob Feller   d. Luis Tiant

49. _____ Who stole 20 bases without getting caught during a season?
   a. Willie Wilson   c. Julio Cruz
   b. Tim Raines   d. Paul Molitor

50. _____ Who was the left-handed pitcher who threw 45 consecutive scoreless innings?
   a. Doc White   c. Lefty Gomez
   b. Walter Johnson   d. Lefty Grove

106. NATIONAL LEAGUE RECORDS

1. _____ Who had a slugging average of .756 one year?
   a. Chuck Klein   c. Rogers Hornsby
   b. Hack Wilson   d. Joe Medwick

2. _____ Who, like Rogers Hornsby of the 1922 Cardinals, had one or more hits in 135 games one year?
   a. Paul Waner   c. Chuck Klein
   b. Pete Rose   d. Honus Wagner

3. _____ Who had 200 or more hits for five consecutive years?
   a. Pete Rose   c. Paul Waner
   b. Chuck Klein   d. Lloyd Waner

4. _____ Who twice had six hits in six at-bats?
   a. Stan Musial   c. Bill Terry
   b. Jim Bottomley   d. Lefty O'Doul

5. _____ Who had 14 hits in two consecutive doubleheaders?
   a. Bill White   c. Terry Moore
   b. Enos Slaughter   d. Marty Marion

6. _____ Who hit for the cycle three times?
   a. Stan Musial   c. Roberto Clemente
   b. Pete Reiser   d. Babe Herman

7. _____ Who led the league in doubles eight times?
   a. Honus Wagner   c. Pete Rose
   b. Stan Musial   d. Paul Waner

8. _____ Who was the left-handed batter who hit 521 career homers?
   a. Duke Snider   c. Mel Ott
   b. Willie McCovey   d. Willie Stargell

9. _____ Who hit 18 career pinch-hit homers?
   a. Gus Bell   c. Jerry Lynch
   b. Red Schoendienst   d. Rusty Staub

10. _____ Who was the switch-hitter who banged 38 home runs one year?
    a. Ted Simmons   c. Reggie Smith
    b. Howard Johnson   d. Pete Rose

11. _____ Who was the pitcher who twice hit seven home runs in a season?
   a. Don Newcombe   c. Don Drysdale
   b. Warren Spahn   d. Ken Brett

12. _____ Who hit 34 home runs at his home grounds one year?
   a. Ted Kluszewski   c. Eddie Mathews
   b. Mel Ott   d. Ralph Kiner

13. _____ Who hit 30 or more home runs for nine consecutive years?
   a. Hank Aaron   c. Willie McCovey
   b. Eddie Mathews   d. Willie Mays

14. _____ Who hit 101 home runs in back-to-back seasons?
   a. Johnny Mize   c. Hack Wilson
   b. Willie Mays   d. Ralph Kiner

15. _____ Who was the left-handed batter who hit 96 home runs in back-to-back years?
   a. Mel Ott   c. Ted Kluszewski
   b. Willie McCovey   d. Eddie Mathews

16. _____ Who hit 17 home runs in one month?
   a. Willie McCovey   c. Willie Mays
   b. Ernie Banks   d. Johnny Mize

17. _____ Who was the Cardinal who hit five home runs in a doubleheader?
   a. Johnny Mize   c. Stan Musial
   b. Rogers Hornsby   d. Joe Cunningham

18. _____ Who was the Padre who hit five home runs in a doubleheader?
   a. Nate Colbert   c. Graig Nettles
   b. Willie McCovey   d. Steve Garvey

19. _____ Who was the Expo who hit pinch-hit homers in both ends of a doubleheader?
   a. Harold Breeden   c. Ellis Valentine
   b. Andre Dawson   d. Larry Parrish

20. _____ Who five times hit three home runs in a senior circuit game?
   a. Joe Morgan   c. Johnny Mize
   b. Ernie Banks   d. Bill Nicholson

21. _____ Who was the pitcher who three times hit two home runs in a game?
   a. Steve Carlton   c. Rick Wise
   b. Don Newcombe   d. Tony Cloninger
22. _____ Who hit for 450 total bases in one season?
   a. Hack Wilson   c. Hank Aaron
   b. Mel Ott   d. Rogers Hornsby
23. _____ Who three times had more than 400 total bases in a season?
   a. Stan Musial   c. Chuck Klein
   b. Hank Aaron   d. Bill Terry
24. _____ Who had 25 total bases in two consecutive games?
   a. George Foster   c. Joe Adcock
   b. Dave Kingman   d. Tony Perez
25. _____ Who was the Pirate who hit four or more long hits in a game four times?
   a. Willie Stargell   c. Roberto Clemente
   b. Ralph Kiner   d. Bob Robertson
26. _____ Who walked 1,799 times?
   a. Jimmy Wynn   c. Joe Morgan
   b. Eddie Stanky   d. Richie Ashburn
27. _____ Who walked 100 times in his rookie year?
   a. Maury Wills   c. Richie Ashburn
   b. Jim Gilliam   d. Willie McCovey
28. _____ Who walked seven consecutive times?
   a. Ralph Kiner   c. Johnny Mize
   b. Willie Mays   d. Mel Ott
29. _____ Who was the right-handed slap hitter who also walked seven consecutive times?
   a. Eddie Stanky   c. Harvey Kuenn
   b. Al Dark   d. Dick Groat
30. _____ Who was the Cardinal who walked at least once in 16 consecutive games?
   a. Joe Adcock   c. Hank Aaron
   b. Jack Clark   d. Billy Bruton
31. _____ Who struck out 1,936 times during his career?
   a. Bobby Bonds   c. Willie Stargell
   b. Dave Kingman   d. Vince DiMaggio
32. _____ Who struck out only 173 times in 18 years?
   a. Tommy Holmes   c. Pete Reiser
   b. Paul Waner   d. Lloyd Waner

33. _____ Who was the pitcher who struck out 62 times in a season?
   a. Jerry Koosman
   b. Bob Buhl
   c. Sandy Koufax
   d. Russ Meyer

34. _____ Who grounded into 30 double plays in one year?
   a. Joe Medwick
   b. Ernie Lombardi
   c. Roy Campanella
   d. Walker Cooper

35. _____ Who stole home 33 times during his career?
   a. Pete Reiser
   b. Jackie Robinson
   c. Max Carey
   d. Pee Wee Reese

36. _____ Who got caught stealing 36 times in one year?
   a. Maury Wills
   b. Ron LeFlore
   c. Miller Huggins
   d. Tim Raines

37. _____ Who pitched 434 innings one year?
   a. Christy Mathewson
   b. Grover Alexander
   c. Joe McGinnity
   d. Dazzy Vance

38. _____ Who was the 22-game winner for the Dodgers who had an .880 winning percentage one year?
   a. Whit Wyatt
   b. Carl Erskine
   c. Preacher Roe
   d. Don Newcombe

39. _____ Who was the pitcher who hit 35 career homers?
   a. Warren Spahn
   b. Don Newcombe
   c. Don Drysdale
   d. Rick Wise

40. _____ Who pitched 90 career shutouts?
   a. Warren Spahn
   b. Grover Alexander
   c. Christy Mathewson
   d. Bob Gibson

41. _____ Who was the pitcher who lost 13 1–0 games?
   a. Burleigh Grimes
   b. Lee Meadows
   c. Bill Hallahan
   d. Bill Lee

42. _____ Who pitched 21 consecutive hitless innings one year?
   a. Don Drysdale
   b. Sal Maglie
   c. Johnny Vander Meer
   d. Ewell Blackwell

43. _____ Who allowed nine career grand slams?
   a. Jerry Reuss
   b. Don Sutton
   c. Robin Roberts
   d. Steve Carlton

44. _____ Who was the Cardinal pitcher who allowed nine walks in a shutout game?
   a. Vinegar Bend Mizell
   b. Dizzy Dean
   c. Howie Pollet
   d. Harry Brecheen

45. _____ Who was the right-hander who struck out 313 batters in one season?
   a. Tom Seaver   c. Dizzy Dean
   b. J. R. Richard   d. Don Drysdale
46. _____ Who hit 56 home runs in a season?
   a. Ralph Kiner   c. Johnny Mize
   b. Willie Mays   d. Hack Wilson
47. _____ Who stole home seven times in one season?
   a. Jackie Robinson   c. Lou Brock
   b. Pete Reiser   d. Maury Wills
48. _____ Who led his league in stolen bases ten times?
   a. Max Carey   c. Lou Brock
   b. Maury Wills   d. Tim Raines
49. _____ Who hit 154 batters during his career?
   a. Bobo Newsom   c. Don Drysdale
   b. Steve Carlton   d. Sam Jones
50. _____ Who is the present-day pitcher whose 19 strikeouts in one game tied Tom Seaver for the most whiffs by a league right-handed pitcher?
   a. David Cone   c. Dwight Gooden
   b. Bill Gullickson   d. Ramon Martinez

107. MAJOR LEAGUE RECORDS

1. _____ Who played the most games in one season?
   a. Pete Rose   c. Bobby Richardson
   b. Maury Wills   d. Rickey Henderson
2. _____ Who was the left-handed batter who hit for the highest single-season batting average?
   a. Bill Terry   c. George Sisler
   b. Ted Williams   d. Joe Jackson
3. _____ Who was the switch-hitter who hit for the highest single-season batting average?
   a. Jimmy Collins   c. Pete Rose
   b. Eddie Murray   d. Mickey Mantle
4. _____ Who scored one or more runs in 18 consecutive games?
   a. Red Rolfe   c. Bobby Richardson
   b. Nellie Fox   d. Red Schoendienst
5. _____ Who was the right-handed batter who got 253 hits in a season?
   a. Rogers Hornsby   c. Heinie Manush
   b. Jimmie Foxx   d. Al Simmons
6. _____ Who had seven hits in a nine-inning game?
   a. Bill Mazeroski   c. Willie Randolph
   b. Johnny Ray   d. Rennie Stennett
7. _____ Who had five hits in his first major league game?
   a. Cecil Travis   c. Casey Stengel
   b. Joe Cronin   d. Bob Nieman
8. _____ Who hit for the cycle in both leagues?
   a. Frank Robinson   c. Nellie Fox
   b. Bob Watson   d. Davey Lopes
9. _____ Who got three hits in one inning?
   a. Sammy White   c. Pee Wee Reese
   b. Gene Stephens   d. Stan Musial
10. _____ Who got two hits in one inning in his first major league game?
   a. Bob Nieman   c. Billy Martin
   b. Bert Campaneris d. Junior Gilliam

11. _____ Who reached base 16 consecutive times?
   a. George Brett   c. Eddie Yost
   b. Ted Williams   d. Garry Templeton

12. _____ Who got nine consecutive pinch-hits?
   a. Dave Philley   c. Del Unser
   b. Rusty Staub   d. Davey Johnson

13. _____ Who was the pitcher who, like Kirby Higbe of the 1941 Brooklyn Dodgers, got eight hits in two consecutive games?
   a. George Earnshaw   c. Red Ruffing
   b. Wes Ferrell   d. Don Newcombe

14. _____ Who sprayed 198 singles in one season?
   a. Willie Wilson   c. Lloyd Waner
   b. Wade Boggs   d. Nelson Fox

15. _____ Who hit six doubles in a doubleheader?
   a. Pete Rose   c. Tris Speaker
   b. Stan Musial   d. Hank Majeski

16. _____ Who hit 36 triples in one season?
   a. Sam Crawford   c. Joe Jackson
   b. J. Owen Wilson   d. Earle Combs

17. _____ Who two times in one season got three triples in a game?
   a. Kiki Cuyler   c. Dave Brain
   b. George Stirnweiss   d. Ty Cobb

18. _____ Who hit 20 pinch-hit home runs?
   a. Johnny Mize   c. Bob Cerv
   b. Rusty Staub   d. Cliff Johnson

19. _____ Who hit 30 or more home runs for 12 consecutive years?
   a. Hank Aaron   c. Babe Ruth
   b. Harmon Killebrew   d. Jimmie Foxx

20. _____ Who hit 20 or more home runs for 20 consecutive years?
   a. Frank Robinson   c. Ted Williams
   b. Hank Aaron   d. Jimmie Foxx

21. _____ Who hit 114 home runs in back-to-back years?
   a. Babe Ruth   c. Willie Mays
   b. Hank Aaron   d. Ralph Kiner

22. _____ Who was the pitcher who hit three home runs in one game?
   a. Tony Cloninger   c. Red Ruffing
   b. Rick Wise   d. Jim Tobin
23. _____ Who was the pitcher who five times hit two home runs in a game?
   a. Bob Lemon   c. Don Newcombe
   b. Wes Ferrell   d. Don Drysdale
24. _____ Who was the part-time player who hit four consecutive home runs in three consecutive games?
   a. George Shuba   c. John Blanchard
   b. Gino Cimoli   d. Chuck Essegian
25. _____ Who was the pitcher who hit home runs in four consecutive games?
   a. Warren Spahn   c. Walter Johnson
   b. Red Lucas   d. Ken Brett
26. _____ Who got six home runs, out of six hits, in six consecutive games? Frank Hurst of the 1929 Phillies turned the trick, too.
   a. Mike Schmidt   c. Moises Alou
   b. Del Ennis   d. Willie Jones
27. _____ Who hit three home runs in his first two games?
   a. Buddy Hassett   c. Joe Cunningham
   b. Dolph Camilli   d. Jim Tobin
28. _____ Who hit a grand slam in his first major league game?
   a. Bobby Bonds   c. Dwayne Murphy
   b. Bobby Murcer   d. Tony Armas
29. _____ Who had 17 total bases in an extra-inning game?
   a. Willie Mays   c. Mike Schmidt
   b. Rudy York   d. Rocky Colavito
30. _____ Who was the Indian who had seven consecutive long hits?
   a. Elmer Smith   c. Al Rosen
   b. Larry Doby   d. Andre Thornton
31. _____ Who was the White Sox who had seven consecutive long hits?
   a. Richie Allen   c. Bill Melton
   b. Earl Sheely   d. Sherm Lollar

32. _____ Who had one or more long hits in 14 consecutive games?
   a. Walker Cooper   c. Sid Gordon
   b. Johnny Mize   d. Paul Waner

33. _____ Who drove home at least one run in 17 consecutive games?
   a. Ray Grimes   c. Taft Wright
   b. George Stirnweiss d. Elmer Valo

34. _____ Who was the right-handed hitter who walked 151 times in a season?
   a. Jimmy Wynn   c. Eddie Yost
   b. Eddie Stanky   d. Jimmy Foxx

35. _____ Who was the Tiger who walked at least once in 18 consecutive games?
   a. Roy Cullenbine   c. Charlie Gehringer
   b. Harvey Kuenn   d. Jake Woods

36. _____ Who struck out only 113 times in a 14-year career?
   a. Luke Appling   c. Earle Combs
   b. Richie Ashburn   d. Joe Sewell

37. _____ Who had 67 sacrifices in one season?
   a. Ray Chapman   c. Nellie Fox
   b. Phil Rizzuto   d. Eddie Yost

38. _____ Who hit 123 career sacrifice flies?
   a. Gil Hodges   c. Frank Robinson
   b. Robin Yount   d. Willie McCovey

39. _____ Who hit 19 sacrifice flies in 1954?
   a. Joe Adcock   c. Andy Pafko
   b. Gil Hodges   d. Eddie Mathews

40. _____ Who pitched for 27 years?
   a. Gaylord Perry   c. Grover Alexander
   b. Phil Niekro   d. Nolan Ryan

41. _____ Who started 37 games in one year but didn't complete one of them?
   a. Steve Bedrosian   c. Vern Bickford
   b. Bob Buhl   d. Joe Cowley

42. _____ Who pitched in 13 consecutive games?
   a. Mike Marshall   c. Bruce Sutter
   b. Rollie Fingers   d. Goose Gossage

43. _____ Who pitched 39 consecutive complete games in one season?
   a. Ed Walsh   c. Joe McGinnity
   b. Jack Chesbro   d. Jack Taylor
44. _____ Who pitched 464 innings in one season?
   a. Vic Willis   c. Joe McGinnity
   b. Ed Walsh   d. Jack Chesbro
45. _____ Who, going into the 1995 season, had registered 434 career saves?
   a. Dave Righetti   c. John Franco
   b. Tom Henke   d. Lee Smith
46. _____ Who, at the start of his career, pitched 25 consecutive scoreless innings?
   a. Hank Borowy   c. Tex Hughson
   b. George McQuillan   d. Howie Pollet
47. _____ Who allowed 11 walks in a shutout win?
   a. Vinegar Bend Mizell   c. Spud Chandler
   b. Lefty Gomez   d. Mario Russo
48. _____ Who pitched 21 consecutive scoreless innings in one game?
   a. Leon Cadore   c. Walter Johnson
   b. Carl Hubbell   d. Joe Oeschger
49. _____ Who pitched a 21-inning game without allowing a walk?
   a. Stan Coveleski   c. Carl Mays
   b. Babe Adams   d. Jim Hunter
50. _____ Who struck out seven consecutive batters in his first major league game?
   a. Mort Cooper   c. Sammy Stewart
   b. Ron Davis   d. Nolan Ryan

108. HIGHEST CAREER FIELDING PERCENTAGE PER POSITION (MINIMUM OF 1,000 GAMES)

American League

The respective positions and percentages are provided. Select the correct choice from the three players who are named.

1. (1B) _____ (.996)
   a. Don Mattingly
   b. Joe Judge
   c. Jim Spencer

2. (2B) _____ (.985)
   a. Bobby Grich
   b. Eddie Collins
   c. Jim Gantner

3. (3B) _____ (.971)
   a. Eddie Yost
   b. Brooks Robinson
   c. George Kell

4. (SS) _____ (.982)
   a. Cal Ripken
   b. Everett Scott
   c. Tony Fernandez

5. (OF) _____ (.991)
   a. Amos Otis
   b. Rocky Colavito
   c. Brian Downing

6. (C) _____ (.993)
   a. Yogi Berra
   b. Bill Freehan
   c. Bill Dickey

7. (P) _____ (3)*
   a. Whitey Ford
   b. Bobby Shantz
   c. Walter Johnson

*The pitcher determination is based upon the most times with the best percentage and most chances.

The respective positions and percentages are provided. Select the correct choice from the players who are named. At first base and at the pitcher's position, there is a tie for the lead, so more than the customary three choices are given.

1. (1B) _____ (.996)
   a. Wes Parker
   b. Steve Garvey
   c. Ted Kluszewski
   d. Charlie Grimm
   e. George Kelly
   f. Frank McCormick
   g. Ed Bouchee

2. (2B) _____ (.990)
   a. Ryne Sandberg
   b. Ken Boswell
   c. Red Schoendienst

3. (3B) _____ (.970)
   a. Willie Jones
   b. Ken Reitz
   c. Ron Santo

4. (SS) _____ (.980)
   a. Rabbit Maranville
   b. Ozzie Smith
   c. Larry Bowa

5. (OF) _____ (.993)
   a. Willie Mays
   b. Terry Puhl
   c. Roberto Clemente

6. (C) _____ (.992)
   a. Roy Campanella
   b. Gabby Hartnett
   c. Johnny Edwards

7. (P) _____ (4)*
   a. Larry Jansen
   b. Johnny Sain
   c. Larry Jackson
   d. Claude Passeau
   e. Warren Spahn
   f. Steve Carlton

*The pitcher determination is based upon the most times with the best percentage and most chances.

109. HIGHEST SEASON FIELDING PERCENTAGE PER POSITION (MINIMUM OF 150 GAMES, EXCEPT THIRD BASE AND CATCHER, 100)

American League

The respective positions and percentages are provided. Select the correct choice from the three players who are named. At the outfield position there is a tie for the lead, so six choices instead of the customary three are given.

1. (1B) _____ (.999)   a. Don Mattingly
                                         b. Mickey Vernon
                                         c. Stuffy McInnis

2. (2B) _____ (.995)   a. Bobby Grich
                                         b. Bobby Doerr
                                         c. Jim Gantner

3. (3B) _____ (.991)   a. Graig Nettles
                                         b. Steve Buchele
                                         c. Brooks Robinson

4. (SS) _____ (.996)   a. Cal Ripken
                                         b. Luis Aparicio
                                         c. Luke Appling

5. (OF) _____ (1.000)   a. Rocky Colavito
                                         b. Dom DiMaggio
                                         c. Tommy Henrich
                                         d. Brian Downing
                                         e. Amos Otis
                                         f. Devon White

6. (C) _____ (1.000)   a. Yogi Berra
                                         b. Buddy Rosar
                                         c. Jim Hegan

7. (P) _____ (1.000)   a. Lefty Grove
                                         b. Bobby Shantz
                                         c. Walter Johnson

National League

The respective positions and percentages are provided. Select the correct choice from the three players who are named. At shortstop and catcher there is a two-way tie for the lead, so six choices are given. At the outfield positions there is a four-way spot. Danny Litwhiler of the 1942 Phillies, Curt Flood of the 1966 Cardinals, and Terry Puhl of the 1979 Astros are three of the four. Select the fourth one, who has been the only outfielder to twice record 1.000 fielding percentages.

1. (1B) _____ (1.000)   a. Gil Hodges
                           b. Steve Garvey
                           c. Orlando Cepeda

2. (2B) _____ (.996)   a. Joe Morgan
                           b. Manny Trillo
                           c. Jose Oquendo

3. (3B) _____ (.983)   a. Mike Schmidt
                           b. Heinie Groh
                           c. Ken Boyer

4. (SS) _____ (.987)   a. Marty Marion
                           b. Pee Wee Reese
                           c. Johnny Logan
                           d. Alvin Dark
                           e. Larry Bowa
                           f. Ozzie Smith

5. (OF) _____ (1.000)   a. Richie Ashburn
                           b. Brett Butler
                           c. Willie Mays

6. (C) _____ (.999)   a. Gary Carter
                           b. Phil Masi
                           c. Wes Westrum
                           d. Tom Pagnozzi
                           e. Bruce Edwards
                           f. Mike Piazza

7. (P) _____ (1.000)   a. Randy Jones
                           b. Mort Cooper
                           c. Johnny Vander Meer

110. ALL-TIME GOLD GLOVE CHAMPS

In the left-hand column we'll provide the National League players who have the most circuit Gold Gloves at their respective positions; in the right-hand column we'll do the same for the top American League players. In between the two names, we'll place in parentheses the all-time high number. All that you have to do is to select the player you think has won the most Gold Gloves. The number that the runner-up recorded will be stated in the answers. Two outfielders are clear-cut winners. The third spot is up for grabs, though. Four outfielders, two in each league, won eight. Therefore, we'll have four outfielders filling the third slot.

1B	Keith Hernandez	(11)	Don Mattingly
2B	Ryne Sandberg	(9)	Frank White
3B	Mike Schmidt	(16)	Brooks Robinson
SS	Ozzie Smith	(13)	Luis Aparicio
OF	Willie Mays	(12)	Al Kaline
OF	Roberto Clemente	(12)	Carl Yastrzemski
OF	Curt Flood	(8)	Paul Blair
OF	Garry Maddox	(8)	Dwayne Murphy
OF	Dale Murphy	(8)	Dwight Evans
OF	Andre Dawson	(8)	Devon White
C	Johnny Bench	(10)	Jim Sundberg
P	Bob Gibson	(16)	Jim Kaat

Three Men on Third

Babe Herman looked like a knightly champion when he stepped into the batter's box—he hit .393 in 1930 and he batted .324 lifetime—but when he played the outfield or ran the bases, he seemed to develop some chinks in his armor.

Fly balls, the stories go, used to either bounce off his head or carom off his shoulders with great regularity. Some baseball observers have said that his glove was a mere ornament on his hand.

His base running didn't help the Brooklyn franchise lose its nickname of "Bums," either. Take the case of the day in 1926, for example, when the Dodgers hosted the Braves. The bases were full of Dodgers when Herman, a rookie at the time, advanced mightily to the plate. Hank DeBerry led off third, Dazzy Vance danced off second, and Chick Fewster leaned off first.

Herman did not disappoint them. He rocketed a ball high off the right-field wall. DeBerry scored easily. Vance could have, too, but he changed his mind after taking a wide turn around third. He retreated to third base where he met Fewster sliding into the "hot corner." In the meantime, Herman got a good start out of the box. He put his head down and raced around the bases with reckless abandon. Sliding into third, with what he thought was a sure triple, he was perplexed to bump into his two teammates. You might call the Dodgers' base running, in that instance, a "comedy of errors," or you might label Herman's aggressive dash an example of a "rookie's mistake."

But the third baseman was confused, too. He knew that two of the runners didn't belong there, but he didn't know which two runners were trespassing. So he did the obvious: he tagged all three of the runners. And the umpire called two of them out. But which two? Who, do you think, had the right to be there?

(Answer appears on page 344.)

Chapter Twenty

THE HALL OF FAME

111. CLUES TO COOPERSTOWN

From Barrow to Youngs

Match the following 50 Hall of Famers with the descriptions that follow.

Jackie Robinson	Red Faber	Max Carey
Zack Wheat	Bob Feller	Frankie Frisch
Herb Pennock	Harry Hooper	Lefty Gomez
Carl Hubbell	Cool Papa Bell	Sam Rice
John McGraw	Nap Lajoie	George Sisler
Bob Lemon	Josh Gibson	Monte Irvin
Bill Dickey	Ed Barrow	Pie Traynor
Hank Greenberg	Eppa Rixey	Ray Schalk
Dazzy Vance	Fred Clarke	Lou Boudreau
Al Simmons	Jesse Haines	Rabbit Maranville
Bill Terry	Babe Ruth	Joe Cronin
Mel Ott	Ross Youngs	Lou Gehrig
Branch Rickey	Johnny Evers	Ted Lyons
Heinie Manush	Satchel Paige	Charlie Gehringer
Frank Baker	Chick Hafey	George Kelly
Jimmy Collins	Edd Roush	Robin Roberts
Dave Bancroft	Goose Goslin	

1. _____ This celebrated National League screwball artist won 253 major league games (24 in succession), pitched a 1–0 18-inning win against the Cardinals in 1933 (it wrapped up the pennant), and gained baseball immortality in the 1934 All-Star Game when he struck out Babe Ruth, Lou Gehrig, Jimmie Foxx, Al Simmons, and Joe Cronin in succession.

2. _____ This slugging American League first baseman scored more than 100 runs in 13 consecutive seasons, batted in more than 100 runs in 13 consecutive seasons, and played in every one of his team's games for 13 consecutive seasons while, at one time or another, leading the league in almost every conceivable batting title.

3. _____ The third best winning percentage (.671) pitcher of all time, he also won 12 league home run titles.

4. _____ Part of a double-play trio immortalized in a famous poem, he had the good judgment to retrieve Al Bridwell's apparent hit and touch second base to force Fred Merkle on a play that pushed the Giants into a one-game playoff that they lost to the Cubs in 1908.

5. _____ A six-time home run champion, he hit more National League round-trippers with one team than any other left-handed batter.

6. _____ This American League outfielder, who won two batting titles (1930–31) and hit .334 lifetime, batted better than .380 four times, and hit better than .300 for four American League teams.

7. _____ Though he never played in a World Series, he twice hit over .400, sported a .340 lifetime average, hit safely a record 257 times in one season, earned the reputation of being the best defensive first baseman of his time, and produced two sons who played in the majors.

8. _____ The last National Leaguer to hit over .400, he has been the Giants' most successful manager since John McGraw: he led New York to three pennants and one world title.

9. _____ A four-time home run champion who lost four peak years to the military service, he was discharged in mid-season of 1945, just in time to lead his team to pennant and World Series victories.

10. _____ Winner of 286 major league games, he claims that his most satisfying victory was his pennant-clinching decision against the Dodgers in 1950.

11. _____ One of the most exciting base runners of all time, he led the Dodgers to six pennants and one World Series victory between 1947–56; however, his greatest contribution came in 1949 when he was named the MVP for leading the league in batting (.342) and stolen bases (37). In that same year he drove home 124 runs and he scored 122 runs.

12. _____ Though he never won a World Series game, he did win 266 lifetime contests, hurled three no-hitters, and pitched 12 one-hitters in his 18-year major league career.

13. _____ In a 22-year career divided between the Phillies and the Reds, he won 266 games, the most victories by a National League southpaw until Warren Spahn recorded 363 triumphs.

14. _____ A pennant-winning manager in his first year, he was sold two years later, by Clark Griffith (his father-in-law), to the Red Sox for $250,000.

15. _____ Untainted catcher for the infamous Black Sox of 1919, he led American League receivers in putouts for nine years; fielding, eight years; and he caught over 100 games a season for 11 consecutive years.

16. _____ One of the four men who have won four consecutive home run titles, he starred in the infield for the Athletics (1908–14) and the Yankees (1916–22).

17. _____ One of the best defensive catchers who ever played the game, one of the best average-hitting catchers who ever played the game (.313), one of the best home run-hitting catchers who ever played the game (202), he played on eight world championship clubs.

18. _____ Shortstop for the "Miracle Braves," he played with five National League teams over a 23-year span, during which time he established the major league shortstop record for putouts (5,139), and placed second in assists (7,354) and total chances (13,124).

19. _____ A three-time 20-game winner, he set a National League record when he led the loop in strikeouts for seven consecutive years.

20. _____ In 21 years of pitching in the American League, his team finished in the first division only five times (its highest finish was third); however this durable right hander won 260 games, a club record.

21. _____ Possessor of a 29-game batting streak, he played 18 years in the Dodgers' outfield while posting a .317 career batting mark and winning the 1918 batting championship with a .335 batting average.

22. _____ This Pirate outfielder, who stole 738 lifetime bases, led the National League in thefts for ten years. In 1922 he stole successfully 51 out of 53 times.

23. _____ A great defensive outfielder with the Reds and Giants (1916–31), he was also an accomplished batter, hitting .323 lifetime and winning batting championships in 1917 and 1919.

24. _____ He played in more games, registered more at-bats, scored more runs, collected more hits, slashed more doubles, slammed more triples, ran more total bases, and batted in more runs than any other Senator player.

25. _____ Second on the Tigers to Ty Cobb in games played, at-bats, runs, hits, doubles, and total bases, he starred in the 1934–35 World Series and won the batting championship in 1937.

26. _____ Though he led the league in only one offensive department (triples, 19, in 1923), he batted .320 lifetime and gained baseball's admiration as the greatest defensive third baseman in National League history.

27. _____ A 240-game winner for the Athletics, Red Sox, and Yankees, he excelled in World Series play with a spotless 5–0 record. He also saved three games in series competition.

28. _____ A .316 lifetime hitter, and manager of "The Gashouse Gang" that won the pennant and series in 1934, he was traded to the Cardinals for Rogers Hornsby.

29. _____ Considered by many to be the greatest third baseman ever to play the game, he revolutionized the style of third base play while compiling a .294 lifetime average and managing the Red Sox to back-to-back pennants in 1903–04.

30. _____ The first successful "boy manager"—he won consecutive pennants from 1901–3 and in 1909—he played 15 years in the Pirates' outfield while recording a .312 lifetime average.

31. _____ A .334-hitting third baseman, he gained greater fame when he led his charges to ten pennants and three World Series victories.

32. _____ Winner of batting championships in 1901, 1903, and 1904, he once hit .422 for the Athletics, the highest single-season batting average in American League history.

33. _____ This .322 lifetime hitter for the Giants batted .300 in nine of his ten years in the majors while leading New York to five pennants and two world titles. At the age of 30, he died of a kidney ailment.

34. _____ Winner of 254 games, he was one of the four White Sox pitchers who won 20 games in 1920. During 15 of his 20 seasons in the majors, his team finished in the second division. He was also the last of the legal spitball pitchers in the American League.

35. _____ He played on five pennant winners with the Senators and the Tigers while compiling a .316 lifetime average. In 1928 he won the batting title with a .379 mark. Eleven times he drove home 100 runs.

36. _____ Though he did not get to the majors until he was 30, this outfielder for the Giants won an RBI title and finished his career with a .293 mark. In the 1951 series he batted .458 and stole home once.

37. _____ First baseman for the Giants, Reds, and Dodgers (1915–32), he batted .297. He once hit three home runs in three consecutive innings. At another time he banged seven home runs in six games.

38. _____ The oldest rookie in the history of the game (42), he posted a 6–1 record in 1948 to help the Indians win the pennant. At the age of 59, he pitched his last game for the Athletics. Dizzy Dean called him the greatest pitcher he had ever seen.

39. _____ This American League left-hander was 6–0 in World Series play and 3–1 in all-star action. He was also a four-time 20-game winner with an overall record of 189–102.

40. _____ The last player-manager who led his team to a pennant and World Series victory, he owns a .295 lifetime average. He had his greatest year in 1948 when he hit .355, got four hits in the playoff game, and won the Most Valuable Player award.

41. _____ He recorded a .317 lifetime average despite poor eyesight. For six consecutive years he batted better than .329. In 1929 the flyhawk, who played with both the Cardinals and the Reds, hit safely ten consecutive times to tie a league record.

42. _____ They called him "Beauty," because in his time he was considered a shortstop without peer. In 1922 he set a record when he handled 984 chances at shortstop for the Giants. He averaged 5.97 chances a game during his major league career.

43. _____ Considered the best defensive outfielder, next to Tris Speaker, during his time, he was responsible for talking Ed Barrow into converting Babe Ruth into an outfielder. Along with Speaker and Duffy Lewis, he played in one of the most famous outfields of all time. A great World Series performer, he turned in his best season's batting marks in 1921 and 1924 with the White Sox.

44. _____ He didn't come up to the majors until he was 27, but he won 210 games before he pitched his last major league ball at the age of 44. In the 1926 World Series he beat the Yankees twice.

45. _____ He was likened to Willie Keeler with the bat, Tris Speaker in the field, and Ty Cobb on the bases. Yet this all-round performer never got a chance to show his skills in the majors. He was limited to 29 summers of Negro ball and 21 winters of off-season play.

46. _____ He won four batting titles and hit almost 800 home runs in the Negro leagues. Twice he hit more than 70 home runs in a season. He died at the age of 35, the year Jackie Robinson was admitted to the major leagues.

47. _____ A player, manager, and general manager, "The Mahatma" reached greatness in the game as an innovative administrator. He established the first farm system with the Cardinals, broke the color line when he signed Jackie Robinson, and created dynasties in St. Louis and Brooklyn.

48. _____ The manager of the 1918 Red Sox world championship team, he is more singularly remembered for having discovered Honus Wagner, converting Babe Ruth into an outfielder, and establishing a dynasty as general manager of the Yankees.

49. _____ Winner of two games in the 1948 World Series and loser of two games in the 1954 World Series, he started out as a third baseman and ended up winning 207 major league games.

50. _____ A .330 lifetime hitter, he won one batting title (Tigers), collected 200 hits four times, and batted .300 for four major league clubs.

From Aaron to Kell

Match the following 50 Hall of Famers with the descriptions that follow.

Hank Aaron	Eddie Collins	Burleigh Grimes
Grover Alexander	Earle Combs	Lefty Grove
Luis Aparicio	Stan Coveleski	Gabby Hartnett
Luke Appling	Sam Crawford	Harry Heilmann
Earl Averill	Kiki Cuyler	Billy Herman
Ernie Banks	Ray Dandridge	Rogers Hornsby
Johnny Bench	Dizzy Dean	Waite Hoyt
Yogi Berra	Ed Delahanty	Jim Hunter
Jim Bottomley	Joe DiMaggio	Reggie Jackson
Mordecai Brown	Don Drysdale	Travis Jackson
Jesse Burkett	Rick Ferrell	Hugh Jennings
Roy Campanella	Elmer Flick	Walter Johnson
Frank Chance	Chief Bender	Addie Joss
Jack Chesbro	Rod Carew	Al Kaline
Roberto Clemente	Whitey Ford	Willie Keeler
Ty Cobb	Jimmie Foxx	George Kell
Mickey Cochrane	Willie McCovey	

1. _____ A winner of 239 games during the regular season and five games in World Series play, he won 20 or more games six consecutive years (1906–11), posted an ERA of 1.04 in 1906—the lowest mark for any pitcher with more than 250 innings of pitching—and he didn't allow an earned run in the 1907–08 series.

2. _____ In 1941 he won his 300th—and last—game with the Boston Red Sox.

3. _____ A multi-time batting champ, he once batted .360 over an eight-year span (1920–27) without winning a crown.

4. _____ A four-time batting champ, he hit safely in 14 consecutive World Series games, and he finished his career with 3,000 hits.

5. _____ He once hit 50 home runs in a season, but he didn't win the home run crown; he finished his regular-season career with a .609 slugging average, and he finished his World Series career with a .609 slugging average.

6. _____ In 1904 he set a record when he struck out 349 opposing batters. That American League mark stood until Nolan Ryan of the 1983 Angels struck out 383 batters.

7. _____ A .281 lifetime hitter, he caught 1,805 games over an 18-year career with three American League teams, some of which were spent handling the pitches of a brother who six times won 20 games.

8. _____ The Cubs have not won a World Series since this .297 career hitter led them to back-to-back crowns (1907–08) as their player-manager.

9. _____ Third on the all-time hit list (3,771), he also won four home run crowns, three of the times with the number of four-base blows he hit corresponding to the number (44) he wore on his back.

10. _____ A three-time winner of the home run crown, he hit more home runs than any other left-handed batter in National League history.

11. _____ He ranks first in World Series games, at-bats, hits, and doubles; second in runs and runs batted in; and third in home runs and walks.

12. _____ A .304 lifetime hitter, he got a career-high 227 hits in 1935, and played in four World Series with the Cubs and Dodgers at three-year intervals (1932–35–38–41).

13. _____ A 300-game winner, he posted ERAs below 2.00 for six consecutive years (1915–20).

14. _____ His lifetime ERA was 1.88, the second all-time low, but unfortunately he died young, at the age of 31.

15. _____ In the 1921 World Series he didn't allow an earned run in 27 innings of pitching, but he won only two of three decisions, losing the final game, 1–0, on an error by Roger Peckinpaugh.

16. _____ A 236-game lifetime winner, he posted the best all-time winning percentage (.690) in modern-day ball.

17. _____ A 210-game lifetime winner, he failed to complete a game in World Series play only one out of ten times, the last time, after completing a record nine games in a row.

18. _____ In 1904 this old Highlander started 51 games, finished 48 contests, and won 41 games, all-time bests.

19. _____ A five-time 20-game winner, he won three games for the Indians in the 1920 World Series, and lost two games for the Senators in the 1925 post-season classic.

20. _____ The second all-time winner with 416 victories, he won the last game of the 1924 World Series, and lost the curtain-caller the following year.

21. _____ He didn't pitch his first full season in the National League until he was 30 years old, yet he went on to win 270 major league games.

22. _____ He was the last National League pitcher (1934) to win 30 games in a season.

23. _____ From 1962–65 he had 40 or more starts every year, and he pitched over 300 innings in each of those seasons.

24. _____ A .341 lifetime hitter, he three times batted .400 in the 1890s before leading the league with a .382 mark for the 1901 Cards.

25. _____ A catcher in the National League for 20 years, he hit 236 career homers, high at his position until Roy Campanella ended up with 242.

26. _____ He was the only player to win batting titles in both leagues, hitting .408 for the 1899 Phillies and .376 for the 1902 Senators.

27. _____ A .327 lifetime batter, he had a career average that was higher than any other player at his position.

28. _____ He led the American League in stolen bases his first nine years (1956–64) in the circuit.

29. _____ He won batting titles in 1936 and 1943, the only ones that a player on his team has won.

30. _____ He hit .333 lifetime but never won a batting crown.

31. _____ Four times he hit more than 20 triples in a season, and twice—once in each league—he won the home run crown.

32. _____ In the 11 full seasons that this .318 career hitter played in the majors, he averaged 104 RBIs a year.

33. _____ A .320 lifetime hitter, he played in five World Series, four of them in the 1930s, and player-managed a team to back-to-back pennants.

34. _____ From 1924 to 1929 this .310 lifetime hitter—who had seasons of most hits, doubles, triples, home runs, and RBIs—averaged 126 runs batted in a year.

35. _____ A middle infielder, he averaged 44 home runs a year from 1957–60.

36. _____ Until Don Mattingly eclipsed it, he held the Yankee team record of 231 hits in a season.

37. _____ Eight years in a row this .345 lifetime hitter collected more than 200 hits.

38. _____ He finished his career one home run shy of 400.

39. _____ This .315 lifetime hitter once (1905) won a batting title with a mark of .306.

40. _____ A second baseman, he hit 301 career homers.

41. _____ This .325 lifetime hitter, in his first five years in the majors, averaged better than one RBI for every game he played.

42. _____ This .312 lifetime hitter became the first manager to lead his team to three consecutive pennants (1907–09); he was also the first of only two skippers to lead his club to three consecutive World Series defeats.

43. _____ A .306 lifetime batter, this infielder hit better than .300 eight straight years and won the batting title in 1949.

44. _____ A defensive standout, this middle infielder played his entire career with one club and posted a .291 lifetime average.

45. _____ In 1921 he won the batting title, outhitting his manager by five points.

46. _____ People who saw him play say that Brooks Robinson couldn't match his defensive skills at third base, but unfortunately he didn't get the opportunity to showcase them in the big leagues.

47. _____ In World Series play he won four-of-four decisions for a West Coast team and one-of-four for an East Coast club.

48. _____ He won the Rookie of the Year Award, two MVP honors, two home run crowns, three RBI titles, and led all catchers with 389 homers.

49. _____ Seven times a batting champ, he ended his career with a .328 lifetime average while setting the batting-mark high with two different teams.

50. _____ He slugged 563 career homers, five round-trippers in one World Series, and enough circuit clouts to win four-base crowns with three different teams.

From Killebrew to Wynn

Match the following 52 Hall of Famers with the descriptions that follow.

Harmon
Killebrew
Ralph Kiner
Chuck Klein
Sandy Koufax
Fred Lindstrom
Mickey Mantle
Juan Marichal
Rube Marquard
Eddie Mathews
Christy
Mathewson
Willie Mays
Joe McGinnity
Joe Medwick
Johnny Mize
Stan Musial
Eddie Plank
Pee Wee Reese
Tom Seaver

Carl Yazstremski
Tris Speaker
Joe Tinker
Rube Waddell
Honus Wagner
Bobby Wallace
Ed Walsh
Willie Stargell
Lloyd Waner
Paul Waner
Ted Williams
Hack Wilson
Billy Williams
Early Wynn
Mike Schmidt
Walter Alston
Charles Comiskey

Clark Griffith
Bucky Harris
Miller Huggins
Brooks Robinson
Frank Robinson
Red Ruffing
Joe Sewell
Duke Snider
Warren Spahn
Joe Morgan
Jim Palmer
Al Lopez
Connie Mack
Joe McCarthy
Bill McKechnie
Wilbert Robinson
Casey Stengel

1. _____ In back-to-back years (1903–04) he pitched more than 400 innings in each season.
2. _____ In his last five years (1962–66) he posted ERAs under 2.00.
3. _____ He finished his career with *300* victories.
4. _____ This 201-game winner pitched in five World Series with the Giants and Dodgers, winning two games and losing five.
5. _____ Six times he won more than 20 games in a season for the Giants.
6. _____ He held the American League single-season strike-out record (349) until Nolan Ryan broke it.

7. _____ Four times—three times in a row—he won 30 or more games in a season.

8. _____ Eight times he won 20 or more games for Connie Mack.

9. _____ The most games he won in a season was 23, but he won 20 or more games in a year a record 13 times.

10. _____ He won six consecutive games in World Series play.

11. _____ He hit more than 500 career homers, including 40 or more in his second, third, and fourth years in the majors.

12. _____ In his first five full seasons in the majors (1929–33) he won four home run crowns.

13. _____ He led the National League in home runs in back-to-back years with two clubs.

14. _____ He played on five consecutive World Series losers before he played on a winning team.

15. _____ A .324 lifetime batter, he led the National League in doubles and RBIs from 1936–38.

16. _____ He hit .365 one year (1957) but finished second to Ted Williams in the batting race.

17. _____ He hit more right-handed home runs (586) than any other player except Willie Mays and Hank Aaron.

18. _____ He averaged 37 home runs a season in his ten-year career.

19. _____ A .333 lifetime hitter, he won batting crowns in 1927, 1934, and 1936.

20. _____ At age 18 he got four hits in a World Series game against Walter Johnson.

21. _____ After the Giants traded him to the Cubs, he promptly proved that his former team had made a mistake by winning three home run titles in his first three years in the Windy City.

22. _____ In the four years that he won home run crowns he averaged 50 circuit clouts a season.

23. _____ From 1953–57 he hit 40 or more home runs in each season.

24. _____ Eight times he hit more than 40 home runs in a season but never hit 50.

25. _____ He broke into Cleveland's lineup after Ray Chapman was killed by a Carl Mays pitch.

26. _____ At the age of 37 this .344 lifetime hitter batted .389.

27. _____ A .327 lifetime batter, he had a career average that was higher than any other player at his position.

28. _____ This .331 lifetime hitter played in four World Series (1942–46) in a five-year period of time.

29. _____ This .316 lifetime batter collected more than 200 hits in four of his first five years in the majors.

30. _____ In his first two league Championship Series (1969–70), this .267 lifetime batter hit .500 and .583.

31. _____ A .344 lifetime hitter, he won a batting title at the age of 40.

32. _____ A .263 lifetime hitter, he played in consecutive World Series from 1906–08.

33. _____ A one-time 40-game winner, he posted the lowest career ERA (1.82) of all time.

34. _____ This super defensive shortstop played 25 years, most of them with the Browns; he was called "Rhody."

35. _____ He won back-to-back pennants with Cincinnati.

36. _____ He won two pennants and finished a runner-up ten times.

37. _____ He won World Series on both coasts, one in the East and three in the West.

38. _____ He won World Series 23 years apart.

39. _____ In 24 years of managing he won nine pennants—one in the National League and eight in the American League—and never finished lower than fourth in the standings.

40. _____ Called "The Tall Tactician," he finished first nine times, but ended up last 17 times.

41. _____ A one-time coach for John McGraw, with whom he played with the Orioles, he later managed Brooklyn to two pennants.

42. _____ Called "The Old Roman," he once managed St. Louis to four straight pennants; he was later the owner of the White Sox during the Black Sox scandal.

43. _____ No stranger to highs and lows, he won ten pennants but finished up his managerial career with four consecutive tenth-place finishes.

44. _____ Called "The Old Fox," he managed just one winner in 20 years, but he also became an owner who presided over three pennant winners and one World Series champ.

45. _____ Called "The Mighty Mite," he twice led one team to three consecutive pennants.

46. _____ Thirteen years in a row he hit 20 or more round-trippers—he slugged 426 lifetime—but he never won a home run crown.

47. _____ He drew more bases on balls than any other National League player, hit more home runs at his position than any other left-handed batter in the senior circuit, played on two world title teams, and got the winning hit of the 1975 fall classic.

48. _____ He won 268 games, posted a 2.86 ERA, chalked up 20 wins eight times, logged an 8–3 record in ALCS and World Series play, and won three Cy Young awards.

49. _____ He also posted a 2.86 ERA, while winning 311 games, copping ten consecutive strikeout titles, and picking up three Cy Young awards in the opposite league.

50. _____ Though he struck out 1,936 times, he batted .282, hit 475 career homers, won two four-base titles, and played on two championship teams, getting 12 hits for one of them.

51. _____ Possessor of the third highest number of hits in the American League, he won three batting crowns, banged 452 career homers, and won the Triple Crown.

52. _____ He hit 548 career homers, won eight four-base crowns, and copped three MVP awards.

112. ARE THEY IN THE HALL OF FAME?

There is not too much difference talent-wise between the players listed below. But 15 of them are in the Hall of Fame, and 15 of them are not. Write a "yes" in front of those who are and a "No" in front of those who aren't.

1. _____ Mel Parnell
2. _____ Earle Combs
3. _____ Gil Hodges
4. _____ Hack Wilson
5. _____ Ernie Lombardi
6. _____ Jim Bunning
7. _____ Minnie Minoso
8. _____ Bobby Doerr
9. _____ Pee Wee Reese
10. _____ Nelson Fox
11. _____ Bucky Walters
12. _____ Tony Oliva
13. _____ Red Schoendienst
14. _____ George Kell
15. _____ Rollie Fingers

16. _____ Rick Ferrell
17. _____ Walker Cooper
18. _____ Mickey Vernon
19. _____ Carl Furillo
20. _____ Dixie Walker
21. _____ Luis Aparicio
22. _____ Lou Boudreau
23. _____ Monte Irvin
24. _____ Hank Sauer
25. _____ Denny McLain
26. _____ Joe Cronin
27. _____ Phil Cavarretta
28. _____ Lefty Gomez
29. _____ Arky Vaughan
30. _____ Hoyt Wilhelm

What Have You Done Lately?

Career-wise, Dusty Rhodes was a less-than-mediocre pinch-hitter, but for one season, 1954, he was probably the best clutch-hitting pinch-hitter in baseball history.

In 1954, the year the Giants won the pennant and swept the Indians in the World Series, Rhodes seemed to come through almost every time he stepped to the plate with men on base in a clutch situation. Actually, he made 15 hits in 45 at bats, in pinch-hitting situations, for a .333 average. Overall, he batted .341 and he belted 15 home runs.

In the World Series that year, he made four hits in six plate appearances. Pinch-hitting, he batted safely all three times he stepped to the plate. All three pinch-hits were timely. In Game One he hit a three-run homer in the bottom of the tenth to provide the winning margin in a 5–2 contest. In Game Two his pinch-hit single tied the score at 1–1. Inserted in left field, he proceeded to hit a long home run en route to a Giant 3–1 win. In Game Three he delivered a pinch-hit single with the bases loaded to score the runs that turned out to be the tying and winning counters.

But after that season his star faded. Four years later, he was out of the big leagues. His seven-year pinch-hitting average was an anemic .212.

Another irony of Rhodes's 1954 performance was that in each one of his pinch-hitting appearances he batted for a Giant star—now a Hall of Famer—who in the 1951 World Series clubbed the ball for a .458 mark and stole home in the opening game.

Who was that Giant superstar of 1951—he got seven hits in the first two games—who bowed in favor of the Giant superstar of 1954?

(Answer appears on page 344.)

Moe the Pro

Moe Drabowsky was just a .426 winning percentage pitcher during his 17-year career but he was a 1.000 winning percentage moundsman in the 1966 fall classic, his only World Series appearance.

In Game One of the Orioles' four-game sweep of the Dodgers, Bird manager Hank Bauer summoned Drabowsky to relieve starter Dave McNally in the third inning with Baltimore clinging tenuously to a 4–2 lead. Drabowsky was superb. He pitched six and two thirds innings of shutout ball en route to the Orioles' 5–2 win. But it was the manner in which Drabowsky stifled the Dodgers that raised the eyebrows of veteran World Series observers. He allowed just one hit, issued two free passes, and struck out *11* batters, a fall classic record for pitchers in relief.

Drabowsky's pitching performance turned out to be the catalyst that the Birds' staff needed. In Game Two, Jim Palmer blanked Los Angeles, 9–0; in Game Three, Wally Bunker zipped the Dodgers, 1–0; and in Game Four, Dave McNally whitewashed manager Walter Alston's men, 1–0. In the last 33⅔ innings of the 1966 Series, Baltimore's staff did not allow the Dodgers a single run.

At one point in Game One, Drabowsky fanned six consecutive Los Angeles batters, another record for relief pitchers in World Series play.

A Cincinnati pitcher of 1919 recorded six consecutive outs via the strikeout route, but he permitted White Sox batters to reach base during the skein. A Giant pitcher topped that performance in 1921 when he got seven consecutive outs in strikeout fashion, but he permitted three Yankee batters to walk during the intervening time.

Can you name either the Red or the Giant pitcher who recorded a World Series first? If you can name both of them you will be a 1.000 winning pitcher—just like Moe Drabowsky!

(Answer appears on page 344.)

Chapter Twenty-one

BASEBALL'S BELIEVE IT OR NOT

WALTER JOHNSON of the Senators *won* the seventh game of the 1924 World Series and *lost* the seventh game of the 1925 fall classic.

RALPH TERRY of the Yankees *lost* the seventh game of the 1960 World Series and *won* the seventh game of the 1962 fall classic.

EDDIE LOPAT of the White Sox, Yankees, and Orioles batted *.211* in 11 seasons and *.211* in five World Series.

JIMMIE FOXX had a *.609* regular-season slugging average and a *.609* World Series slugging average.

STAN MUSIAL had 3,630 career hits, *1,815* of them on the road and *1,815* of them at home.

EDDIE SANICKI of the 1949 Phillies had three hits—all of them home runs.

WARREN SPAHN had *363* lifetime wins and *363* career hits.

DUTCH LEONARD of the 1916 Red Sox retired only one St. Louis batter before being taken out. The next day he started again and didn't allow *one* hit.

ART SHAMSKY of the Reds didn't enter one particular game in 1966 until the eighth inning, yet he hit three home runs in that extra-inning contest.

KENT MERCKER, Mark Wohlers, and Alejandro Pena of the 1991 Braves teamed up to pitch the sixth combined no-hitter in history, and the first ever in the National League.

335

TONY GWYNN has hit .300 for all 13 of his full-time seasons in the big leagues. The highlight of his career was the .394 he hit in 1994.

His next best season was his .370 average in 1987. It was the highest mark in the National League since Stan Musial of the 1948 Cardinals batted .375.

The following year, he batted .313, the lowest average ever by a National League batting crown winner.

DALE MURPHY of the Atlanta Braves hit 36 home runs in each season from 1982 to 1984. In 1985 he was off his norm—he hit 37.

DALE MURPHY did big things in back-to-back years. For example, he won RBI and MVP titles in 1982 and 1983, he won slugging average crowns in 1983 and 1984, and he won home run honors in 1984 and 1985.

STEVE BEDROSIAN of the 1985 Atlanta Braves started 37 games but didn't finish one of them. That's a major league record.

Two years later, with the Phillies, he finished 40 games that Philadelphia won—as a reliever.

His 5–3 record and 40 saves earned him the National League's Cy Young Award that year.

BO JACKSON's first major league home run, with Kansas City in 1986, was the longest in the history of Royal Stadium.

MYRIL HOAG of the 1934 Yankees in the first game of a doubleheader stroked six singles in six at-bats, a major league record for a nine-inning game, in a 15–3 win over the Red Sox.

In the second game manager Joe McCarthy moved up Hoag from seventh to second place in the line-up. But Hoag didn't elevate his performance. He got only one hit in five at-bats—a single.

It's pretty difficult to win a triple title, but it's three times more difficult for three men on the same team to tie for the triple title.

But that's what happened in 1957 when HARRY SIMPSON, GIL MCDOUGALD, and HANK BAUER of the Yankees each hit nine.

JACKIE JENSEN won the RBI title in the American League in both 1958 and 1959, but he didn't hit a triple in either one of those seasons.

In each of his other nine major league seasons, he did hit triples, including a league-leading 11 in 1956.

REGGIE JACKSON of the 1977 Yankees, who hit three home runs in Game Six of that year's fall classic, clubbed them off three different pitchers, throwing three different pitches: Burt Hooten of the Dodgers threw him a slider, Elias Sosa served him a sinking fastball, and Charlie Hough offered him a knuckleball.

ROCKY COLAVITO of the 1959 Indians led the American League in home runs. But after the season he was traded to the Tigers for Harvey Kuenn, who had led the junior circuit in batting.

TED WILLIAMS of the 1957 Red Sox was the only American League player to hit three home runs in each of two different games in the same season. The "Splendid Splinter" hit 38 home runs that year—at the age of 39.

DARRELL EVANS of the 1985 Tigers led the American League in home runs with 40 at the age of 38. He was the oldest player in the major leagues to win a four-base crown.

Ironically, the 1985 home run title was his first and only one.

Baseball's three greatest home run hitters—HANK AARON (755), BABE RUTH (714), and WILLIE MAYS (660)—each ended up his career in the same city in which he started it—but with different franchises.

Aaron got to the major leagues with the 1954 Milwaukee Braves, and he concluded it with the 1976 Milwaukee

Brewers. Ruth came to the big leagues with the 1914 Boston Red Sox, and he exited with the 1935 Boston Braves. Willie Mays broke in with the 1951 New York Giants, and he bowed out with the 1973 New York Mets.

WILLIE MAYS was both the youngest and oldest player to hit 50 or more home runs in a season. He was 24 years old when he hit 51 four-base blows with the New York Giants in 1955, and he was 34 years old when he blasted 52 round-trippers with the San Francisco Giants in 1965.

That made him the only player in history to hit 50 home runs in a season ten years apart.

JOE JACKSON of the 1911 Indians hit a record .408 as a rookie. But he didn't win the batting title. Ty Cobb, who batted .420, did.

"Shoeless Joe" of the 1920 White Sox batted a major league record .382 for a final major league season. But he finished third in the batting race, behind George Sisler and Tris Speaker, respectively.

Jackson never won a batting title, despite the fact that he hit .356 lifetime, third on the all-time list.

TY COBB of the 1911 Tigers hit only eight homers, but he drove home 144 runs, a record number for any player with fewer than ten round-trippers in a season.

Brothers MATTY and FELIPE ALOU did something that no other two brothers in baseball have done: they finished one-two in the 1966 batting race.

They share another, though dubious, distinction. On December 3, 1973, they were each sold by the Yankees to National League teams in separate transactions. Matty was dealt to the Cardinals and Felipe was moved to the Expos.

NORM CASH of the 1961 Tigers won the batting title with an average of .361. He was the last Tiger to do so. It was also the last time that he hit .300 in the majors.

TED WILLIAMS never got 200 hits in a season. The most he ever got was 194 in 1949.

338

LOU GEHRIG stole 102 career bases. Lou Brock stole 938. But Gehrig stole home 15 times. Brock never stole home.

ROBERTO CLEMENTE of the 1960 and 1971 Pittsburgh Pirates played in a total of 14 World Series games (the only ones in which he ever participated), and he batted safely in all 14 contests.

GROVER ALEXANDER won a National League record-tying 373 career games. But he never pitched a no-hitter.

On the other hand, Charles "Bumpus" Jones, with two lifetime victories, and Bobo Holloman, with three, each pitched a hitless game.

JOE DIMAGGIO hit safely in 56 consecutive games to set a record in 1941. The "Yankee Clipper" was stopped one night in Cleveland when Indian third baseman Kenny Keltner made two sensational stops and throws to get him by an eyelash at first base.

DiMaggio then went on to hit safely in 17 additional consecutive games. Overall, he batted safely in 73 of 74 games, almost half the total of 154 at that time.

Joe was no stranger to long batting streaks, though. In 1935, with the San Francisco Seals of the Pacific Coast League, he batted safely in 61 consecutive games to set a league mark.

ANSWERS SECTION

Inner-Chapter Answers

Introduction: Warren Sandell, who according to the *New York Times* "has a propensity to throw home-run pitches," never made it to the major leagues.

Ruth's Shadow: Lou Gehrig

The Shot Heard 'Round the World: Larry Jansen

The Asterisk Pitcher: Hank Aaron, the runner on first base, thought that Joe Adcock's game-winning hit had remained in play; so, when he saw Felix Mantilla racing toward home, he assumed that the one run would automatically bring the game to an end. Consequently, shortly after rounding second base, he stopped and headed for the dugout. Adcock, who had not noticed Aaron's error in judgment, naturally passed his teammate. Since the hitter had illegally passed the base runner, he was ruled out by the umpire. Aaron, on the other hand, could have been called out for illegally running the base paths. If both runners had been called out before Mantilla crossed home plate, no run would count because the third out would have been recorded before the winning run scored. But Mantilla did score and the Braves did win.

And Harvey Haddix has become an asterisk!

Exceptions to the Rule: Bob Cain, pitcher; Bob Swift, catcher; and Bill Stewart, umpire

The Mystery Death: Willard Hershberger

A Checkered Career: Hank Gowdy

Classic Comebacks: Gaylord Perry (Giants) and Ray Washburn (Cardinals); Jim Maloney (Reds) and Don Wilson (Astros)

Baseball's Number Game: Vic Willis

The Fateful Farewell: Al Gionfriddo was Furillo's pinch-runner, Eddie Miksis was Reiser's, and Eddie Miksis was the fielder.

The Iron Horse: Wally Pipp

To Catch a Thief: Bob O'Farrell

Two Strikes Against Him: Joe Sewell

Where Are the Iron Men: The pitchers are Steve Blass and Nelson Briles of the 1971 Pirates and Burt Hooton and Don Sutton of the 1977 Dodgers. Blass recorded the two complete games.

The Trivia Tandem: Larry McWilliams (starter) and Gene Garber (reliever)

The Black Sox: Ray Schalk, catcher, Eddie Collins, second baseman; and Red Faber, pitcher

The Shoe Polish Plays: Nippy Jones and Cleon Jones

The Shutout Series: Red Ames (Giants) and Chief Bender (Athletics)

A Man for All Seasons: Ed Barrow

Three Men on Third: Dazzy Vance, since there was no force, had rightful possession of the bag. Chick Fewster and Babe Herman, who were the trespassers, were declared out. Since that day, whenever someone says, "The Dodgers have three men on base," a listener with a keen sense of wit will invariably say, "Which one?"

What Have You Done lately: Monte Irvin

Moe the Pro: Hod Eller (Reds) and Jesse Barnes (Giants)

Chapter One Answers

1. The National League

1. Dave Justice (.313)
2. Carlos Garcia
3. Mike Piazza (1993)
4. Andy Benes
5. Rod Beck (Giants)
6. Mark Portugal
7. Fred McGriff (1989 Blue Jays)
8. Moises Alou (.339)
9. Lenny Dykstra
10. Jose Rijo
11. Darryl Kile
12. Mark Whiten
13. Raul Mondesi
14. Robby Thompson (second base, 1993)
15. Tom Browning (Reds)
16. Bret Saberhagen (Mets)
17. Ken Hill
18. Fred McGriff
19. Gary Sheffield (Padres to Marlins)
20. Marquis Grissom (Expos)
21. John Franco (1994–95)
22. Mickey Morandini
23. Tom Browning (1985)
24. Tony Gwynn (1984, 1987–89, and 1994–95 Padres)
25. Matt Williams (Giants)
26. Darryl Strawberry (252)
27. Jeff Bagwell (1991)
28. Jay Bell (Pirates)
29. Deion Sanders (Atlanta Falcons and Braves, 1992)
30. Barry Larkin (Reds)
31. Joe Orsulak (22)
32. Kurt Abbott
33. Tom Glavine
34. Chris Hammond
35. Bobby Bonilla
36. Kevin Stocker (1993)
37. Sammy Sosa (1993)
38. Hal Morris
39. Craig Biggio
40. Barry Larkin (1993)
41. Ozzie Smith (Cardinals)
42. Dante Bichette
43. Mike Piazza (1993)
44. Tony Gwynn
45. Darren Lewis (Giants)
46. Javier Lopez (Braves, 24)
47. Jeff Blauser
48. Pedro Martinez
49. Jeff Kent (21 and 80)
50. Dave Hollins (1992)
51. Darren Daulton
52. Gregg Jeffries (1993–94)
53. Jeff Bagwell
54. Al Martin
55. Ray Lankford
56. Walt Weiss
57. Raul Mondesi

58. Tony Gwynn
59. Matt Williams
60. Mark Portugal
61. Barry Bonds (1990, 1992–93 Giants)
62. Bip Roberts (Padres)
63. Ramon Martinez (22)
64. David Nied
65. Tom Henke
66. Steve Cook
67. John Hudek (Astros)
68. John Smiley
69. Bret Boone
70. Randy Myers (Cubs)
71. Curt Schilling
72. Bret Saberhagen
73. Mel Rojas
74. Bryan Harvey (46 with 1991 Angels and 45 with 1993 Marlins)
75. Steve Avery (23)
76. Ryan Klesko (Braves)
77. Danny Jackson
78. Wil Cordero (15)
79. Todd Hundley (Mets)
80. Lenny Dykstra
81. Mark Grace
82. Tom Browning
83. Ken Caminiti (Astros)
84. Tony Gwynn (1994)
85. Ozzie Smith (shortstop)
86. Marvin Freeman
87. Eric Karros
88. Phil Plantier (1993 Padres)
89. Barry Bonds (Bobby)
90. Darryl Strawberry (1987–88 Mets)
91. Ramon Martinez
92. Allen Watson (1993)
93. Joze Guzman (1993 Cubs)
94. Brett Butler
95. Tom Pagnozzi (Cardinals)
96. John Wetteland (1993)
97. Robb Nen (1993 Rangers and 1994 Marlins)
98. John Smoltz
99. Greg Maddux (1994 Braves)
100. Ken Hill

2. The American League

1. Ken Griffey Jr. (1993 Mariners)
2. J. T. Snow (Jack)
3. Wally Joyner (1986–87 Angels)
4. Roger Clemens (1986–87 Red Sox)
5. Kenny Rogers (Rangers)
6. Bobby Witt (1990 Rangers)
7. Scott Erickson
8. Greg Vaughn
9. Dave Winfield (Yankees, Angels, Blue Jays, Twins, and Indians)
10. Jimmy Key (Yankees)
11. Albert Belle (1995 Indians)
12. Mo Vaughn
13. Cal Ripken (1983 and 1991)

14. Brady Anderson (Orioles)
15. John Valentin (Red Sox)
16. Scott Cooper
17. Marty Cordova (Twins)
18. Paul O'Neill (Yankees)
19. Joe Carter
20. Frank Thomas (1993–94 White Sox)
21. Carlos Baerga (1992–93 Indians)
22. Bob Hamelin (1994–95 Royals)
23. Cal Eldred (1992)
24. Rick Aguilera
25. Mark Langston
26. Dennis Eckersley
27. Randy Johnson (308 with 1993 Mariners)
28. Albert Belle (Indians)
29. Ivan Rodriguez (Rangers)
30. John Olerud (.363 with the 1993 Blue Jays)
31. Edgar Martinez (1992 and 1995)
32. Dennis Eckersley (1992)
33. Tony Fernandez
34. Kirby Puckett (1989)
35. Ricky Bones (1994)
36. Jeff Montgomery
37. Dennis Martinez (Indians)
38. Jason Bere
39. Juan Guzman (Blue Jays)
40. Jack McDowell (1992–93)
41. Mike Henneman
42. Jose Canseco (1988 A's)
43. Chris Hoiles (1993)
44. Mike Stanley (1993 Yankees)
45. Cal Ripken
46. Harold Baines (Bill Veeck)
47. Mike Mussina
48. Jose Canseco (Rangers)
49. Cecil Fielder
50. Don Mattingly (1984 and 1985)
51. Cal Ripken (Orioles)
52. Frank Thomas (41 in 1993)
53. Albert Belle (1992–95)
54. Garret Anderson (Angels)
55. Cal Eldred (1993 Brewers)
56. Mark Langston
57. Mark McGwire (1987 A's)
58. Ken Griffey, Jr.
59. Juan Gonzalez (Rangers)
60. Otis Nixon
61. Chris Bosio
62. Rickey Henderson (1980, 1982–83 A's)
63. Lee Smith
64. Chuck Knoblauch
65. David Cone (Royals)
66. Dennis Martinez
67. Dave Winfield (Twins)
68. Albert Belle
69. Kenny Lofton
70. Tim Raines
71. Duane Ward (676 to 664)
72. Rickey Henderson (93 in 1988)
73. Wade Boggs (Yankees)

74. Lou Whitaker
75. Aaron Sele
76. Rafael Palmeiro
77. Tim Naehring
78. Roger Clemens (1986)
79. Cecil Fielder (1990)
80. Mike Blowers
81. Wade Boggs (1983–89 Red Sox)
82. Tony Phillips
83. Paul O'Neill (1994)
84. Paul Molitor (Blue Jays)
85. Robin Ventura
86. Eddie Murray
87. Kirby Puckett
88. Tim Salmon
89. Mark McGwire (1987–90)
90. Pat Hentgen (Blue Jays)
91. Jay Buhner
92. Felix Fermin
93. Randy Johnson (6–10)
94. Ken Ryan
95. Don Mattingly
96. Paul Molitor (1993)
97. Paul Molitor (1993)
98. Joe Carter
99. Devon White
100. Juan Guzman

3. Present-Day Gold Glove Champs

1. Don Mattingly (Grace and Galarraga have two each.)
2. Robby Alomar (Lind, Thompson, and Biggio have won one.)
3. Gary Gaetti (Wallach and Williams have copped three awards.)
4. Ozzie Smith (Trammell and Fernandez have each won two.)
5. Andre Dawson (Winfield* has won five in the American League.)
6. Kirby Puckett (Gwynn trails with five.)
7. Devon White (Bonds is one behind with five.)
8. All of the contestants at this position have won three.**
9. Mark Langston (Maddux won five in a row from 1990 to 1994.

** Pena also won one Gold Glove in the American League, so his overall total is four.
* Winfield also won two Gold Gloves in the National League, so his overall total is seven.

They Went to School At . . .

1. b	8. r	15. s	22. a
2. d	9. u	16. j	23. h
3. k	10. w	17. f	24. g
4. q	11. x	18. o	25. c
5. v	12. i	19. n	
6. p	13. t	20. y	
7. l	14. e	21. m	

5. How Good Is .300?

Batting Champs

1. Mickey Mantle (.298)
2. Tommy Davis (.294)
3. Norm Cash (.271)
4. Hal Chase (.291)
5. George Stirnweiss (.268)
6. Carl Yastrzemski (.285)
7. Pete Runnels (.291)
8. Bobby Avila (.281)
9. Harry Walker (.296)
10. Dick Groat (.286)
11. Lou Boudreau (.295)
12. Mickey Vernon (.286)
13. Debs Garms (.293)
14. Heinie Zimmerman (.295)
15. Pete Reiser (.295)
16. Larry Doyle (.290)
17. Ferris Fain (.290)
18. Alex Johnson (.288)
19. Phil Cavarretta (.293)
20. Carl Furillo (.299)

.300 Hitters

1. Johnny Pesky (.307)
2. Enos Slaughter (.300)
3. Joe Cronin (.302)
4. Mel Ott (.304)
5. Bill Dickey (.313)
6. Lloyd Waner (.316)
7. Bob Meusel (.309)
8. Joe Jackson (.356)
9. Hack Wilson (.307)
10. Earl Averill (.318)
11. Sam Rice (.322)
12. Dale Mitchell (.312)
13. Hank Greenberg (.313)
14. Eddie Collins (.333)
15. Earle Combs (.325)
16. Babe Herman (.324)
17. Kiki Cuyler (.321)
18. Frankie Frisch (.316)
19. Pie Traynor (.320)
20. Mickey Cochrane (.320)

6. Who Did It Twice?

National League

1. Willie Mays
2. Harry Walker
3. Dixie Walker
4. Carl Furillo
5. Jackie Robinson

1. Lefty O'Doul
2. Tommy Davis
3. Henry Aaron
4. Ernie Lombardi
5. Richie Ashburn

1. George Kell
2. Al Kaline
3. Norm Cash
4. Mickey Mantle
5. Harvey Kuenn

1. Jimmie Foxx
2. Luke Appling
3. Mickey Vernon
4. Pete Runnels
5. Ferris Fain

7. The Fabulous Fifties

1. Roger Maris
2. Babe Ruth
3. Babe Ruth
4. Jimmie Foxx
5. Hank Greenberg
6. Hack Wilson
7. Babe Ruth
8. Babe Ruth
9. Ralph Kiner
10. Mickey Mantle

11. Mickey Mantle
12. Willie Mays
13. George Foster
14. Both answers can be
15. Johnny Mize or Ralph Kiner
16. Willie Mays
17. Cecil Fielder
18. Jimmie Foxx
19. Albert Belle

8. The (500) Home Run Club

1. Hank Aaron
2. Babe Ruth
3. Willie Mays
4. Frank Robinson
5. Harmon Killebrew
6. Reggie Jackson
7. Mike Schmidt
8. Mickey Mantle
9. Jimmie Foxx

10. Ted Williams or Willie McCovey
11. Ted Williams or Willie McCovey
12. Eddie Mathews or Ernie Banks
13. Eddie Mathews or Ernie Banks
14. Mel Ott

9. They Hit for Power and Average

National League

1. Heinie Zimmerman
2. Rogers Hornsby
3. Rogers Hornsby
4. Chuck Klein
5. Joe Medwick
6. Johnny Mize

American League

1. Nap Lajoie
2. Ty Cobb
3. Babe Ruth
4. Jimmie Foxx
5. Lou Gehrig
6. Ted Williams
7. Ted Williams
8. Ted Williams
9. Mickey Mantle
10. Frank Robinson
11. Carl Yastrzemski

10. The 3,000-Hit Club

1. Pete Rose
2. Ty Cobb
3. Hank Aaron
4. Stan Musial
5. Tris Speaker
6. Carl Yastrzemski
7. Cap Anson
8. Honus Wagner
9. Eddie Collins
10. Willie Mays
11. Nap Lajoie
12. George Brett
13. Paul Waner
14. Robin Yount
15. Dave Winfield
16. Eddie Murray
17. Rod Carew
18. Lou Brock
19. Al Kaline
20. Roberto Clemente

11. Triple Crown Winners

1. Nap Lajoie
2. Ty Cobb
3. Rogers Hornsby
4. Rogers Hornsby
5. Chuck Klein or Jimmie Foxx
6. Chuck Klein or Jimmie Foxx
7. Lou Gehrig
8. Joe Medwick
9. Ted Williams
10. Ted Williams
11. Mickey Mantle
12. Frank Robinson
13. Carl Yastrzemski

12. Highest Lifetime Average for Position

National League

1. Bill Terry
2. Rogers Hornsby
3. Honus Wagner
4. Pie Traynor
5. Riggs Stephenson
6. Paul Waner
7. Lefty O'Doul
8. Eugene Hargrave

American League

1. Lou Gehrig and George Sisler
2. Nap Lajoie
3. Cecil Travis
4. Frank Baker
5. Ty Cobb
6. Joe Jackson
7. Ted Williams
8. Mickey Cochrane

13. Highest Single Season Average for Position

National League

1. Bill Terry
2. Rogers Hornsby
3. Arky Vaughan
4. Fred Lindstrom
5. Lefty O'Doul
6. Tony Gwynn
7. Babe Herman
8. Chief Meyers

American League

1. George Sisler
2. Nap Lajoie
3. Luke Appling
4. George Brett
5. Ty Cobb
6. Joe Jackson
7. Ted Williams
8. Bill Dickey

14. The Year They Hit the Heights

1. Rogers Hornsby
2. Ty Cobb
3. Ted Williams
4. Babe Ruth
5. Joe DiMaggio
6. Stan Musial
7. Mickey Mantle
8. Roberto Clemente
9. Jackie Robinson
10. Charlie Keller

15. Matching Averages

1. Ty Cobb
2. Rogers Hornsby
3. Tris Speaker
4. Babe Ruth
5. Bill Terry
6. Stan Musial
7. Honus Wagner
8. Jimmie Foxx
9. Mickey Cochrane
10. Mel Ott

16. Once Is Not Enough

1. Lou Gehrig
2. Rocky Colavito
3. Mark Whiten
4. Gil Hodges
5. Pat Seerey
6. Joe Adcock
7. Mike Schmidt
8. Willie Mays
9. Bob Horner

17. National League Home Run Kings

1. Mike Schmidt
2. Ralph Kiner
3. Mel Ott
4. Johnny Mize
5. Eddie Mathews or Johnny Bench
6. Eddie Mathews or Johnny Bench
7. Barry Bonds or Duke Snider or Fred McGriff*
8. Barry Bonds or Duke Snider or Fred McGriff*
9. Barry Bonds or Duke Snider or Fred McGriff*

18. American League Home Run Kings

1. Babe Ruth
2. Harmon Killebrew
3.–8. Any combination of Jimmie Foxx, Frank Baker, Hank Greenberg, Reggie Jackson, Ted Williams, and Mickey Mantle
9.–10. Either Lou Gehrig or Jim Rice

*Fred McGriff also won one four-base crown in the American League with the 1989 Blue Jays.

11.–16. Any combination of Frank Howard, Jose Canseco, Joe DiMaggio, Gorman Thomas, Juan Gonzalez, and Dick Allen

17.–20. Any combination of Roger Maris, George Scott, Graig Nettles, and Carl Yastrzemski

19. Would You Pinch-Hit?

1. No (.294)
2. No (.283)
3. No (.290)
4. No (.289)
5. Yes (.326)
6. No (.270)
7. Yes (.304)
8. No (.272)
9. Yes (.312)
10. Yes (.296)
11. Yes (.286)
12. Yes (.284)
13. No (.269)
14. No (.261)
15. Yes (.287)
16. Same (.276)
17. Yes (.304)
18. No (.264)
19. Yes (.293)
20. Yes (.273)

20. Decades of Batting Champs

National League

1. Pirates
2. Reds
3. Phillies
4. Reds
5. Cubs
6. Dodgers
7. Reds
8. Braves
9. Expos
10. Padres

American League

1. Senators
2. Indians
3. Tigers
4. White Sox
5. Yankees
6. Athletics
7. Red Sox
8. Angels
9. Red Sox
10. Rangers

21. Sub-.320 Batting Leaders

1. Terry Pendleton
2. Rod Carew
3. Frank Robinson
4. Tony Gwynn
5. George Stirnweiss
6. Elmer Flick
7. Carl Yastrzemski

22. .390-Plus Runners-up

1. Joe Jackson
2. Ty Cobb
3. Babe Ruth
4. Babe Herman
5. Al Simmons

23. Stepping into the Box

1. L
2. R
3. S
4. R
5. S
6. L
7. S
8. R
9. L
10. S
11. R
12. L
13. L
14. R
15. L
16. L
17. R
18. R
19. S
20. S
21. L
22. R
23. S
24. L
25. R
26. S
27. R
28. L
29. S
30. S

Chapter Three Answers

24. Famous Home Run Pitches

1. Ralph Terry
2. Robin Roberts
3. Ralph Branca
4. Don Newcombe
5. Jack Billingham
6. Al Downing
7. Howie Pollet
8. Barney Schultz
9. Bob Lemon
10. Bob Purkey
11. Dennis Eckersley
12. Charlie Leibrandt
13. Mitch Williams

25. The Pitching Masters

1. Cy Young
2. Walter Johnson
3. Christy Mathewson or Grover Alexander
4. Christy Mathewson or Grover Alexander
5. Warren Spahn
6. Steve Carlton
7. Eddie Plank
8. Nolan Ryan or Don Sutton
9. Nolan Ryan or Don Sutton
10. Phil Niekro
11. Gaylord Perry
12. Tom Seaver
13. Lefty Grove or Early Wynn
14. Lefty Grove or Early Wynn

The Perfect Game

1. Tom Browning
2. Kenny Rogers
3. Ernie Shore
4. Jim Hunter
5. Dennis Martinez
6. Jim Bunning
7. Cy Young
8. Addie Joss
9. Sandy Koufax
10. Don Larsen
11. Charlie Robertson
12. Mike Witt
13. Len Barker

27. Multiple No-Hitters

1. Nolan Ryan
2. Sandy Koufax
3. Bob Feller or Jim Maloney
4. Bob Feller or Jim Maloney

5–15. Any combination of the following: Johnny Vander Meer, Steve Busby, Ken Holtzman, Don Wilson, Dean Chance, Jim Bunning, Warren Spahn, Sam Jones, Carl Erskine, Allie Reynolds, Virgil Trucks

28. Back-to-Back 20-Game Winners

1. h
2. s
3. p
4. n
5. w
6. d
7. v
8. t
9. k
10. m
11. f
12. q
13. o
14. e
15. x
16. j
17. a
18. i
19. c
20. u
21. g
22. r
23. b
24. l
25. y
26. z

29. The Flamethrowers

1. Nolan Ryan
2. Sandy Koufax
3. Mickey Lolich
4. Sam McDowell
5. Bob Feller
6. Steve Carlton
7. Walter Johnson
8. Rube Waddell
9. Vida Blue
10. J. R. Richard
11. Mike Scott
12. Randy Johnson

30. Blue-Chip Pitchers

1. Whitey Ford (.690)
2. Allie Reynolds (.630)
3. Jim Palmer (.638)
4. Mort Cooper (.631)
5. Tom Seaver (.603)
6. Vic Raschi (.667)
7. Sal Maglie (.657)
8. Dizzy Dean (.644)
9. Sandy Koufax (.655)
10. Lefty Gomez (.649)

31. 200 Times a Loser

1. Cy Young
2. Bobo Newsom
3. Walter Johnson
4. Warren Spahn
5. Grover Alexander
6. Red Ruffing
7. Paul Derringer
8. Robin Roberts
9. Bob Friend
10. Early Wynn

32. Winding Up

1. L
2. L
3. R
4. L
5. R
6. R
7. L
8. L
9. R
10. R
11. R
12. R
13. L
14. L
15. R
16. R
17. L
18. L
19. R
20. L
21. L
22. L
23. R
24. R
25. R
26. R
27. L
28. R
29. L
30. L

33. Good-Hitting Pitchers

1. Jack Bentley (1923 Giants)
2. Jack Tobin (1942 Braves)
3. Ken Brett (1973 Phillies)
4. Red Ruffing
5. Don Newcombe (Brooklyn Dodgers)
6. Dave McNally (1969–70 Orioles)
7. Tom Hughes (1906 Senators)
8. Babe Ruth
9. Mike Cuellar (1970 Orioles)
10. Vic Raschi (1953 Yankees)
11. Allie Reynolds (1947, 1949, 1953 Yankees)
12. Tony Cloninger (1966 Braves)
13. Bob Gibson (Cardinals)
14. Joe Wood
15. Bucky Walters
16. Don Drysdale (1958, 1965 Los Angeles Dodgers)
17. Wes Ferrell
18. Red Lucas
19. George Uhle
20. Walter Johnson (1925 Senators)
21. Andy Messersmith
22. Lewis Wiltse
23. Warren Spahn
24. Bob Lemon
25. Cy Young

Chapter Four Answers

34. Four Bases to Score

1. d
2. c
3. b
4. b
5. a
6. b
7. d (1910, 1913, and 1917)
8. a (1939–40)
9. c
10. d
11. a
12. a
13. c (50 in 1995)
14. d
15. d
16. d (170–161)
17. a
18. c (for the 1948 Indians)
19. d
20. c
21. c (1951–52)
22. c (1962–63)
23. d
24. d
25. b
26. c
27. a
28. b
29. c (.401 in 1930)
30. d
31. a
32. d
33. c (.407 in 1920 and .420 in 1922)
34. b (30–7 in 1934)
35. a (.349)
36. d
37. a (41)
38. a (33–25 in 1925)
39. a
40. b (51 in 1947)
41. a (9)
42. c (36)
43. b
44. c
45. b
46. b (1973)
47. b
48. c
49. b
50. d
51. d
52. d
53. c (1946–52)
54. d (1968)
55. a
56. b (.422 in 1901)
57. a
58. c (1922)
59. b
60. d
61. d (1964)
62. d
63. a
64. b
65. b (Indians)
66. c
67. d
68. c (1226)
69. c (1964)

70. d
71. d (Hunter was 5–3 in series play.)
72. a (1915)
73. c
74. c (1952)
75. d
76. d
77. c (1961)

35. From Ruth to Reggie

1. Hank Greenberg
2. Johnny Allen (1937)
3. Earl Averill
4. Bob Feller
5. Frank Robinson
6. Hank Greenberg
7. Chris Chambliss
8. Hank Borowy
9. Phil Masi
10. Joe McCarthy
11. Joe Gordon
12. Rocky Colavito
13. Stu Miller
14. Lou Boudreau
15. Ted Williams
16. Cal Abrams
17. Bobo Holloman (Browns, 1953)
18. Chuck Stobbs
19. Johnny Antonelli
20. Willie Mays
21. Hank Aaron
22. Vic Wertz
23. Pat Dobson
24. Tommy Byrne
25. Gil McDougald
26. Sal Maglie
27. Yogi Berra
28. Tony Kubek
29. Pirates (1925)
30. Harry Heilmann (.403 in 1923)
31. Casey Stengel
32. Tom Zachary
33. Tracy Stallard
34. Luis Arroyo
35. Johnny Blanchard
36. Frank Lary
37. Casey Stengel
38. Willie Davis
39. First Base
40. Happy Chandler
41. Frank Robinson
42. Norm Siebern
43. Al Rosen
44. Don Demeter
45. Bill McKechnie
46. Ken Harrelson
47. Denny McLain (31–6 in 1968)
48. Nippy Jones
49. Cleon Jones
50. Curt Flood
51. Rod Carew (1972)
52. Gene Tenace (1972)
53. Dick Williams
54. Howard Ehmke
55. Phillies (1930)
56. Allie Reynolds
57. Philadelphia (Jimmie Foxx, A's; Chuck Klein, Phillies)
58. Bill Terry
59. Jerome and Paul Dean
60. Bobby Brown (1947, 1949–51)
61. Lefty O'Doul (254, 1929) and Bill Terry (254, 1930)
62. Spud Chandler (.717)

63. Whitey Ford (8)
64. Bobby Richardson (209, 1962)
65. Duke Snider (1956)
66. Reggie Jackson (1980 Yankees)
67. Johnny Burnett (1932 Indians)
68. Bump Hadley (1937)
69. Jeff Heath
70. Maury Wills
71. Sandy Koufax (1966)
72. Charlie Grimm
73. Yogi Berra
74. Johnny Edwards
75. Rogers Hornsby
76. Lou Gehrig (1931)
77. Jack Coombs (13, 1910 Athletics)
78. Joe Morgan

Chapter Seven Answers

36. Baseball's Who's Who

1. Walter Johnson
2. Bill McKechnie (Pirates, 1925; Cardinals, 1928; and Reds, 1939–40)
3. Al Kaline of the Tigers, who was 20 in 1955
4. Ted Williams of the Red Sox, who was 40 in 1958
5. Mike Higgins of the 1938 Red Sox
6. Walt Dropo of the 1952 Tigers
7. Joe Jackson (1920)
8. Ty Cobb, whose .401 for the Tigers in 1922 finished second to George Sisler's .420
9. Tom Zachary of the 1929 Yankees
10. "Iron Man" Joe McGinnity of the 1903 Giants
11. Casey Stengel
12. Jimmie Foxx (A's, 1932–33; and Red Sox, 1938)
13. Dizzy Dean
14. Harry Heilmann of the 1921, 1923, 1925, and 1927 Tigers
15. Ted Williams of the 1941–42, 1947–48, and 1957–58 Red Sox
16. Eddie Robinson (1948)
17. Ralph Houk
18. Joe McCarthy
19. Casey Stengel
20. Johnny Frederick of the 1932 Dodgers
21. Joe Cronin of the 1943 Red Sox
22. Ed Reulbach of the 1906–08 Cubs
23. Lefty Grove of the 1929–31 Athletics
24. Grover Alexander
25. Mel Ott of the 1932, 1934, and 1937 Giants
26. Ralph Kiner of the 1947–48, and 1952 Pirates
27. Wes Ferrell
28. Walter Johnson
29. Luke Appling (1936 and 1943)
30. Mark Littell
31. Hal Newhouser (1944–45)
32. Rube Bressler
33. Harmon Killebrew
34. Hank Aaron
35. Norm Cash
36. Dave Winfield (Blue Jays)
37. Red Ruffing
38. Red Lucas
39. Lefty Grove
40. Jimmie Foxx: batting, 1933 (Athletics) and 1938 (Red Sox); home runs,

1932–33, 1935 (Athletics) and 1939 (Red Sox).
41. Mickey Mantle (1956)
42. Roy Face
43. Ted Williams (1941–42 and 1947)
44. Cy Young
45. Jim Bottomley
46. Roger Cramer
47. Mike Marshall of the 1974 Dodgers
48. Steve Carlton of the 1972, 1977, 1980, and 1982 Phillies
49. Greg Maddux of the 1992 Cubs and 1993–95 Atlanta Braves
50. Fred Lynn of the 1975 Red Sox
51. Mark Davis of the 1989 Padres
52. Mike Schmidt of the 1974–76 Phillies
53. Frank Thomas of the 1993–94 White Sox
54. Barry Bonds of the 1992 Pirates and 1993 San Francisco Giants
55. Gaylord Perry (1972 Indians and 1978 Padres)
56. Tony Gwynn, who hit .394 for the Padres in 1994
57. Pete Rose
58. Ferguson Jenkins (1967–72)
59. Gaylord Perry of the Giants, Indians, and Padres
60. Jim Palmer of the Orioles
61. Sparky Lyle
62. Phil Niekro (21–20) of the 1979 Braves
63. Rod Carew (.388 with the Twins and .339 with the Angels)
64. Tom Seaver of the 1968–76 Mets

37. Matching Names

1.	Bobby Thomson	11.	Honus Wagner
2.	Allie Reynolds	12.	Tris Speaker
3.	Ted Williams	13.	Babe Ruth
4.	Johnny Mize	14.	Walter Johnson
5.	Dom DiMaggio	15.	Lou Gehrig
6.	Casey Stengel	16.	Carl Hubbell
7.	Tommy Henrich	17.	Mickey Mantle
8.	Vernon Law	18.	Luke Appling
9.	Joe DiMaggio	19.	Paul Waner
10.	Ty Cobb	20.	Frankie Frisch

38. First Names

1.	Bill	11.	Charles Dillon
2.	Paul	12.	Fred
3.	Jerome	13.	Harry
4.	Larry	14.	Leroy
5.	Elwin	15.	Enos
6.	George	16.	Charles
7.	Joe	17.	Edward
8.	Johnny	18.	Leon
9.	Lynwood	19.	Robert
10.	Edwin	20.	James

39. Middle Names

1.	"The Hat"	7.	"The Lip"
2.	"The Man"	8.	"The Whip"
3.	"The Cat"	9.	"King Kong"
4.	"The Dutch Master"	10.	"Puddin' Head"
5.	"The Barber"	11.	"The Crow"
6.	"Louisiana Lightning"	12.	"Home Run"

13. "Poosh 'Em Up"
14. "The Kid"
15. "Pie"
16. "Bobo"

17. "Birdie"
18. "Twinkletoes"
19. "Three Finger"
20. "Pee Wee"

40. Last Names

1. Medwick
2. Crawford
3. Jackson
4. Wood
5. Dugan
6. Piniella
7. Greenberg
8. Cochrane
9. Feller
10. Grimm

11. Reiser
12. Bottomley
13. Doby
14. Newhouser
15. Houk
16. Keeler
17. Murphy
18. Turner
19. Jones
20. Hubbell

41. Preset-Day Players

1. c	5. t	9. k	13. p	17. l
2. f	6. r	10. b	14. e	18. i
3. g	7. j	11. s	15. q	19. h
4. n	8. a	12. m	16. o	20. d

42. Did They or Didn't They?

1. False (Don Drysdale hit seven twice.)
2. False (Johnny Bench .389)
3. True (1955)
4. False (Don Newcombe, 1956)
5. True (1990 and 1992 Pirates; 1993 San Francisco Giants)
6. True
7. True (51 in 1955 and 52 in 1965)
8. True
9. False (Don Mattingly, 1985)
10. True
11. True (1951, 1953, and 1955)
12. False (Hank Aaron)
13. True
14. True (1966)
15. False (Dan Bankhead did, too.)
16. True (1969, 1973, 1977–78)
17. True (.300 for 1980 Yankees)
18. False (Joe Black, 1952)
19. False (Elston Howard, 1963)
20. True (1949)
21. False (Lou Brock did not.)
22. True (Burt Hooton, Elias Sosa, and Charlie Hough)
23. True
24. False (Frank Robinson, 1966)
25. True
26. False (Larry Doby, 1948)
27. False (Jim Gilliam, 1953)
28. True (1957)
29. False (Jimmie Foxx, 50 in 1938)
30. False (Marshall Bridges, 1962)
31. True
32. False (Vida Blue, 301 in 1971)
33. True (7)
34. False (Mudcat Grant, 1965)
35. True (Maury Wills, Jim Gilliam, John Roseboro, Tommy Davis, Willie Davis, and Lou Johnson)
36. False (Mickey Lolich, 1968)
37. False (Willie Wilson, 705 in 1980)
38. True (284)
39. True (the 1950s, 1960s, 1970s, and 1980s)
40. False (Rod Carew, .328)
41. True (1965–67)
42. False (Max Carey had 738; Wills, 586.)

43. True
44. True
45. True (.302–.298)
46. False (Roberto Cle-
mente, 1964–65)
47. True (1955)
48. False (He won two AL
titles, 1972 and 1974.)
49. True (1985)
50. True (1980)

43. The Trailblazers

1. Thompson-Brown
2. Roberts
3. Thomas
4. Howard
5. Trice
6. Doby
7. Banks-Baker
8. Black
9. Green
10. Paula
11. Robinson
12. Jethroe
13. Alston-Lawrence
14. Thompson-Irvin
15. Virgil
16. Hairston

44. Black Clouters

1.–3. Willie Mays, Hank
Aaron, or Reggie
Jackson
4.–5. Willie McCovey or
Jim Rice
6.–12. Any combination of
Larry Doby, Dick
Allen, Willie Stargell,
Ernie Banks, George
Foster, Fred McGriff,
or Cecil Fielder

13.–22. Any combination of
Frank Robinson,
George Scott, Ben
Oglivie, Jesse Bar-
field, Andre Daw-
son, Ken Griffey,
Darryl Strawberry,
Kevin Mitchell,
Barry Bonds, or
Albert Belle

45. Single-Season Sluggers

1. Willie Mays
2. George Foster
3. Willie Mays
4. Frank Robinson
5. Hank Aaron
6. George Bell
7. Ken Griffey
8. Frank Thomas
9. Reggie Jackson
10. Darryl Strawberry

11. Nate Colbert
12. Andre Dawson
13. Andres Galarraga
14. Gary Sheffield

46. National League Batting Champs

1. Robinson
2. Mays
3. Aaron
4. Aaron
5. Clemente
6. Davis
7. Davis
8. Clemente
9. Clemente
10. Alou
11. Clemente
12. Carty
13. Williams
14. Garr
15. Madlock
16. Madlock
17. Parker
18. Parker
19. Madlock
20. Oliver
21. Madlock
22. Gwynn
23. McGee
24. Raines
25. Gwynn
26. Gwynn
27. Gwynn
28. McGee
29. Pendleton
30. Sheffield
31. Galarraga
32. Gwynn
33. Gwynn

47. American League Batting Champs

1. Oliva
2. Oliva
3. Robinson
4. Carew
5. Johnson
6. Oliva
7. Carew
8. Carew
9. Carew
10. Carew
11. Carew
12. Carew
13. Wilson
14. Puckett
15. Franco
16. Martinez
17. Martinez

48. Rookies of the Year

1. Robinson
2. Newcombe
3. Jethroe
4. Mays
5. Black
6. Gilliam

49. The Hall of Fame

1–25. Any combination of
the following players:
Jackie Robinson
Roy Campanella
Satchel Paige
Buck Leonard
Josh Gibson
Cool Papa Bell
Roberto Clemente
Monte Irvin
Judy Johnson
Ernie Banks
John "Pop" Lloyd
Martin Dihigo

Willie Mays
Oscar Charleston
Hank Aaron
Lou Brock
Bob Gibson
Juan Marichal
Frank Robinson
Willie McCovey
Ray Dandridge
Billy Williams
Willie Stargell
Leon Day
Reggie Jackson

50. South of the Border: Yesterday I

1. Bobby Avila (1954 Indians)
2. Fernando Valenzuela (1981 Los Angeles Dodgers)
3. Al Lopez (1954 Indians and 1959 White Sox)
4. Roger Moret (1973 and 1975)
5. Luis Aparicio (1956 White Sox)
6. Mike Gonzalez (1912–32, excepting 1913, 1922–23, and 1930, Boston Braves, Reds, Cardinals, New York Giants, and Cubs)
7. Orlando Cepeda (1958 San Francisco Giants)
8. Tony Perez (1975 Reds)
9. Zoilo Versalles (1965 Twins)
10. Roberto Clemente (1966 Pirates)

51. South of the Border: Yesterday II

1. Ed Figueroa (1978 Yankees)
2. Juan Marichal (1963 and 1968 San Francisco Giants)
3. Juan Nieves (1987 Brewers)
4. Willie Hernandez (1984 Tigers)
5. Pedro Ramos (1958–61 Washington Senators and Minnesota Twins)
6. Chico Carrasquel (1950)
7. Tony Oliva (1964 Twins)
8. Adolph Luque (1923 Reds)
9. Luis Tiant (1968 Indians; 1973–74 and 1976 Red Sox)
10. Hector Lopez (1960 Yankees)

52. South of the Border: Today I

1. Benito Santiago (Padres)
2. Tony Fernandez (.982)
3. Raul Mondesi
4. Ozzie Guillen (1985 White Sox)
5. Andres Galarraga (1993 Rockies)
6. Julio Franco (1991 Rangers)
7. Edgar Martinez (1992 Mariners)
8. Jose Canseco (A's)
9. Juan Gonzalez (1992–93 Rangers)
10. Robby Alomar (Blue Jays)

53. South of the Border: Today II

1. Carlos Baerga (1992–93 Indians)
2. Ruben Sierra
3. Devon White
4. Danny Tartabull
5. Jose Rijo
6. Sammy Sosa
7. Dennis Martinez
8. Juan Guzman
9. Chili Davis
10. Bernie Williams

54. One-Town Men

1. Luke Appling
2. Brooks Robinson
3. Bill Terry
4. Stan Hack
5. Walter Johnson
6. Mel Ott
7. Al Kaline
8. Ernie Banks
9. Cecil Travis
10. Pee Wee Reese

55. The First Inning

1. Charlie Grimm
2. Jimmy Dykes
3. Lou Boudreau
4. Bill Rigney
5. Walter Alston
6. Harry Lavagetto
7. Mickey Vernon
8. Bill Rigney
9. Harry Craft
10. Casey Stengel
11. Bobby Bragan
12. Bob Kennedy
13. Joe Gordon
14. Joe Schultz
15. Gene Mauch
16. Preston Gomez
17. Dave Bristol
18. Ted Williams
19. Darrell Johnson
20. Roy Hartsfield
21. Don Baylor
22. Rene Lachemann

56. The Last Inning

1. Charlie Grimm
2. Marty Marion
3. Eddie Joost
4. Bill Rigney
5. Walter Alston
6. Harry Lavagetto
7. Bobby Bragan
8. Luke Appling
9. Joe Schultz
10. Ted Williams

57. Major League Owners

1. e
2. h
3. j
4. c
5. p
6. o
7. t
8. k
9. n
10. b
11. f
12. s
13. m
14. a
15. q
16. g
17. l
18. i
19. d
20. r

58. The Missing Link

1. Yogi Berra
2. Charlie Keller
3. Terry Moore
4. Duffy Lewis
5. Earle Combs
6. Carl Furillo
7. Ted Williams
8. Lou Piniella
9. Don Mueller
10. Matty Alou
11. Dick Sisler
12. Roger Maris
13. Jackie Jensen
14. Vic Wertz
15. Sid Gordon
16. Pete Reiser
17. Al Simmons
18. Harry Heilmann
19. Casey Stengel
20. Frank Robinson
21. Reggie Smith
22. Al Kaline
23. Joe Rudi
24. Cesar Cedeno
25. Jimmy Wynn
26. Greg Luzinski
27. Tom Brunansky
28. Dave Henderson
29. Joe Carter
30. Ron Gant

59. Who Played Third

1. Brooks Robinson
2. Sal Bando
3. Mike Schmidt
4. Ron Cey
5. Red Rolfe
6. Jim Tabor
7. Harry Lavagetto
8. Whitey Kurowski
9. Ken Keltner
10. Hank Majeski
11. Johnny Pesky
12. Billy Cox

13. Willie Jones
14. Hank Thompson
15. Gil McDougald
16. Al Rosen
17. Bobby Adams
18. Eddie Mathews
19. Don Hoak
20. Clete Boyer
21. Al Smith

22. Ken Boyer
23. Ron Santo
24. Billy Werber
25. Eddie Yost
26. Gary Gaetti
27. Carney Lansford
28. Vance Law
29. Terry Pendleton
30. Kelly Gruber

60. Brother Combinations

1. Vince
2. Wes
3. Mort
4. Norm
5. Virgil
6. Paul
7. Jim
8. Joe
9. Harry
10. Christy
11. Jesus
12. Eddie
13. Frank
14. Billy
15. Ken

16. Emil
17. Bill
18. Tommie
19. Lloyd
20. Hector
21. Fred
22. Dave
23. Faye
24. Ed
25. Charlie
26. Roberto
27. Billy
28. Ozzie
29. Carlos
30. Pedro

61. No Handicap

1. Red Ruffing
2. William "Dummy" Hoy
3. Mordecai "Three-Finger" Brown
4. Pete Gray

5. Jim Abbott
6. John Olerud
7. John Hiller
8. Jim Eisenreich

62. Baseball Tragedies

1. Ed Delahanty
2. Ray Chapman
3. Lou Gehrig
4. Harry Agganis
5. Kenny Hubbs or Jim Umbricht
6. Kenny Hubbs or Jim Umbricht
7. Roberto Clemente
8. Don Wilson
9. Danny Frisella
10. Lyman Bostock
11. Thurman Munson

63. No Untouchables

1. Athletics
2. Giants
3. White Sox
4. Indians
5. Yankees
6. Senators
7. White Sox
8. Dodgers
9. White Sox
10. Red Sox
11. Dodgers
12. Cubs
13. Cardinals
14. Pirates
15. Giants
16. Tigers
17. Cubs
18. Red Sox
19. Pirates
20. Braves
21. Indians
22. Brewers
23. Mets
24. Red Sox
25. Yankees

64. When Did They Come Up?

1930s–1940s

1. Joe DiMaggio
2. Tommy Henrich
3. Joe Gordon
4. Ted Williams
5. Dom DiMaggio
6. Stan Musial
7. Warren Spahn
8. George Kell
9. Eddie Yost
10. Red Shoendienst

1940s–1950s

1. Yogi Berra
2. Jackie Robinson
3. Richie Ashburn
4. Jerry Coleman
5. Whitey Ford
6. Willie Mays
7. Eddie Mathews
8. Al Kaline
9. Hank Aaron
10. Rocky Colavito

1950s–1960s

1. Frank Robinson
2. Roger Maris
3. Ron Fairly
4. Maury Wills
5. Juan Marichal
6. Carl Yastrzemski
7. Ed Kranepool
8. Pete Rose
9. Mel Stottlemyre
10. Catfish Hunter

1960s–1970s

1. George Scott
2. Rod Carew
3. Bobby Bonds
4. Thurman Munson
5. Cesar Cedeno
6. Chris Speier
7. Mike Schmidt
8. Dave Parker
9. Jim Rice
10. Fred Lynn

1970s–1990s

1. Rick Sutcliffe
2. Eddie Murray
3. Paul Molitor
4. Rickey Henderson
5. Harold Baines
6. Cal Ripken
7. Wade Boggs
8. Joe Carter
9. Billy Hatcher
10. Jose Canseco
11. Will Clark
12. Ron Gant
13. Craig Biggio
14. Ken Griffey
15. Carlos Baerga

Chapter Thirteen Answers

65. Opening Day Highlights

1. b. (1940 Indians)
2. e.
3. i.
4. j. (1959 White Sox)
5. g. (1954 Reds)
6. f. (1988 Blue Jays)
7. h. (1994 Cubs)
8. d.
9. a.
10. c. (1950 Yankees)

66. Whom Did They Precede?

1. d
2. c
3. b
4. a
5. c
6. a
7. b
8. d
9. a
10. a

67. Whom Did They Succeed?

1. d
2. b
3. a
4. c
5. d
6. a
7. c
8. b
9. a
10. c

68. Chips off the Old Block

1. George Sisler
2. Mike Tresh
3. Jim Hegan
4. Gus Bell
5. Dolph Camilli
6. Max Lanier
7. Ray Boone
8. Maury Wills
9. Roy Smalley
10. Paul "Dizzy" Trout

69. Current Chips off the Old Block

1. Sandy Alomar, Sr.
2. Ed Sprague
3. Mel Stottlemyre
4. Bobby Bonds
5. Bob Boone
6. Hal McRae
7. Ken Griffey, Sr.
8. Dick Nen
9. Felipe Alou
10. Randy Hundley

70. The Gas House Gang

1. d
2. f
3. h
4. i
5. a
6. j
7. b
8. e
9. g
10. c

71. The Year of ———

1. The Hitless Wonders
2. Merkle's Boner
3. Home Run Baker
4. The Miracle Braves
5. The Black Sox
6. Alex's Biggest Strikeout
7. Murderers' Row
8. The Wild Hoss of the Osage
9. The Babe Calls His Shot
10. The Gas House Gang
11. Ernie's Snooze
12. Mickey's Passed Ball
13. Pesky's Pause
14. Gionfriddo's Gem
15. Feller's Pick-off (?)
16. The Whiz Kids
17. The Miracle of Coogan's Bluff
18. Billy the Kid
19. Mays's Miracle Catch
20. Sandy's Snatch
21. Larsen's Perfect Game
22. The Go-Go Sox
23. Maz's Sudden Shot
24. The M&M Boys
25. The Amazin' Ones

72. The Men at the Mike

1. g
2. i
3. f
4. n
5. j
6. p

7. a	12. c
8. m	13. h
9. e	14. k
10. l	15. d
11. b	16. o

73. Pen Names

1. Del Rice	11. Carl Reynolds
2. Wes Parker	12. Babe Adams
3. Fred Winchell	13. Bill Dailey
4. Woody Woodward	14. Don Gross
5. Frank Sullivan	15. Babe Young
6. Hal Schumacher	16. Hal Smith
7. Dick Williams	17. Babe Twombly
8. Pat Meany	18. Roxie Lawson
9. Art Fowler	19. Ray Murray
10. Jack Graham	20. Johnny Powers

74. Matching Moguls

1. e	8. x	15. b	22. u
2. h	9. aa	16. d	23. o
3. t	10. bb	17. z	24. n
4. v	11. i	18. w	25. c
5. a	12. s	19. r	26. y
6. m	13. g	20. l	27. k
7. q	14. f	21. p	28. j

75. A Star Is Born

1. d	6. e
2. f	7. h
3. i	8. a
4. j	9. c
5. g	10. b

76. The National Pastime

Alabama to Georgia

1. c	6. j
2. e	7. i
3. h	8. d
4. b	9. f
5. g	10. a

Hawaii to Maryland

1. c	6. e
2. g	7. i
3. j	8. d
4. a	9. b
5. f	

Massachusetts to New Jersey

1. j	6. g
2. h	7. c
3. e	8. i
4. b	9. f
5. a	10. d

New Mexico to South Carolina

1. c	6. e
2. g	7. d
3. i	8. h
4. j	9. b
5. a	10. f

South Dakota to Wyoming

1. e	5. b
2. a	6. g
3. j	7. c
4. i	

77. The International Pastime

1. d
2. j
3. g
4. c
5. p
6. r
7. i
8. e
9. m
10. f
11. n
12. a
13. o
14. q
15. k
16. h
17. l
18. b

78. Big-League Bloopers

1. Mickey Owen
2. Jay Howell
3. Ted Williams
4. Jack McDowell
5. Herb Washington
6. Fred Merkle (1908)
7. Babe Ruth (1926)
8. Joe DiMaggio
9. Lonnie Smith
10. Darrell Evans
11. Marv Throneberry (1962 Mets)
12. Hank Gowdy (1924)
13. Babe Herman (1926 Brooklyn Dodgers)
14. Steve Lyons
15. Jose Canseco (1993 Rangers)
16. Kevin Kennedy (1993 Rangers)
17. Phil Rizzuto
18. Casey Stengel
19. Mickey Mantle
20. Jimmy Piersall
21. Clyde Sukeforth
22. Pee Wee Reese
23. Lou Piniella
24. Fred Snodgrass
25. Dave Winfield

79. Quick Quizzing the Managers

I.

1. Lou Boudreau (24)
2. Roger Peckinpaugh (23)
3. Joe Cronin (26)
4. Tom Sheehan (66)
5. Burt Shotton (62)

II.

1. Casey Stengel
2. Joe McCarthy
3. Connie Mack
4. John McGraw
5. Walter Alston

III.

1. e
2. c
3. a
4. b
5. d

IV.

1. Joe McCarthy
2. Frank Chance or Billy Southworth
3. Frank Chance or Billy Southworth
4. John McGraw
5. Al Lopez

V.

1. Sparky Anderson
2. Tommy Lasorda
3. Tom Kelly or Cito Gaston
4. Tom Kelly or Cito Gaston
5. Davey Johnson

80. Did They or Didn't They . . . Manage?

1. Joe Adcock
2. Joe Gordon
3. Kerby Farrell
4. Bill Dickey
5. Bucky Walters
6. Phil Cavarretta
7. Christy Mathewson
8. Luke Appling
9. Eddie Joost
10. Mickey Vernon
11. Red Rolfe
12. Ben Chapman
13. Jim Lemon
14. Freddie Fitzsimmons
15. Bob Elliott
16. Eddie Lopat
17. Johnny Pesky
18. Dick Sisler
19. Mel McGaha
20. Eddie Stanky

81. Post-War World Series Winners

National League

1. Eddie Dyer
2. Leo Durocher
3. Walter Alston
4. Fred Haney
5. Danny Murtaugh
6. Johnny Keane
7. Red Schoendienst
8. Gil Hodges
9. Sparky Anderson
10. Chuck Tanner
11. Dallas Green
12. Tom Lasorda
13. Whitey Herzog
14. Davey Johnson
15. Lou Piniella
16. Bobby Cox

American League

1. Bucky Harris
2. Lou Boudreau
3. Casey Stengel
4. Ralph Houk
5. Hank Bauer
6. Mayo Smith
7. Earl Weaver
8. Dick Williams
9. Al Dark
10. Billy Martin
11. Bob Lemon
12. Joe Altobelli
13. Sparky Anderson
14. Dick Howser
15. Tom Kelly
16. Tony La Russa
17. Cito Gaston

82. Back-to-Back Pennant Winners

1. Casey Stengel
2. Chuck Dressen
3. Walter Alston
4. Casey Stengel
5. Fred Haney
6. Ralph Houk
7. Walter Alston
8. Red Schoendienst
9. Earl Weaver
10. Dick Williams
11. Sparky Anderson
12. Billy Martin
13. Tom Lasorda
14. Tony La Russa
15. Bobby Cox
16. Cito Gaston

83. You're Hired to Be Fired

1. e	6. i	11. d	16. p	21. x
2. g	7. h	12. k	17. s	22. u
3. b	8. m	13. f	18. o	23. y
4. c	9. j	14. q	19. r	24. v
5. a	10. l	15. t	20. n	25. w

84. Managers in Search of a Pennant

1. Red Rolfe	6. Bobby Bragan
2. Eddie Stanky	7. Harry Walker
3. Bill Rigney	8. Mel Ott
4. Birdie Tebbetts	9. Gene Mauch
5. Mike Higgins	10. Paul Richards

85. Managerial Half Truths

1. F (Ed Barrow, 1918)	22. T (1961–63)
2. T (1933)	23. F (3–3)
3. T (1948)	24. F (1961 Reds)
4. T	25. F (John McGraw of the
5. T	1911–13 Giants also)
6. F (Hughie Jennings, 1907–09, too)	26. T (1906)
7. F (Al Dark, 1962)	27. F (Whitey Herzog, 1982)
8. F (1946, as an interim skipper)	28. T
9. F (Tom Lasorda, 1977–78)	29. T (in 1902, when he won a pennant, the World Series had not yet been established.)
10. F (Tommy Lasorda, 1981, also)	30. F (Paul Owens, 1983)
11. T (8½ years to 7½ years)	31. T (.875–.700)
12. T	32. T (6)
13. T (1907–08)	33. F (Sparky Anderson did it, too.)
14. T	34. F (Red Schoendienst, in 1967–68, did it also.)
15. F (He was the playing manager.)	35. T
16. T (1954 Indians and 1959 White Sox)	36. F (Fred Clarke, 1909; Bill McKechnie, 1925; and Chuck Tanner, 1979)
17. F (George Stallings, 1914)	37. F (Mayo Smith, 1968)
18. T (1924–25)	38. T (2–1)
19. T (27)	39. F (1976–77 Yankees)
20. T (660–754)	40. F (Billy Southworth, 1942–44)
21. F (Browns, 1933–37 and 1952)	41. T (1944)

42. T (1974–75)
43. T
44. T (Cardinals, 1942–44; Braves, 1948)
45. F (1920 Indians)
46. F (1–3)
47. F (Joe Cronin)
48. T (1966 Orioles)
49. T (He was 4–3 in 1926, his only series as a manager.)
50. F (Appling did not.)
51. T
52. F (Bob Lemon managed the 1978 winners.)
53. T (1987, 1991 Twins)
54. F (.571 to .667)
55. F (Bobby Cox of the 1991–92 Braves)
56. F (Tony La Russa of the 1988–90 A's)
57. F (1–2 and .385)
58. T (He won in 1989 and he lost in 1990.)
59. F (Lou Piniella)
60. F
61. F
62. T (1978–81 Angels and 1986–88 White Sox)
63. T (1982–85 Blue Jays)
64. F
65. T (1989)

86. All-Star Game Standouts

1. Hank Aaron
2. Brooks Robinson
3. Stan Musial
4. Dwight Gooden (19 years, seven months, 24 days)
5. Satchel Paige (47 years, seven days)
6. Pete Rose, (first, second, third, left, and right field)
7. Charlie Gehringer
8. Terry Moore
9. Willie Jones
10. Ted Williams (1946)
11. Mickey Mantle (1954–60)
12. Joe Morgan (1970, 1972–77)
13. Phil Cavarretta (1944)
14. Dave Winfield
15. Rod Carew (1978)
16. Roberto Clemente (1967)
17. George Brett
18. Joe DiMaggio
19. Pie Traynor (1934)
20. Tony Oliva (1967)
21. Goose Gossage
22. Don Drysdale
23. Lefty Gomez (1935)
24. Whitey Ford
25. Atlee Hammaker (1983)
26. Tom Glavine (1992)
27. Jim Palmer
28. Steve Garvey
29. Nelson Fox
30. Ozzie Smith
31. Brooks Robinson
32. Yogi Berra
33. Willie Mays

87. Who's Who

1. Babe Ruth
2. Carl Hubbell
3. Frankie Frisch
4. Lefty Gomez
5. Lefty Gomez
6. Joe Medwick
7. Dizzy Dean
8. Earl Averill
9. Ted Williams
10. Arky Vaughan
11. Mickey Owen
12. Johnny Vander Meer
13. Vince DiMaggio
14. Phil Cavarretta
15. Ted Williams
16. Rip Sewell
17. Vic Raschi
18. Jackie Robinson

19. Roy Campanella
20. Don Newcombe
21. Larry Doby
22. Red Schoendienst
23. Ted Williams
24. Hank Sauer
25. Satchel Paige
26. Al Rosen
27. Stan Musial
28. Ken Boyer
29. Hank Aaron
30. Willlie Mays
31. Willie Mays
32. Stan Musial
33. Johnny Callison
34. Maury Wills
35. Tony Perez
36. Ferguson Jenkins
37. Willie McCovey
38. Reggie Jackson
39. Frank Robinson
40. Steve Garvey
41. Carl Yastrzemski
42. Steve Garvey
43. Lee Mazzilli
44. Mike Schmidt
45. Dave Concepcion
46. Fred Lynn
47. Fernando Valenzuela
48. Steve Garvey
49. Lou Whitaker
50. Tim Raines
51. Terry Steinbach
52. Nolan Ryan
53. Julio Franco
54. Cal Ripken
55. Ken Griffey, Jr.
56. Moises Alou

88. From Bando to Washington

1. Claudell Washington (20 years, one month, and five days)
2. Will Clark (1989)
3. Bill North (1974–75 A's, 1978 Los Angeles Dodgers)
4. Reggie Jackson
5. Jerry Martin (1978 Phillies)
6. Richie Hebner
7. Jim Palmer (Orioles)
8. Pete Rose (42 years, five months, 24 days)
9. Devon White (1986 Angels; 1991–93 Blue Jays)
10. Jay Johnstone (1976 Phillies)
11. Will Clark (1989 San Francisco Giants)
12. Gary Gaetti (1987 Twins)
13. George Brett
14. Bob Robertson (1971 Pirates)
15. Paul Blair (1969 Orioles)
16. Paul Popovich (1974 Pirates)
17. Paul Molitor (1993 Blue Jays)
18. Mike Cuellar (1970 Orioles)
19. Phil Niekro
20. Sal Bando (1974 A's)

89. From Baylor to Wynn

1. Dave Stewart
2. Jim Hunter
3. Dennis Eckersley
4. Jim Palmer
5. Bert Blyleven (19 years, five months, 29 days)
6. Phil Niekro (43 years, six months, eight days)
7. Cesar Geronimo (1975 Reds)
8. Will Clark (1989 San Francisco Giants)
9. Steve Garvey
10. Don Baylor (1982 Angels)
11. Pedro Guerrero
12. Tony Taylor (1972 Tigers)
13. Rickey Henderson
14. Darryl Strawberry (1986 Mets)
15. Frank Thomas (1993 White Sox)
16. Joe Morgan

17. Hal McRae
18. Reggie Jackson (1972 A's)
19. Bob Robertson (1971 Pirates)

20. Bob Robertson (1971 Pirates)

90. From Anderson to Wynn

1. Billy Martin (1970 Twins, 1972 Tigers, 1976–77 Yankees, and 1981 A's)
2. Earl Weaver
3. Sparky Anderson (1970, 1972, 1975–76 Reds, and 1984 Tigers)
4. Mike Cuellar (1974 Orioles)
5. Wes Gardner (1988 Red Sox)
6. Jim Palmer
7. Dwight Gooden (1988 Mets)
8. Juan Guzman (1993 Blue Jays)
9. Dennis Eckersley
10. Steve Carlton
11. Dennis Eckersley
12. Eric Show (1984 Padres)
13. Jerry Reuss
14. Roger Clemens (1986 Red Sox)
15. Jim Hunter
16. Dave McNally (1969 Orioles)
17. Steve Avery (1991–92 Braves)
18. George Brett
19. Pete Rose
20. Ron Gant (1992 Braves)

91. From Bando to Yastrzemski

1. Fred Lynn (.611 for the 1982 Angels)
2. Brooks Robinson (.583 for the 1970 Orioles)
3. Frank White (.545 for the 1980 Royals)
4. Chris Chambliss (.524 for the 1976 Yankees)
5. Brooks Robinson (.500 for the 1969 Orioles)
6. Tony Oliva (.500 for the 1970 Twins)
7. Sal Bando (.500 for the 1975 A's)
8. Bob Watson (.500 for the 1980 Yankees)
9. Graig Nettles (.500 for the 1981 Yankees)
10. Jerry Mumphrey (.500 for the 1981 Yankees)

92. From Baker to Zisk

1. Jay Johnstone (.778 for the 1976 Phillies)
2. Will Clark (.650 for the 1989 San Francisco Giants)
3. Darrell Porter (.556 for the 1982 Cardinals)
4. Ozzie Smith (.556 for the 1982 Cardinals)
5. Art Shamsky (.538 for the 1969 Mets)
6. Terry Puhl (.526 for the 1980 Astros)
7. Willie Stargell (.500 for the 1970 Pirates)
8. Richie Zisk (.500 for the 1975 Pirates)

93. From Aaron to Staub

1. George Brett
2. Steve Garvey
3. Reggie Jackson
4.–8. Any combination of the following: Sal Bando, Graig Nettles, Gary Matthews, Greg Luzinski, and Johnny Bench
9.–16. Any combination of the following: Jeff Leonard, Lenny Dykstra, Boog Powell, Bill Madlock, Bob Robertson, Ron Cey, Willie Stargell, and Jose Canseco
17.–27. Any combination of the following: Hank Aaron, Rusty Staub, George Foster, Al Oliver, Tony Perez, Pete Rose, Richie Hebner, Jay Bell, Dave Justice, John Olerud, and Jim Rice
28.–30. Any combination of the following: Kirk Gibson, Kirby Puckett, and Rickey Henderson

94. Championship Series Game Winners

National League

1. Pete Rose
2. Bob Tolan
3. Richie Hebner
4. Manny Sanguillen
5. Johnny Bench
6. Pete Rose
7. Bill Russell
8. Bill Russell
9. Willie Stargell
10. Dave Parker
11. Garry Maddox
12. Jerry White
13. Rick Monday
14. Ken Oberkfell
15. Mike Schmidt
16. Steve Garvey
17. Glenn Davis
18. Lenny Dykstra
19. Alan Ashby
20. Gary Carter
21. Jeff Leonard
22. Robby Thompson
23. Lenny Dykstra

American League

1. Paul Blair
2. Curt Motton
3. Paul Blair
4. Gene Tenace
5. Bert Campaneris
6. Bobby Grich
7. Sal Bando
8. Reggie Jackson
9. Chris Chambliss
10. Thurman Munson
11. Roy White
12. John Lowenstein
13. Larry Harlow
14. George Brett
15. Paul Molitor
16. Cecil Cooper
17. Tito Landrum
18. Johnny Grubb
19. Bobby Grich
20. Dave Henderson
21. Pat Sheridan
22. Mike Pagliarulo
23. Harold Baines
24. Robby Alomar

Chapter Seventeen

95. World Series Standouts

I.

1. Yogi Berra
2. Pee Wee Reese, Elston Howard
3. Casey Stengel
4. Billy Hatcher (1990 Reds)
5. Pepper Martin
6. Bobby Richardson
7. Hank Bauer
8. Lou Gehrig (1928)
9. Willie Wilson
10. Mickey Mantle

II.

1. Whitey Ford
2. Darold Knowles
3. Christy Mathewson
4. Bob Gibson
5. Bill Bevens
6. Carl Mays
7. Jim Lonborg (1967)
8. Jim Palmer (20)
9. Harry Brecheen
10. Babe Ruth

III.

1. Cubs
2. Athletics
3. Red Sox
4. Giants
5. Yankees
6. Athletics
7. Yankees
8. Yankees
9. Yankees
10. A's
11. Reds
12. Yankees
13. Blue Jays

IV.

1. Al Gionfriddo
2. Billy Cox
3. Willie Mays
4. Sandy Amoros
5. Mickey Mantle
6. Eddie Mathews
7. Bill Virdon
8. Tommie Agee
9. Brooks Robinson
10. Dick Green
11. Graig Nettles
12. Kirby Puckett

V.

1. Harry Brecheen
2. Johnny Podres
3. Don Larsen
4. Lew Burdette
5. Bob Turley
6. Whitey Ford
7. Sandy Koufax

8. Bob Gibson
9. Mickey Lolich
10. Jim Hunter
11. Jack Morris

12. Bret Saberhagen
13. Dave Stewart
14. Jose Rijo
15. Jimmy Key

96. World Series Players

1. Richie Ashburn
2. Ted Williams
3. Al Kaline
4. Chili Davis
5. Harvey Kuenn
6. Johnny Logan
7. Ted Kluszewski
8. Mike Greenwell
9. Vada Pinson
10. Felipe Alou

11. Tony Pena
12. Gus Bell
13. Walker Cooper
14. Ray Sadecki
15. Bob Allison
16. Steve Howe
17. Satchel Paige
18. Bill White
19. Frank Torre
20. Terry Mulholland

97. Two-Team World Series Players

1. Mariano Duncan (Reds, 1990; Phils, 1993)
2. Gino Cimoli (Dodgers, 1956; Pirates, 1960)
3. Lenny Dykstra (Mets, 1986; Phillies, 1993)
4. Tommy Holmes (Braves, 1948; Brooklyn Dodgers, 1952)
5. Bill Skowron (Yankees 1955–58, 1961–62; Los Angeles Dodgers, 1963)
6. Roger Maris (Yankees, 1960–64; Cardinals, 1967–68)
7. Al Dark (Braves, 1948; New York Giants, 1951 and 1954)
8. Kirk Gibson (Tigers, 1984; Los Angeles Dodgers, 1988)
9. Mickey Cochrane (Athletics, 1929–31; Tigers, 1934–35)
10. Reggie Smith (Red Sox, 1967; Los Angeles Dodgers, 1977–78)
11. Joe Gordon (Yankees, 1938–39, 1941–43; Indians, 1948)
12. Johnny Sain (Braves, 1948; Yankees, 1951–53)
13. Enos Slaughter (Cardinals, 1942, 1946; Yankees, 1956–58)
14. Brian Harper (Cardinals, 1985; Twins, 1991)

15. Orlando Cepeda (San Francisco Giants, 1962; Cardinals, 1967–68)
16. Rickey Henderson (A's, 1989–90; Blue Jays, 1993)
17. Luis Aparicio (White Sox, 1959; Orioles, 1966)
18. Jack Morris (Tigers, 1984; Twins, 1991; Blue Jays, 1992)
19. Dick Groat (Pirates, 1960; Cardinals, 1964)
20. Frank Robinson (Reds, 1961; Orioles, 1966)

98. Mound Classics

1. Johnny Sain
2. Allie Reynolds
3. Preacher Roe
4. Vic Raschi
5. Clem Labine
6. Lew Burdette
7. Bob Shaw, Billy Pierce, and Dick Donovan
8. Ralph Terry
9. Don Drysdale
10. Wally Bunker
11. Dave McNally
12. Jack Billingham and Clay Carroll
13. Bruce Hurst
14. Jack Morris
15. Tom Glavine

99. Seventh-Game Winners

1. Johnny Podres
2. Johnny Kucks
3. Lew Burdette
4. Ralph Terry
5. Bob Gibson
6. Bob Gibson
7. Mickey Lolich
8. Steve Blass
9. Ken Holtzman
10. Joaquin Andujar
11. Bret Saberhagen
12. Frank Viola

100. World Series Shorts

Three-Game Winners

1. Stan Coveleski
2. Harry Brecheen
3. Lew Burdette
4. Bob Gibson
5. Mickey Lolich

Individual Records

1. Lefty Grove
2. Whitey Ford
3. Bob Gibson
4. Christy Mathewson
5. Lefty Gomez

Home Run Hitters	Career Records
1. Mickey Mantle	1. Eddie Collins and Lou Brock
2. Babe Ruth	
3. Yogi Berra	2. Yogi Berra
4. Duke Snider	3. Thurman Munson (1976–77 Yankees)
5. Lou Gehrig	4. Frank Isbell
	5. Bobby Richardson (1960–64 Yankees)

101. Four Homers in One Series

1. Babe Ruth
2. Lou Gehrig
3. Duke Snider
4. Duke Snider
5. Hank Bauer
6. Gene Tenace
7. Willie Aikens
8. Lenny Dykstra

102. World Series Chronology

1. Jimmy Sebring (Pirates)
2. Christy Mathewson
3. Ed Walsh (White Sox)
4. Harry Steinfeldt
5. Orval Overall
6. Babe Adams
7. Jack Coombs (Athletics)
8. Frank Baker
9. Joe Wood
10. Jack Lapp
11. Johnny Evers
12. George "Rube" Foster
13. Babe Ruth (13⅓)
14. Red Faber
15. Charlie Pick
16. Dickie Kerr
17. Elmer Smith (Indians)
18. Waite Hoyt (Yankees)
19. Art Nehf
20. Babe Ruth (1923 Yankees)
21. Earl McNeely
22. Walter Johnson
23. Jesse Haines
24. Babe Ruth
25. Bill Sherdel
26. Al Simmons
27. Jack Quinn
28. Pepper Martin
29. Tony Lazzeri
30. Mel Ott
31. Frankie Frisch
32. Goose Goslin
33. Carl Hubbell
34. Cliff Melton
35. Red Ruffing
36. Monte Pearson
37. Bucky Walters

38. Whit Wyatt
39. Whitey Kurowski
40. Spud Chandler
41. Mort Cooper
42. Hank Borowy
43. Enos Slaughter
44. Hugh Casey
45. Bob Feller
46. Tommy Henrich
47. Whitey Ford
48. Hank Bauer
49. Johnny Mize
50. Carl Erskine
51. Vic Wertz
52. Gil Hodges
53. Enos Slaughter
54. Lew Burdette
55. Bob Turley
56. Chuck Essegian
57. Roy Face
58. Whitey Ford
59. Don Larsen
60. Harry Bright
61. Tim McCarver (1964 Cardinals)
62. Claude Osteen
63. Dave McNally (Game One)
64. Bob Gibson
65. Mickey Lolich
66. Al Weis
67. Brooks Robinson
68. Roberto Clemente
69. Jim Hunter
70. Ken Holtzman
71. Ken Holtzman
72. Tony Perez
73. Johnny Bench
74. Thurman Munson
75. Brian Doyle
76. Phil Garner
77. Tug McGraw
78. Steve Yeager
79. Robin Yount
80. Eddie Murray
81. Kirk Gibson
82. Bret Saberhagen
83. Ray Knight
84. Frank Viola
85. Orel Hershiser
86. Rickey Henderson
87. Jose Rijo
88. Jack Morris
89. Dave Winfield
90. Joe Carter
91. Tom Glavine

103. World Series Multiple Choice

1. c (Yankees)
2. b (Yankees)
3. d (1936–39 Yankees)
4. c (1914 Braves-1928 Cards)
5. b (1965 Twins-1982 Cards)
6. c (1951 Giants-1973 Mets)
7. d (1914 Athletics-1932 Yankees)
8. a (19 years before the 1987 series)
9. d (44 with 1983 Phillies)
10. b (1960–62, 1964 Yankees)
11. b (1972–73 A's)
12. c (1982 Brewers)

13. b (1934–35 Tigers)
14. c
15. a (1934 Tigers)
16. d (1939 Yankees)
17. b (1952, 1955 Dodgers)
18. b (1977–78 Yankees)
19. d (1926–28 Yankees)
20. b (1906 Tigers: four doubles)
21. a (1960 Yankees)
22. d (1925 Pirates)
23. b (1955 Yankees)
24. c (1906–08, 1910 Cubs)
25. b (1929–30 Athletics)
26. c (1972–74 A's)
27. d (1936–39, 1941, 1943 Yankees)
28. a (1964, 1967–68 Cards)
29. b (1955–58 and 1961–64 Yankees)
30. d (1905, 1914 Athletics)
31. b (1934 Tigers)
32. a (1949 Dodgers)
33. b (1956 Yankees)
34. d (1924 Senators)
35. b (Yankees)
36. a (Giants and Cards)
37. d (Yankees)
38. b (Yankees)
39. b (Dodgers)
40. d (Yankees)
41. d (Yankees)
42. b (Yankees)
43. d (Yankees)
44. b (27 for the 1924 Senators)
45. a (26 for the 1933 Senators)
46. c (Giants)
47. a (Yankees)
48. c (1925 Pirates, 1928 Cards, 1939–40 Reds)
49. c (Yankees)
50. b

104. World Series Clues Who's Who

1. Christy Mathewson
2. Red Ruffing
3. Herb Pennock
4. Allie Reynolds
5. Rollie Fingers (1972–74 A's)
6. Moe Drabowsky (1966)
7. Ross Youngs
8. Lou Brock (1968 Cards)
9. Emil "Irish" Meusel
10. Paul Molitor
11. Dick Hughes
12. Edd Roush
13. Fred Lindstrom (1924 Giants)
14. Frankie Frisch
15. Dave McNally
16. Goose Goslin
17. Ray Schalk
18. Sherry Smith (Dodgers)
19. Patsy Dougherty (1903)
20. Bill Abstein
21. Red Faber
22. Grove Alexander (Cards)
23. Jesse Barnes
24. Rogers Hornsby (1926 Cards)
25. Fred Snodgrass
26. Mickey Cochrane (1934–35 Tigers)

27. Mort Cooper (1944)
28. Sparky Anderson (1975–76 Reds)
29. Ken Brett (1967 Red Sox)
30. Sandy Koufax (1965 Dodgers)
31. Lou Brock (Cards)
32. Goose Goslin (Senators)
33. Thurman Munson (Yankees)
34. Dusty Rhodes (1954 Giants)
35. Duke Snider (Dodgers)
36. Ed Reulbach
37. Thurman Munson
38. Roger Peckinpaugh
39. Ralph Houk (1961–63 Yankees)
40. Vic Raschi (1949–50 Yankees)
41. Allie Reynolds (Yankees)
42. Bob Kuzava
43. Eddie Plank (Athletics)
44. Mickey Lolich (Tigers)
45. Walter Johnson (Senators)
46. Art Nehf
47. Claude Passeau
48. Monte Irvin (Giants)
49. Mickey Owen (Dodgers)
50. Yogi Berra (Yankees)
51. Bill Bevens
52. Hal Schumacher
53. George Pipgras
54. Clarence Mitchell (1920 Dodgers)
55. Jim Lonborg
56. Ray Kremer
57. Billy Martin (Yankees)
58. Mort Cooper (Cards)
59. Dick Hall
60. Jack Billingham
61. Kiki Cuyler
62. Enos Slaughter
63. Harry Walker (Cards)
64. Willie Aikens (Royals)
65. Rusty Staub (Mets)
66. Dave McNally (Orioles)
67. Tommie Agee
68. Willie Horton
69. Joe Pepitone (1963 Yankees)
70. Curt Flood
71. Deacon Phillippe (1903 Pirates)
72. Joe Wood (1912 Red Sox)
73. Jack Coombs (Athletics)
74. Bucky Harris (Senators)
75. Herb Pennock (1927 Yankees)
76. Yogi Berra

Chicago Cubs

1. True (Chance, .296; Cavarretta, .293; and Grimm, .290)
2. True
3. False (1,125–1,259)
4. False (Harry Steinfeldt)
5. True (.304)
6. True (1975–76)
7. Hack Wilson
8. Sammy Sosa
9. Bill "Swish" Nicholson
10. Chuck Klein
11. Billy Williams
12. Andy Pafko
13. b
14. c
15. a
16. a
17. b
18. d (1917)
19. c
20. c
21. a (1967–72)
22. d (1906)
23. c
24. b
25. b (1906–08)

Montreal Expos

1. f (1970–74)
2. d (1974–76)
3. a
4. e (1969)
5. c (1970–74)
6. b
7. b (1994)
8. b (1987)
9. a
10. a
11. d
12. c
13. True
14. False (less than one season)
15. True (1985)
16. Ross Grimsley (1978)
17. Bill Stoneman (1971)
18. Woodie Fryman
19. Jeff Reardon
20. Mike Marshall (1972–73)
21. Carl Morton
22. Bill Stoneman (1969 and 1972)
23. Charlie Lea
24. Steve Rogers
25. Mike Torrez (1974)

New York Mets

1. True (1963)
2. False (Al Weis)
3. False (.238)
4. False (Jim Fregosi did.)
5. True (1962–79)
6. True
7. Bobby Bonilla (1994)
8. Darryl Strawberry (1987–88)
9. Cleon Jones (1969)
10. Richie Ashburn (1962)
11. Joe Orsulak
12. Ron Swoboda (1969)
13. a
14. b
15. c
16. c (1969 and 1971)
17. a (1972)
18. c
19. b (1965)
20. a
21. b (1986)
22. b (1994)
23. b
24. d
25. a (1984–86)

Philadelphia Phillies

1. True (1992–94)
2. False (Juan Samuel had 701 official at-bats in his rookie 1984 season.)
3. True (.305 in 1975)
4. True
5. False (Mike Goliat)
6. False (25–37)
7. Lenny Dykstra (1993)
8. Gavvy Cravath (1913–15, 1917–19)
9. Chuck Klein (Hack Wilson had a record 190 RBIs that year.)
10. Lefty O'Doul (1929)
11. Dick Sisler
12. Richie Ashburn (1955 and 1958)
13. c
14. b
15. a
16. a (1911)
17. d (1945)
18. c (1909)
19. b (1950)
20. a (266)
21. d
22. c
23. a (1964)
24. b (1972–73)
25. a (1967)

Pittsburgh Pirates

1. Dale Long (1956)
2. Bill Mazeroski
3. Arky Vaughan
4. Pie Traynor

5. Hank Greenberg
6. Honus Wagner
7. f
8. a
9. d
10. c
11. b
12. e
13. a
14. c
15. d

16. False (eephus pitch)
17. False (197–230)
18. True (1960)
19. False (Harvey Haddix)
20. False (Phil Niekro, 1977–80 Braves)
21. True (.750 in 1968)
22. True (3–2 in 1903)
23. True
24. False (Denny Neagle)
25. True

St. Louis Cardinals

1. a
2. d
3. b (1978–94)
4. c (1964)
5. a
6. b (1950)
7. False (Tony Gwynn, 1987–89 Padres)
8. True (1937)
9. False (.300)
10. False (Maury Wills stole 104 bases in 1962.)
11. True
12. False (Flood didn't.)
13. Bob O'Farrell

14. Walker Cooper (1942–44)
15. Tom Pagnozzi (1992–94)
16. e
17. d
18. i (1931)
19. b (1933–36)
20. h
21. f
22. c (1946)
23. a (The shutouts came in 1968.)
24. j
25. g

Atlanta Braves

1. d
2. d (1973)
3. b (1994)
4. a (1960–64 Yankees)
5. b (Hank Aaron also hit 47 homers in 1971.)
6. c

7. True
8. False (335–398)
9. False (Ralph Garr)
10. True (26–27 in 1982–83)
11. True (1964)
12. True (1975–76 Reds)
13. Joe Torre
14. Earl Williams

15. Ozzie Virgil (1987)
16. b
17. d (1979)
18. e
19. c (1992–95)
20. j

21. h
22. g
23. f
24. a
25. i (Houston, 1979–80)

Cincinnati Reds

1. f (1953–56)
2. c (1975–76)
3. e (1989–93)
4. d
5. b
6. a
7. c
8. b (1976–77)
9. a (1905)
10. a
11. c (1917 and 1919)
12. d
13. True (1970 and 1972)

14. True (1926)
15. True (.306)
16. Johnny Vander Meer
17. Joe Nuxhall
18. Jim Maloney
19. Bucky Walters
20. Paul Derringer
21. Ewell Blackwell
22. Jose Rijo
23. Jack Billingham
24. Joey Jay
25. John Franco

Houston Astros

1. Lee May (1972–74)
2. Nellie Fox
3. Craig Biggio (1994)
4. Doug Rader
5. Joe Pepitone
6. Joe Morgan
7. b
8. c
9. e
10. d
11. f
12. a (1979)
13. a (1963–64)
14. b
15. d (1976)

16. True (21 in 1979)
17. True (1967 and 1969)
18. False (Reds)
19. True (1969)
20. True (1990 Pirates)
21. False (1978 Braves)
22. False (Jim Deshaies did it.)
23. True
24. False (He pitched one for the Angels.)
25. False (J. R. Richard struck out 313 in 1979.)

Los Angeles Dodgers

1. c (1978)
2. d
3. f (1960–65)
4. e (316)
5. a (1949–55)
6. b
7. b
8. a
9. a
10. c (1982–83, 1985)
11. a (1968–70 Senators)
12. a (1962)
13. False (He ended his career with the Twins.)
14. True (1993–94)
15. False (His highest season average was 240; his career mark was .214.)
16. Don Drysdale
17. Fernando Valenzuela
18. Al Downing
19. Orel Hershiser (1985)
20. Don Sutton
21. Tommy John
22. Johnny Podres
23. Ron Perranoski
24. Phil Regan
25. Claude Osteen

San Diego Padres

1. True (38 in 1970)
2. True (1984)
3. True (1989–90 and 1990 Padres; 1992 Reds)
4. True (1972 and 1973)
5. False (272)
6. True (1992)
7. Tony Gwynn
8. Dave Winfield
9. Ollie Brown
10. Dave Kingman (1977)
11. Eddie Williams
12. Bob Tolan
13. c
14. a
15. b (Bob)
16. a (1976)
17. d (1972 Indians, 1978 Padres)
18. c (1971)
19. c
20. a (1974–76)
21. c
22. c
23. c
24. c (1977–78)
25. c

San Francisco Giants

1. b
2. a (1962)
3. d
4. c (1994)

5. b (Giants, Cardinals, and Braves)
6. a (1974–76 in Philadelphia, San Francisco, and Atlanta)
7. True
8. False (Bobby Bonds did it in 1970.)
9. False (51–52)
10. False (.191)
11. False (He won one with the Tigers.)
12. True (1963)
13. Tom Haller (1966)
14. Ed Bailey (1962–63)
15. Bob Brenly (1986)
16. c (1976)
17. e
18. g (1963–69)
19. h
20. b
21. f
22. a
23. d
24. i
25. j

Baltimore Orioles

1. Jim Gentile
2. Davey Johnson
3. Luis Aparicio
4. Brooks Robinson
5. Cal Ripken
6. Vern Stephens
7. b
8. d (Red Sox, A's, and Padres)
9. f
10. c
11. a
12. e
13. b
14. a
15. c
16. False (Steve Stone, 25 in 1980)
17. False (Dave McNally)
18. False (Jim Palmer, 20)
19. False (Milt Pappas)
20. True (1967)
21. False (He lost 21.)
22. True (1979)
23. True
24. True
25. True

Boston Red Sox

1. c
2. e (1960 and 1962)
3. f (the 1944 Browns)
4. d
5. b (1903)
6. a (1983 and 1985–88)
7. d (1931)
8. b
9. c (1973)
10. a (1954)
11. d
12. b

13. True (1915–16)
14. True
15. True
16. Cy Young (1904)
17. Jim Lonborg
18. Dave Sisler
19. Dick Radatz

20. Denny Galehouse
21. Babe Ruth (1916)
22. Lefty Grove (1941)
23. Red Ruffing
24. Joe Wood
25. Ernie Shore

Cleveland Indians

1. Hal Trosky (1936)
2. Bill Wambsganss
3. Ray Boone
4. Kenny Keltner
5. Carlos Baerga (1992–93)
6. Vic Wertz
7. b (in 1905)
8. c
9. e
10. f (.357 in 1994)
11. d
12. a (1948)
13. b
14. c (Bob Feller, Bob
    Lemon, Gene Bearden,
    Mike Garcia, Early
    Wynn, and Herb Score)

15. d (1990)
16. True (31 in 1920)
17. False (20–9 in 1956)
18. True
19. True
20. False
21. True
22. False (Nolan Ryan,
    7; Feller and Jim
    Maloney, 3)
23. False (Jim didn't.)
24. True (from 1929–32)
25. True

Detroit Tigers

1. b (1937–38)
2. d (.361 in 1961)
3. a (1961)
4. d
5. b (for Cleveland's
   Rocky Colavito)
6. c (1990–92)
7. True
8. True

9. False (.297)
10. False (Jim Northrup hit
    the ball.)
11. True (1950)
12. False (Al Kaline, 20)
13. Rudy York (1937)
14. Mickey Cochrane
15. Bill Freehan
16. d (1976)

17. f (1968–69)
18. g (308 in 1971)
19. i
20. e
21. a

22. h (1952)
23. j (1944–46)
24. b (1934)
25. c (He was 21–20 in 1907.)

Milwaukee Brewers

1. True (1975)
2. True (1987)
3. True (3,142)
4. False (207 with 1987 Royals)
5. True (1986)
6. False (25 in 1977)
7. Hank Aaron (1975–76)
8. Rob Deer (1986)
9. Gorman Thomas
10. Tommy Harper
11. Ben Oglivie
12. Robin Yount

13. b
14. a
15. c
16. c
17. d (1987)
18. a
19. a
20. b
21. a
22. b (1981)
23. c (1982)
24. d
25. a

New York Yankees

1. Babe Dahlgren (1939)
2. Billy Martin
3. Phil Rizzuto
4. Frank Baker (1911–14 Athletics)
5. Don Mattingly
6. Bill Skowron
7. c (1939–40)
8. f (1958)
9. a
10. b
11. d
12. e
13. a (1936)

14. c (1956)
15. d
16. True
17. False (Dale Mitchell)
18. False (Bob Kuzava)
19. True (10 and 8)
20. False (Wes Ferrell)
21. True
22. True (2)
23. False (David Cone)
24. False (Reverse Page and Murphy.)
25. False (Lyle didn't.)

Toronto Blue Jays

1. b (1993)
2. c
3. d
4. f
5. e
6. a
7. c
8. d (1987)
9. b (1987)
10. b
11. a
12. c (1977)
13. True (1977)
14. True (1979)
15. False
16. Juan Guzman
17. Dave Stieb (1984)
18. Jimmy Key (1985)
19. Mark Eichhorn (1986)
20. Tom Henke (1985–87)
21. Pat Hentgen
22. Pete Vuckovich (1977)
23. Todd Stottlemyre (1992–94)
24. Bill Singer (1970)
25. Dave Lemanczyk (13–16)

California Angels

1. a
2. d
3. a
4. d
5. b
6. c (1986–87)
7. False (Reggie Jackson, 39 in 1982)
8. False (Mickey Rivers, 70 in 1975)
9. False (Rod Carew, .339 in 1983)
10. False (Bonds was traded to the Angels by the Yankees.)
11. True (1973)
12. True
13. Bob Boone
14. Bob Rodgers (8 years)
15. Jeff Torborg
16. c (1964)
17. d (1962)
18. h (1963)
19. f
20. a
21. b
22. i
23. g
24. e
25. j (33)

Chicago White Sox

1. d (1993)
2. b
3. f (1936)
4. e (with 33 homers in 1971)
5. a

6. c (1985)
7. d
8. c (1963)
9. b (1921–25)
10. a (1937)
11. d (.353 in 1974 with the Braves)
12. b (188)
13. b (In 1920 Red Faber won 23 games; Claude Williams, 22; Ed Cicotte and Dickie Kerr, 21.)
14. a
15. c (Tom)
16. Charlie Robertson (1922)
17. Ed Walsh (1908)
18. Ted Lyons
19. Monty Stratton
20. Dickie Kerr
21. Claude Williams
22. Wilbur Wood (He was 24–20 in 1973.)
23. Billy Pierce
24. Red Faber (1917)
25. Ed Lopat (1949–53)

Kansas City Royals

1. c (36 in 1985)
2. a
3. b (1971–79)
4. d (1979)
5. d (1986–87 Angels)
6. a (1987 and 1991 Twins)
7. True (1969)
8. False (Hal McRae, 1982)
9. True (Thirteen of his first 21 were within the playing confines.)
10. False
11. True (1980)
12. True
13. Jim Sundberg (1986)
14. Darrell Porter
15. John Wathan
16. b
17. f
18. e
19. c (1977)
20. g
21. d (21 in 1985)
22. j (1985)
23. h
24. i (1977)
25. a (1988–94)

Minnesota Twins

1. c
2. b (1982)
3. d
4. a
5. f
6. e
7. d
8. a (1986)
9. d
10. c
11. a
12. b

13. True
14. False (Roseboro, 249; Battey, .270)
15. True (33–26)
16. Jim Kaat (25 in 1966)
17. Bert Blyleven (258 in 1973)
18. Dave Boswell
19. Jim Perry
20. Camilo Pascual (1962–63)
21. Mudcat Grant
22. Dean Chance
23. Ron Perranoski
24. Al Worthington
25. Scott Erickson

Oakland A's

1. Gene Tenace (1972–74 A's, 1982 Cards)
2. Bert Campaneris (1964 Kansas City Athletics)
3. Alfredo Griffin
4. Sal Bando
5. Carney Lansford
6. Mark McGwire (1987 and 1992)
7. b (1981)
8. f (1965)
9. e
10. d
11. c
12. a
13. d
14. b (.256)
15. a (19)
16. True
17. True (22)
18. True
19. True (1985)
20. False (He won 21 in 1973.)
21. True (4–1)
22. False (Bob Welch, 27 in 1990)
23. True (0–3)
24. False (Darold Knowles)
25. True (6)

Seattle Mariners

1. True
2. True (1987)
3. True (1984)
4. True
5. True (Tampa)
6. False (He has won two: 1992 and 1995)
7. Tom Paciorek
8. Ken Griffey, Jr.
9. Jay Buhner (1995)
10. Richie Zisk
11. Danny Tartabull
12. Willie Horton
13. b
14. c
15. a
16. a
17. c
18. c
19. a

20. a
21. b
22. d

23. b
24. d
25. c

Texas Rangers

1. c
2. d
3. e
4. b
5. f
6. a
7. c
8. a
9. d
10. d
11. c
12. a
13. True (1974–83, 1988–89)
14. False

15. True (1980 Royals and 1982 Cardinals)
16. Ferguson Jenkins
17. Doyle Alexander
18. Dock Ellis (Pirates, 1971; Yankees, 1976)
19. Mitch Williams
20. Nolan Ryan (1989)
21. Charlie Hough
22. Bobby Witt
23. Tom Henke
24. Bert Blyleven
25. Gaylord Perry

105. American League Records

1. b (1901 Athletics)
2. c (Tigers)
3. d (1985 Red Sox)
4. c (1929–33 Athletics)
5. c Sam Crawford (Tigers)
6. a (Yankees)
7. d (1991 Twins)
8. c (1985 Red Sox)
9. c (1926 Indians)
10. b (Senators-Twins-Royals)
11. b
12. a (1988 Blue Jays)
13. c Rube Waddell (1904 Athletics)
14. b (1951 Yankees)
15. a (1987 Brewers)
16. b (1922 Browns)
17. a
18. c
19. c (1946 Indians)
20. a (1937 Tigers)
21. d (1937 Yankees)
22. d (1941 White Sox)
23. c (1936 Yankees)
24. b (1992 A's)
25. b (1957 Red Sox)
26. a (Yankees)
27. c (1992 White Sox)
28. b (1932 Athletics)
29. b (1908 Tigers)
30. d (1936–37)
31. d (1968–69)
32. a (1950 Yankees)
33. d
34. c (1960)
35. a (1939)
36. c (1932 Senators)
37. c (1980 Royals)
38. c (1916)
39. c (1986 Red Sox)
40. d (1929–32 Athletics)
41. d (1904 White Sox)
42. b (1918 Senators)
43. a (Red Sox, Yankees, Rangers, and White Sox)
44. c
45. a (Tigers)
46. b (1955 Indians)
47. d (1982–93 Orioles)
48. b (1938 Indians)
49. d (1994 Blue Jays)
50. a (1904 White Sox)

106. National League Records

1. c (1925 Cards)
2. c (1930 Phillies)
3. b (1929–33 Phillies)
4. b (1924, 1931 Cards)
5. a (1961 Cards)
6. d (Dodgers and Cubs)
7. a
8. b (Giants and Padres)

9. c (Reds and Pirates)
10. b (1991 Mets)
11. c (1958, 1965 Dodgers)
12. a (1954 Reds)
13. b (1953–61 Braves)
14. d (1949–50 Pirates)
15. c (1954–55 Reds)
16. c (Giants: August 1965)
17. c (1954)
18. a (1972)
19. a (1973)
20. c
21. b (Dodgers)
22. d (1922 Cards)
23. c (Phillies)
24. c (1954 Braves)
25. a (Pirates)
26. c
27. b (1953 Dodgers)
28. d (1943 Giants)
29. a (1950 Giants)
30. b (1987)

31. c
32. d
33. a (1968 Mets)
34. b (1938 Braves)
35. c (Pirates-Dodgers)
36. c (1914 Cards)
37. c (1903 Giants)
38. c (1951)
39. a
40. b (Phillies-Cubs-Cards)
41. b (Cards-Phils-Pirates)
42. c (1938 Reds)
43. a
44. a (1958 Cards)
45. b (1979 Astros)
46. d (1930 Cubs)
47. b (1946 Dodgers)
48. a (Pirates)
49. c (Brooklyn-Los
    Angeles Dodgers)
50. a (1991 Mets)

107. Major League Records

1. b (165 for the 1962 Los
   Angeles Dodgers)
2. c (.420 for the 1922
   Browns)
3. d (.365 for the 1957
   Yankees)
4. a (1939 Yankees)
5. d (1925 Athletics)
6. d (1975 Pirates)
7. a (1933 Senators)
8. b (Astros-Red Sox)
9. b (1953 Red Sox)
10. c (1950 Yankees; Ross
    Morman of the 1986
    White Sox and Chad

   Kreuter of the 1988
   Rangers subsequently re-
   peated Martin's feat.)
11. b (1957 Red Sox)
12. a (1958–59 Phillies)
13. a (1931 Athletics)
14. c (1927 Pirates)
15. d (1948 Athletics)
16. b (1912 Pirates)
17. c
18. d
19. d (Athletics-Red Sox)
20. b (Braves)
21. a (1927–28 Yankees)
22. d (1942 Braves)

23. b (Indians-Red Sox)
24. c (1961 Yankees)
25. d (1973 Phillies)
26. c (1993 Expos)
27. c (1954 Cards)
28. a (1968 Giants)
29. c (1976 Phillies)
30. a (1921)
31. b (1926)
32. d (1927 Pirates)
33. a (1922 Cubs)
34. c (1956 Senators)
35. a (1947)
36. d (Indians-Yankees)
37. a (1917 Indians)
38. b (Brewers)
39. a (Brooklyn Dodgers)
40. d
41. a (1985 Braves)
42. a (1974 Los Angeles Dodgers*)
43. d (1904 Browns)
44. b (1908 White Sox)
45. d
46. b (1907 Athletics)
47. b (1941 Yankees)
48. d (1920 Braves)
49. b (1914 Pirates)
50. c (1978 Orioles)

108. Highest Career Fielding Percentage per Position

American League

1. a
2. c
3. b
4. c
5. a
6. b
7. c

National League

1. a and b
2. a
3. b
4. c
5. b
6. c
7. c and d

109. Highest Season Fielding Percentage per Position

American League

1. c (1921 Red Sox)
2. a (1973 Orioles)
3. b (1991 Rangers)
4. a (1990 Orioles)

* Dale Mahorcik of the 1986 Rangers has since tied this mark.

5. a (1965 Indians) and d
   (1982 Angels)

6. b (1946 Athletics)
7. c (1913 Senators)

National League

1. b (1984 Padres)
2. c (1990 Cardinals)
3. b (1924 Giants)
4. e (1971–72 Phillies) and f
   (1987, 1991 Cardinals)

5. b (1991, 1993 Los
   Angeles Dodgers)
6. c (1950 Giants) and d
   (1992 Cardinals)
7. a (1976 Padres)

110. All-Time Gold Glove Champs

1. Keith Hernandez (Mattingly has nine.)
2. Ryne Sandberg (White got eight.)
3. Brooks Robinson (Schmidt racked up ten.)
4. Ozzie Smith (Aparicio had nine.)
5. Willie Mays (Kaline registered seven.)
6. Roberto Clemente (Yastrzemski recorded six.)

7. Paul Blair (Flood had seven.)
8. Garry Maddox (Murphy got six.)
9. Dwight Evans (Murphy recorded five.)
10. Andre Dawson (White trails with six).
11. Johnny Bench (Sundberg got six.)
12. Jim Kaat (Gibson had a creditable nine.)

110. Clues to Cooperstown

From Barrow to Youngs

1. Carl Hubbell
2. Lou Gehrig
3. Babe Ruth
4. Johnny Evers
5. Mel Ott
6. Al Simmons
7. George Sisler
8. Bill Terry
9. Hank Greenberg
10. Robin Roberts
11. Jackie Robinson
12. Bob Feller
13. Eppa Rixey
14. Joe Cronin
15. Ray Schalk
16. Frank Baker
17. Bill Dickey
18. Rabbit Maranville
19. Dazzy Vance
20. Ted Lyons
21. Zack Wheat
22. Max Carey
23. Edd Roush
24. Sam Rice
25. Charlie Gehringer
26. Pie Traynor
27. Herb Pennock
28. Frankie Frisch
29. Jimmy Collins
30. Fred Clarke
31. John McGraw
32. Nap Lajoie
33. Ross Youngs
34. Red Faber
35. Goose Goslin
36. Monte Irvin
37. George Kelly
38. Satchel Paige
39. Lefty Gomez
40. Lou Boudreau
41. Chick Hafey
42. Dave Bancroft
43. Harry Hooper
44. Jesse Haines
45. Cool Papa Bell
46. Josh Gibson
47. Branch Rickey
48. Ed Barrow
49. Bob Lemon
50. Heinie Manush

From Aaron to Kell

1. Modercai "Three Finger" Brown
2. Lefty Grove
3. Ty Cobb
4. Roberto Clemente
5. Jimmie Foxx
6. Rube Waddell
7. Rick Ferrell
8. Frank Chance
9. Hank Aaron

10. Willie McCovey
11. Yogi Berra
12. Billy Herman
13. Grover Alexander
14. Addie Joss
15. Waite Hoyt
16. Whitey Ford
17. Chief Bender
18. Jack Chesbro
19. Stan Coveleski
20. Walter Johnson
21. Burleigh Grimes
22. Dizzy Dean (1934 Cards)
23. Don Drysdale
24. Jesse Burkett
25. Gabby Hartnett
26. Ed Delahanty
27. Honus Wagner
28. Luis Aparicio
29. Luke Appling (White Sox)
30. Eddie Collins

31. Sam Crawford
32. Earl Averill
33. Mickey Cochrane
34. Jim Bottomley
35. Ernie Banks
36. Earle Combs (1927)
37. Willie Keeler
38. Al Kaline
39. Elmer Flick
40. Rogers Hornsby
41. Joe DiMaggio
42. Hughie Jennings (Tigers)
43. George Kell
44. Travis Jackson (Giants)
45. Harry Heilmann
46. Ray Dandridge
47. Jim Hunter
48. Johnny Bench
49. Rod Carew (Twins and Angels)
50. Reggie Jackson (A's, Yankees, and Angels)

From Killebrew to Wynn

1. Joe McGinnity
2. Sandy Koufax
3. Early Wynn
4. Rube Marquard
5. Juan Marichal
6. Rube Waddell
7. Christy Mathewson
8. Eddie Plank
9. Warren Spahn
10. Red Ruffing
11. Eddie Mathews
12. Chuck Klein
13. Johnny Mize (1939–40 Cards and 1948–49 Giants)

14. Pee Wee Reese
15. Joe Medwick
16. Mickey Mantle
17. Frank Robinson
18. Ralph Kiner
19. Paul Waner
20. Fred Lindstrom
21. Hack Wilson
22. Willie Mays
23. Duke Snider
24. Harmon Killebrew
25. Joe Sewell
26. Tris Speaker
27. Honus Wagner
28. Stan Musial

29. Lloyd Waner
30. Brooks Robinson
31. Ted Williams
32. Joe Tinker
33. Ed Walsh
34. Bobby Wallace
35. Bill McKechnie
36. Al Lopez
37. Walter Alston
38. Bucky Harris
39. Joe McCarthy
40. Connie Mack
41. Wilbert Robinson

42. Charles Comiskey
43. Casey Stengel
44. Clark Griffith
45. Miller Huggins (Yankees, 1921–23 and 1926–28)
46. Billy Williams
47. Joe Morgan
48. Jim Palmer
49. Tom Seaver
50. Willie Stargell
51. Carl Yastrzemski
52. Mike Schmidt

112. Are They in the Hall of Fame?

1. No
2. Yes
3. No
4. Yes
5. Yes
6. No
7. No
8. Yes
9. Yes
10. No

11. No
12. No
13. No
14. Yes
15. Yes
16. Yes
17. No
18. No
19. No
20. No

21. Yes
22. Yes
23. Yes
24. No
25. No
26. Yes
27. No
28. Yes
29. Yes
30. Yes

⊘ SIGNET (0451)

FIND THE ANSWERS!

☐ **THE V.C. ANDREWS TRIVIA AND QUIZ BOOK by Stephen J. Spignesi.** A companion to the books, the plots, the characters, the steamy scenes, and the movies—plus interviews, a super crossword puzzle, and much more! (179250—$3.99)

☐ **THE COMPLETE BOOK OF MAGIC AND WITCHCRAFT by Kathryn Paulsen.** The unique guide to everything you need to know to become a witch—with all the ancient and modern recipes, spells, and incantations essential for magic, witchcraft and sorcery. (168321—$4.99)

☐ **HOW TO BUY YOUR NEW CAR FOR A ROCK-BOTTOM PRICE by Dr. Leslie R. Sachs.** Get the lowdown from the man who went undercover as a car salesman to learn the tricks of the trade. What you don't know about buying a car could cost you thousands. (149610—$4.99)

☐ **THE AMATEUR MAGICIAN'S HANDBOOK by Henry Hay.** Fourth revised edition. A professional magician teaches you hundreds of the tricks of his trade in this unsurpassed, illustrated guide. (155025—$5.99)

Prices slightly higher in Canada

Buy them at your local bookstore or use this convenient coupon for ordering.

PENGUIN USA
P.O. Box 999 — Dept. #17109
Bergenfield, New Jersey 07621

Please send me the books I have checked above.
I am enclosing $_____ (please add $2.00 to cover postage and handling). Send check or money order (no cash or C.O.D.'s) or charge by Mastercard or VISA (with a $15.00 minimum). Prices and numbers are subject to change without notice.

Card #_____ Exp. Date _____
Signature_____
Name_____
Address_____
City _____ State _____ Zip Code _____

For faster service when ordering by credit card call **1-800-253-6476**

Allow a minimum of 4-6 weeks for delivery. This offer is subject to change without notice.

① SIGNET BOOKS   (0451)

PLAY TO WIN!

☐ **SCARNE ON CARDS by John Scarne.** Acclaimed as "The Card Player's Bible," this book gives the complete rules of card games ranging from poker and blackjack to hearts and cribbage. Also describes professional cardshark tricks and sets guiding principles and central strategies that can make you a winner at the game of your choice. (167651—$5.99)

☐ **SCARNE ON CARD TRICKS by John Scarne.** This volume includes 150 sure-fire time-tested, performance-perfected master card tricks. The tricks require no sleight-of-hand and are all explained and demonstrated. (158644—$5.99)

☐ **WINNING AT CASINO GAMBLING by Terence Reese.** A fascinating guide to the dos and don'ts of casino gambling. You'll learn everything from the basic rules of each game to the smartest bets to place and which to avoid. (167775—$4.99)

☐ **HOYLE'S RULES OF GAMES by Albert H. Morehead and Geoffrey Mott-Smith.** Revised edition. Authoritative rules and instructions for playing hundreds of indoor games. New bridge bidding and scoring rules. (163095—$4.99)

Prices slightly higher in Canada

Buy them at your local bookstore or use this convenient coupon for ordering.

PENGUIN USA
P.O. Box 999 — Dept. #17109
Bergenfield, New Jersey 07621

Please send me the books I have checked above.
I am enclosing $_____ (please add $2.00 to cover postage and handling). Send check or money order (no cash or C.O.D.'s) or charge by Mastercard or VISA (with a $15.00 minimum). Prices and numbers are subject to change without notice.

Card #_____ Exp. Date _____
Signature_____
Name_____
Address_____
City _____ State _____ Zip Code _____

For faster service when ordering by credit card call **1-800-253-6476**

Allow a minimum of 4-6 weeks for delivery. This offer is subject to change without notice.